D1209370

Bartolomé Murillo 1617–1682

COVER ILLUSTRATION
The Return of the Prodigal Son (National Gallery of Art, Washington)

This exhibition has been made possible through the support of

We are grateful to Her Majesty's Government for its help in agreeing to indemnify this exhibition under the National Heritage Act 1980.

Bartolomé Esteban Murillo

1617–1682

MUSEO DEL PRADO MADRID 1982

ROYAL ACADEMY OF ARTS LONDON 1983

Catalogue published in association with
WEIDENFELD AND NICOLSON LONDON

House editor *Vicky Hayward*
Designed by *Trevor Vincent*
for George Weidenfeld and Nicolson Limited
91 Clapham High Street, London SW4 7TA

ISBN 0 297 78193 6 (casebound)
0 297 78194 4 (paperback)

Set in Monophoto Sabon and printed by
BAS Printers Limited, Over Wallop, Hampshire
Colour separations by Newsele Litho Ltd., Italy
Colour printed in Italy by Printers Srl for L.E.G.O., Vicenza

Contents

B.A.T Industries is delighted to be associated with the Royal Academy in presenting the Murillo Exhibition at Burlington House. It is a splendid testimony to the initiative, enthusiasm and energy of Norman Rosenthal of the Royal Academy and Manuela Mena Marqués of the Prado Museum in Madrid. Their collaboration has resulted in the bringing together of the largest collection ever mounted of the works of this Spanish Master.

This is not the first time we have been involved in fine arts sponsorship. Last year B.A.T Industries' American holding company, BATUS, provided substantial support to a U.S. tour of the Phillips Collection, which has its home in Washington D.C. This tour was so successful that BATUS proposes to support another U.S. tour in 1983 – though, very fittingly, this time the paintings will be drawn from the Royal Academy's own collection.

I wish the Murillo Exhibition every success, and great enjoyment to everyone who comes to see it.

PATRICK SHEEHY
Chairman B.A.T Industries p.l.c.

Foreword

In *The Golden Age of Spanish Painting*, the catalogue of the memorable Royal Academy Winter Exhibition in 1976, the distinguished Spanish art historian Prof. Alfonso Pérez Sánchez, until recently Deputy Director of the Prado Museum in Madrid, wrote that Murillo was 'one of the Spanish artists most in need of critical appraisal'. In the eighteenth and nineteenth centuries Murillo was regarded as one of the greatest artists who ever lived and he was certainly one of the most popular. But in our century, especially, his reputation began to sink beneath the weight of his popular success and the appearance of reproductions of his work in all manner of guises – transferred on to plates, printed on chocolate boxes and, above all, used as mass-produced religious images – damaged his reputation in serious cultural circles.

We are thus all the more happy and proud to participate with our friends in the Prado in this, the first ever full-scale exhibition of Murillo's art, presented to give us all an opportunity to reassess the merits of this remarkable artist; on the one hand to perceive his qualities as a highly sophisticated painter and on the other to appreciate his excellence as a truly popular artist, whose gentle imagination has always attracted wide appeal. It is good to be reminded that these two qualities are not always mutually exclusive. Perhaps the gentleness and human tolerance which characterize his art are less appreciated precisely because such qualities seem so hard to achieve in art today.

The exhibition came about in the first instance as the result of a suggestion made at a meeting organized by the British Council in Madrid in 1978 between the then Director of the Prado, Prof. José M. Pita Andrade, and our Exhibitions Secretary, Norman Rosenthal. The idea was welcomed both in Madrid and in London and work began at once. The choice of paintings and drawings, made by Prof. Pérez Sánchez together with Norman Rosenthal, was based on the monumental catalogue raisonné of the paintings of Murillo that appeared in 1981, written by the doyen of Spanish art historians, Prof. Diego Angulo Iñiguez, a former director of the Prado. He has been unfailingly helpful in every way and has further honoured us by writing an essay in the catalogue. Our thanks are due also to the Spanish Ministry of Culture and its two successive Directors General, Señor Xavier Tusell Gómez and his successor Señor Alfredo Pérez de Armiñán, who have supported the project throughout, providing funds for the restoration of very many important paintings. The Director of the Museo del Prado Dr. Federico Sopeña and the Director of the Museo de Bellas Artes in Seville Dr. Enrique Pareja López have been extraordinarily generous with loans, and Prof. Enrique Valdivieso in Seville has been unfailingly helpful.

Here perhaps is the appropriate place to pay tribute to that great friend of the Royal Academy, His Excellency the late Prof. Xavier de Salas, Hon. CBE, Corresponding Member of the Royal Academy and Chairman of the Trustees of the Prado, who gave us every encouragement in this as in so many other projects in the past; rarely has the Royal Academy had so true a friend.

Dña. Manuela Mena Marqués, Deputy Director of the Museo del Prado, has worked tirelessly on the organization of the exhibition and her commitment and assistance have been most warmly appreciated. In England, Mrs. Enriqueta Harris Frankfort, Sir Ellis Waterhouse, Philip Troutman and Eric Young have given freely of their advice, as have Prof. John Elliott, Prof. Jonathan Brown and Prof. Edward Sullivan in the United States. The English version of the catalogue has been edited with exemplary skill by Jane Martineau.

Murillo was much collected in England, especially in the eighteenth and nineteenth centuries, and although certain important works in English collections have sadly not been made available, English museums and private collections have been most generous with their loans. An exhibition of this quality could not have been realized without the generosity and support of many other museums and collections in France, the German Democratic Republic, the German Federal Republic, Italy, the Netherlands, the Republic of Ireland, Switzerland and the United States.

Finally our warmest thanks must go to British American Tobacco for their generous financial assistance. Their two successive Chairmen, Sir Peter Macadam and his successor, Mr Patrick Sheehy, as well as Mr Richard Haddon, Head of Public Affairs, have committed themselves enthusiastically to this venture.

1982 was the tercentenary of Murillo's death and the exhibition was first shown at the Prado Museum to commemorate this anniversary. The exhibition has been a huge success in Madrid and has drawn many hundreds of thousands of visitors to the Prado. Murillo, we know, is a great national hero in Spain, but he has also been much loved in England. We hope, therefore, that this exhibition will find an immediate response here and lead to a rediscovery of Murillo's special qualities, which so endeared him to our ancestors.

HUGH CASSON
President of the Royal Academy

Editorial Note

The following drawings will not be shown at the Royal Academy of Arts:
Cat. D10, D11, D15.

The following catalogue entries are by Manuela Mena Marqués:
3, 4, 5, 8, 9, 10, 11, 18, 19, 20, 21, 25, 27, 31, 32, 33, 34, 35, 36, 37, 38, 39, 47, 48, 49, 50, 51, 52, 53, 54, 55, 56, 57, 59, 60, 63, 69, 70, 72, 73, 74, 75, 76.
The following catalogue entries are by Enrique Valdivieso:
1, 2, 6, 7, 12, 13, 14, 15, 16, 17, 22, 23, 24, 26, 28, 29, 30, 40, 41, 42, 43, 44, 45, 46, 58, 61, 62, 64, 65, 66, 67, 68, 71, 77.

The catalogue entries are arranged in chronological order for both the paintings and drawings.
All paintings are in oil on canvas.

The dimensions are given in centimetres to the nearest 0·5 cm for the paintings and in millimetres for the drawings; height precedes width.

References beneath catalogue entries are to works in the general bibliography; exhibition catalogues are indicated by location and date. Additional references cite in full publications that are of importance for a particular catalogue entry; these titles are not repeated in the bibliography.

EXHIBITION ORGANIZERS
Manuela Mena Marqués,
Deputy Director, Museo del Prado
Norman Rosenthal,
Exhibitions Secretary, Royal Academy of Arts

EDITOR OF THE ENGLISH CATALOGUE
Jane Martineau

TRANSLATORS
Anthony Edgkins
'Murillo: his Life and Work' translated by *Edward Sullivan*

EXHIBITION ASSISTANT
Annette Bradshaw

Murillo: his Life and Work

Diego Angulo Iñiguez

Bartolomé Esteban Murillo was born in Seville and baptized there on 1 January 1618. His father was Bartolomé Esteban, a barber-surgeon who was often referred to by his university titles *bachiller* and *licenciado*. His mother, María Pérez Murillo, was from a family of silversmiths and painters. Bartolomé was the youngest of 14 children and was born when his parents had been married for 30 years.

Although he sometimes used his father's surname Esteban, he more often signed his name and is referred to by that of his mother, Murillo. When he was nine years old both his parents died within six months of each other; he was then taken into the house of one of his older sisters who, like her mother, had married a barber-surgeon.

Upon reaching the age of 15, Bartolomé applied for permission to go to the New World where he had several close relatives. We do not know if he had already started his apprenticeship, nor do we know if he ever made the trip. In any case, it was at about this time that he began his training with the painter Juan del Castillo, a relative of his mother.

In 1645, at the age of 27, he married the 22-year old Beatriz Cabrera who came from a family of silversmiths. It was then that Bartolomé began to paint his first major work, the series of pictures for the cloister of the monastery of San Francisco. From then on he constantly received important commissions. Murillo's marriage lasted some 20 years; in 1663 his wife died and he remained a widower until his death 20 years later. The couple had nine children, although only four were living at the time of their mother's death. Francisca, the painter's only daughter, entered the Dominican convent of the Madre de Dios at an early age and took the name Sor Francisca de Santa Rosa, after the first saint of the Americas. Murillo often painted this saint, perhaps in honour of his daughter. Four years before the artist's own death in 1678, his son Gabriel, then aged 20, left for America; and the following year José, his eldest son, died shortly before reaching his thirtieth year. Only Gaspar, the painter's youngest son, then aged 20, was with Murillo at the time of his death. Gaspar had decided on a career in the Church at an early age and he later became a canon of the Cathedral of Seville.

In contrast to his sad and increasingly lonely private life, Murillo's professional career was filled with triumphs. He was given major commissions in Seville even before he reached the age of 30 and he continued to receive them until the time of his death. Death surprised him literally with his brushes in hand, resulting from a fall from a scaffold in the Capuchin church at Cádiz where he was painting the high altarpiece. It is almost certain that he compensated for the sadness of his family life by painting a world fashioned in his dreams, inhabited by cherubs playing on a sea of clouds, saints in mystical transport, or the smiling, laughing children of Seville.

fig. 1 Murillo *The Last Supper* (Santa María la Blanca, Seville)

In his mature period, after painting his *Vision of St. Antony* (fig. 5) for Seville Cathedral and shortly before the death of his wife, Murillo felt the impulse to teach the art of painting. In 1660 he was co-founder of the Academy of Seville of which he served as first president together with Francisco de Herrera the Younger, although the latter soon left Seville for Madrid. Murillo considered neither de Herrera nor the youthful and successful Valdés Leal, who had also joined the Academy, appropriate as masters to direct the artistic training of young pupils. He therefore decided, after only a few years at the Academy, to leave and teach in his own studio.

The earliest known work by Murillo, *The Virgin Presenting the Rosary to St. Dominic* (Cat. 1) in the Archbishop's Palace, Seville, belongs stylistically to the first quarter of the seventeenth century. The face of the Virgin resembles those painted by his teacher Juan del Castillo and the background, with its crowd of angels, reflects Murillo's admiration for

fig. 2 Juan de Roelas *The Martyrdom of St. Andrew* (Museo de Bellas Artes, Seville)

Juan de Roelas (d. 1625; fig. 2), the painter who introduced Venetian colour to the School of Seville. But the putti in the foreground already show Murillo's preference for movement. There is a profound difference in style between this work (the exact date of which is uncertain, although it cannot have been painted much after 1640 when the artist was 22 years old) and that of the series made in 1646 for the cloister of the monastery of San Francisco. Murillo's first biographer, Antonio Palomino, accounted for this turn towards a naturalistic style by stating that the artist had followed the advice of his fellow Sevillian Velázquez, whom he had visited in Madrid at this date. Although the possibility of such a journey cannot be excluded, we must also remember that Palomino in his youth had heard other artists say of Murillo that 'he had spent that entire time closed up in his house studying things as they looked in nature and thus acquired the ability to paint them'. Certainly Murillo could easily have learned the new style he employed for the San Francisco paintings in Seville, especially by looking at the work of Zurbarán. It is clear that by this time he had abandoned the Renaissance tradition and turned to a naturalistic style.

San Diego Giving Food to the Poor (Cat. 4) is a good example of the painter's ability to capture the likeness of his models. Although Christian charity is the theme of this series, it could also be read as a realistic record of medicants taking advantage of the benevolence of the monks. Here we see for the first time what was to remain one of Murillo's chosen subjects throughout his life: child beggars, gathered around a large cauldron in the centre of the picture. The artist's interest in light effects and volumetric forms derived from Zurbarán. The figures in *St. Giles before Pope Gregory* IX (Raleigh, North Carolina) could almost be painted by Zurbarán himself. In *The Death of St. Clare* (fig. 3), the abrupt division between the divine apparition and the saint's cell is also close to Zurbarán; but although the cell is dark, the procession of female saints is brilliantly lit and heralds the inimitable style and distinctive beauty of the mature Murillo. It is clear that with this painting a new star had arisen in the Sevillian artistic orbit. In the episode of *St. Salvador of Horta*, the principle figures are set against a brilliantly lit background; a stylistic novelty that had important consequences for the artist's later pictures.

The Franciscans of Seville had their martyrs, but in the series of paintings commissioned from Murillo no scene of death was depicted. Instead he concentrated on the virtues of neighbourly love, as in the episodes of San Diego and San Junípero and on the love of God, as in the scene of the *Levitation of St. Giles*, usually known as *The Angels' Kitchen* (fig. 4).

The interest in light and shade effects which so preoccupied Murillo in the San Francisco series is continued in some of his later works, such as the *Adoration of the Shepherds* in the Prado (Cat. 18), a painting which also shows his strong bent toward naturalism. Yet in *The Last Supper* painted for Santa María la Blanca (1650; fig. 1) Murillo goes beyond Zurbaránesque chiaroscuro and creates an interior in which the lighting effects are created by artificial light. Murillo's early interest in strong chiaroscuro, which he derived from Zurbarán, is surprisingly archaic, especially if we consider that by the mid-seventeenth century the other major Sevillian painters of the preceding generation (Velázquez, Alonso Cano) had abandoned this style. On the other hand, chiaroscuro light effects remained a hallmark of the Valencian School as represented by Espinosa until about 1670. As far as Murillo's *Last Supper* is concerned, we must also remember that at about this time (*c.* 1650) Fra Juan Ricci, working in Madrid, painted his *Last Supper of St. Benedict* (Prado) in which the light is provided by a candle. Dutch painters also continued to employ this technique.

fig. 3 Murillo *The Death of St. Clare* (Gemäldegalerie, Dresden)

fig. 4 Murillo *The Angels' Kitchen* (Musée du Louvre, Paris)

In *The Vision of St. Antony* (Seville Cathedral, fig. 5), Murillo abandoned the very large figures and balanced composition of such painters as Zurbarán and Herrera the Elder. A heavenly glory appears at the upper left, opposite the saint, creating a torrent of obliquely slanting light which is typically baroque. The light creates a greater distance between the saint's outstretched arms and the descending Child outlined against a luminous background, against

fig. 5 Murillo *The Vision of St. Antony of Padua* (Seville Cathedral)

which angels are silhouetted. In striving for a natural effect the artist imagined the earthly zone to be bathed in shadow, abandoning the strong Zurbaránesque light which had previously lent a sculpturesque precision to objects. In looking for the roots of this transformation in Murillo's art we might consider the work of Herrera the Younger who had recently returned from Italy.

A further marked development is evident in Murillo's *Birth of the Virgin* in the Louvre (fig. 7, 1660). This painting is surprising in its use of light when compared to his earlier work. The illumination of the small glory of angels in the upper portion as well as that in the scene at the left of the composition creates a framing effect for the main group in the centre, which is intensely highlighted. A young woman and a chair placed in the foreground act as foils to the intense luminosity of the central group.

The influence of Dutch painting and especially of Rembrandt's school is obvious in Murillo's treatment of light and shadow. The aesthetic links between Spain and the Netherlands at that time are often overlooked due to the breakdown of political relations between the two countries. We must remember that the Marquis of Villamanrique, a friend of Murillo, already owned a painting by Rembrandt in 1665, which he exhibited at the inauguration of the church of

fig. 6 Francisco de Herrera the Younger
The Ecstasy of St. Francis (Seville Cathedral)

fig. 7 Murillo *The Birth of the Virgin*
(Musée du Louvre, Paris)

fig. 8 Torre Farfán *La Giralda engalanada*; the tower of Seville Cathedral decorated in honour of the canonization of San Fernando (engraving in *Fiestas . . . al nuevo culto del . . . San Fernando*, 1675)

Santa María la Blanca. Five years later, Murillo painted the *Portrait of Josua van Belle* (Cat. 62) who later became a burghermaster of Rotterdam. The light effects in the *Birth of the Virgin* are more varied than in the *Vision of St. Antony* and there is something of the mysterious enchantment of Rembrandt's pictures in the background. The composition of the central group, set at an angle and obviously Rubensian in inspiration, is a convincing evocation of daily life (not unlike that found in Ghirlandaio's *Birth of the Virgin* in S. Maria Novella, Florence).

In 1665, the small church of Santa María la Blanca was inaugurated. It had undergone a total transformation and Murillo executed four lunettes for it. The church had originally been a synagogue but had been completely refurbished; marble columns and white stucco decoration, intended to remind the visitor (especially when he looked up at the cupola) of the miracle of an August snowfall after which the church was named, had been added. The two larger lunettes painted to go below the cupola in the central nave illustrate the history of the founding of the church of Santa Maria Maggiore in Rome. This church was under the protection of King Philip IV; Santa María la Blanca served as its Sevillian counterpart.

The first painting represents *The Dream of the Patrician* (Cat. 36) in which the Virgin appeared to the patrician and his wife, bidding them to erect a church on the Esquiline Hill, where they were to find the plan for the church traced in snow. In the Roman church itself there is an old mosaic which shows the patrician and his wife asleep in their bed, but Murillo depicted them as if they had fallen asleep while reading from the book on the table; their sleep is languorous, their somnolence emphasized by the white dog who has also curled up to rest. The inclusion of an animal was a favourite device of the painter (see, for example, *The Holy Family with a Little Bird*, Cat. 8). The woman's body, like that of the dog's, forms an oval shape as she sleeps, and the heavy arm of the patrician expresses his total exhaustion. The shadowy atmosphere of the scene contrasts happily with the light of the heavenly apparition.

If this scene takes place amidst shadows, its companion, representing *The Patrician John and his Wife before Pope Liberius* (Cat. 37), is bathed in strong light. The painting consists of two parts: the group in the foreground, and the far distant procession. In the former the painter created a strong contrast of light and shade, the Pope's profile being silhouetted against the light coming from the left and lighting the patrician's wife and the cleric; it is painted very freely. In the background procession this sketchy technique is even more pronounced, with some figures placed in shadow and others strongly lit.

The other two lunettes were placed at the heads of the side aisles and represent the *Triumph of the Eucharist*, also known as *Faith* (Cat. 39), and *The Immaculate Conception* (Cat. 38). This last subject was obviously chosen because the great celebrations accompanying the inauguration of Santa María la Blanca were also celebrating the pontifical brief of 1661, which declared in favour of the Immaculate Conception of the Virgin. The festivities were not limited to those celebrated within the church itself, but continued outside; in the plaza in front of the church altars were set up and façades of the houses were adorned with paintings by Murillo and other famous artists.

The last two great cycles by Murillo were those for the

fig. 9 Murillo *The Vision of St. Francis at the Portiuncula* (Wallraf-Richartz Museum, Cologne)

fig. 10 Murillo *The Virgin and Child in Glory with Saints* (Wallace Collection, London)

Capuchin monastery and the Hospital de la Caridad. The series for the Capuchin monastery comprises the paintings for the high altar and those for the altars of the side chapels; most of these paintings are now in the museum at Seville. The frame of the high altarpiece was sober, in accordance with the severe rules of the order for which it was made, and in marked contrast to the richly decorated altars that were normal in Seville at the time. The large central painting represents the *Vision of St. Francis at the Portiuncula* (fig. 9) now in Cologne; at either side and below were small pictures of various saints. The sketch of *The Virgin and Child in Glory with the Saints* in the Wallace Collection, London (fig. 10), may have been a first idea for a part of the altar that was later abandoned.

The dedication of one of the principal paintings in the altarpiece to SS Justa and Rufina originated from the story of their having been martyred in the Roman amphitheatre located in that part of the city. They were the patron saints of potters. At the beginning of the nineteenth century Goya was commissioned by the chapter of Seville Cathedral to paint SS Justa and Rufina. In this work he included a lion which, although apparently gentle, serves as a reminder of their martyrdom. Murillo, however, preferred to allude to a more recent event: the saints' miraculous intervention at the time of the earthquake of 1504 when the tower of the Cathedral was put in grave danger. Around 1600 the Cathedral chapter commissioned a painting of this miracle from the artist Miguel de Esquivel, a work still in the Cathedral (fig. 89). Esquivel painted the Giralda tower as a massive edifice, but Murillo transformed it into an attenuated spire held by the saints (Cat. 41).

fig. 11 Juan Martínez Montañés *The Adoration of the Shepherds* (Convento de San Isidoro del Campo, Santiponce, Seville)

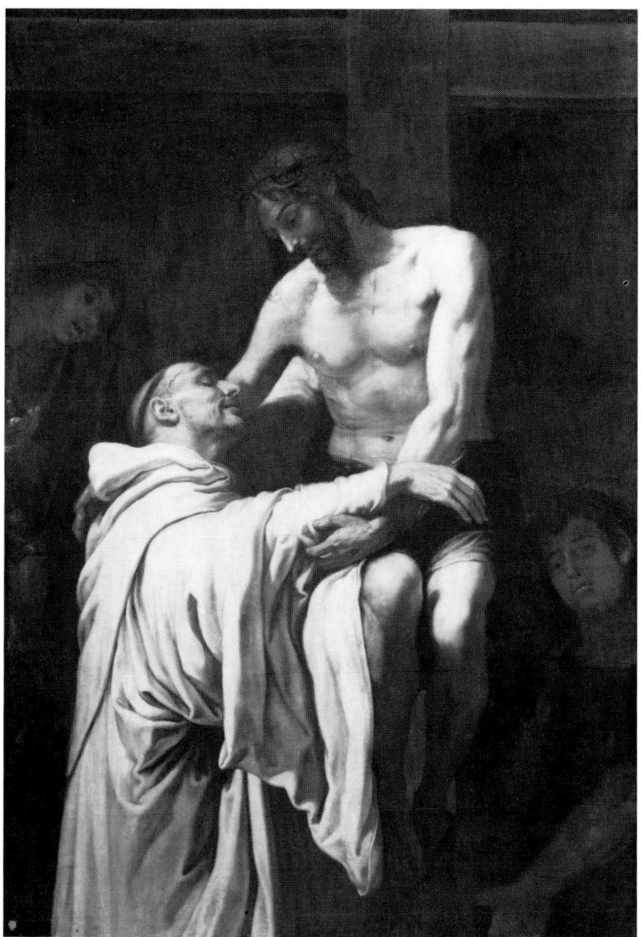

fig. 12 Francisco Ribalta *St. Bernard Embracing the Crucified Christ* (Museo del Prado, Madrid)

fig. 13 Francisco Ribalta *St. Francis Embracing the Crucified Christ* (Museo de Bellas Artes, Valencia)

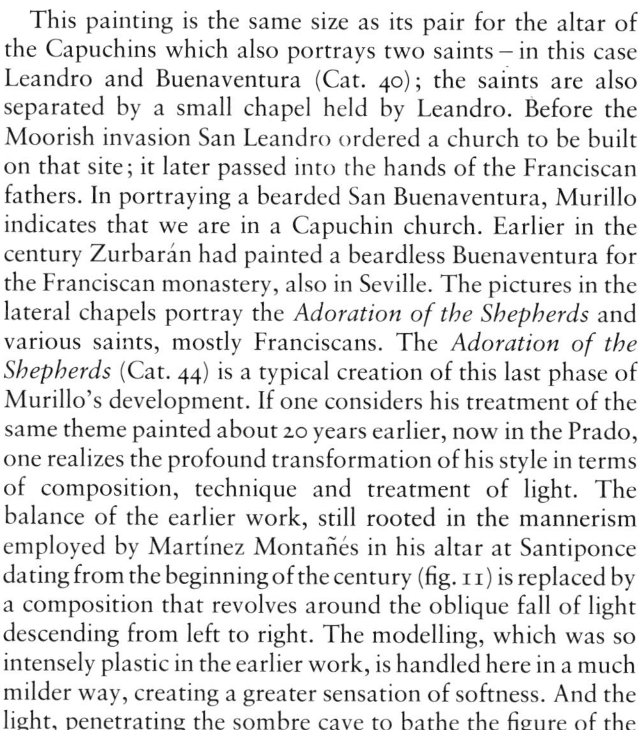

This painting is the same size as its pair for the altar of the Capuchins which also portrays two saints – in this case Leandro and Buenaventura (Cat. 40); the saints are also separated by a small chapel held by Leandro. Before the Moorish invasion San Leandro ordered a church to be built on that site; it later passed into the hands of the Franciscan fathers. In portraying a bearded San Buenaventura, Murillo indicates that we are in a Capuchin church. Earlier in the century Zurbarán had painted a beardless Buenaventura for the Franciscan monastery, also in Seville. The pictures in the lateral chapels portray the *Adoration of the Shepherds* and various saints, mostly Franciscans. The *Adoration of the Shepherds* (Cat. 44) is a typical creation of this last phase of Murillo's development. If one considers his treatment of the same theme painted about 20 years earlier, now in the Prado, one realizes the profound transformation of his style in terms of composition, technique and treatment of light. The balance of the earlier work, still rooted in the mannerism employed by Martínez Montañés in his altar at Santiponce dating from the beginning of the century (fig. 11) is replaced by a composition that revolves around the oblique fall of light descending from left to right. The modelling, which was so intensely plastic in the earlier work, is handled here in a much milder way, creating a greater sensation of softness. And the light, penetrating the sombre cave to bathe the figure of the Christ Child resting on his white cloth, falls delicately on the shepherds, creating strong chiaroscuro effects, and highlighting the superbly realized form of the young shepherdess and that of the old man in the middle ground.

The theme of *St. Francis Embracing the Crucified Christ* (Cat. 43) was a favourite one of the Capuchins, who dedicated one of the chapels in their church to him. The iconographic theme of Christ extending one of his arms from the cross dates from a much earlier period. In Valencia, the place of origin of several of the founders of the Capuchin monastery in Seville, Francisco Ribalta painted *St. Bernard Embracing the Crucified Christ* (fig. 12) in the first half of the seventeenth century. He also painted *St. Francis Embracing the Crucified Christ* (fig. 13) for the Valencian Capuchins, the same theme that the Capuchins of Seville later commissioned from Murillo. Ribalta, who was indirectly influenced by Michelangelo via the Italian artists working at the Escorial, depicted Christ with a large, muscular body, and an equally massive St. Francis. The panther, symbol of worldly pleasures, is seen at the saint's feet. Murillo created more attenuated elegant figures, the proportions are finer and the panther has been replaced by a globe, a symbol of the world which the saint is pushing away lightly with his foot. His body, elevated by the love which suffuses his face, is gently embraced by Christ. While it is possible that the panther, as painted by

fig. 14 Murillo *The Vision of St. Félix of Cantalicio* (Museo de Bellas Artes, Seville)

Ribalta, represented the earthly riches that Christ's disciples should eschew, its animal body also evokes other earthly delights. The orb pushed away by Francis seems to be more in accordance with the text of St. Luke which is held aloft by cherubs and reads: '*Qui non renuntiat omnibus qui possidet non potest meus esse discipulus*' ('He who does not renounce all his goods cannot be my disciple').

The two other Franciscan subjects chosen for the altars of the side chapels were *St. Antony* and *St. Félix of Cantalicio* (fig. 14). They are both good examples of Murillo's pictorial technique in this later phase of his career.

Whereas St. Antony represents the early Franciscans, St. Félix of Cantalicio, patron of the Franciscan lay brothers, represents this new branch of the order. He had been canonized at the time that the Capuchins of Seville took charge of the old chapel of SS Justa and Rufina over which the church was built. Murillo chose to portray the same episode that had been painted at the time of St. Félix's beatification in his burial chapel in Rome – the miraculous apparition of the Virgin to deliver the Christ Child into the arms of the saint. According to the great French iconographer Emile Mâle, it was Murillo who created the definitive version of this subject. Because of the presence of the Virgin, the composition of this painting is more complex than that of the *St. Antony*. The composition of the *St. Félix*, like the *St. Antony* in Seville Cathedral, is typically baroque in its diagonal emphasis and simplified setting. The intense luminosity of the Virgin, who emerges from the glory behind her, carries the lighting effects used by Murillo in the pictures for Santa María la Blanca even further.

The subject of *St. Thomas of Villanueva* (Cat. 42) does not belong to Franciscan iconography; St. Thomas was an Augustinian but he had been Archbishop of Valencia, the native city of many of the founders of the Sevillian Capuchin monastery, and the painting was made to honour the memory of these men. Murillo took such interest in this picture that, as Palomino tells us, he would refer to it as 'my painting'. Certainly the artist had reason to be proud of this work. The deeply recessed background is composed of classicizing architectural elements; in the foreground the figures are strongly contrasted by light; in the middle ground the monumental column and the swag of drapery around it emerge in bold relief against the background, which is strongly illuminated to serve as a halo for St. Thomas. Beyond the arch on the right we see a glimpse of a

fig. 15 Juan de Valdés Leal *Portrait of Miguel de Mañara* (Hospital de la Caridad, Seville)

fig. 16 Church of the Hospital de la Caridad, Seville; interior; altarpiece by Pedro Rolán

Renaissance façade that is very different from the highly ornamental Seville buildings of the time. In the centre the figure of the saint with his finely attenuated face stands majestically with his left hand holding his crook while with his right hand he proffers a coin. His expression is a combination of love and pity for the beggar, who contrasts dramatically with the fine figure of St. Thomas. At the lower left we see a beautifully composed group of a mother and young child, who are happy to have received the saint's charity. Although the face of the mother is virtually lost in shadow, the child's delight, a theme always dear to Murillo, is illuminated. There is a large open book on the table at the left, a reminder of St. Thomas of Villanueva's fame as a theologian (he had preached before Emperor Charles V); it also implies that charity comes before scholarship.

The last great series painted by Murillo, for the Hospital de la Caridad, presents a more unified programme than that executed for the Capuchins. It illustrates the two preoccupations of Miguel de Mañara, the Hospital's founder (fig. 15): love of the unfortunate and disdain of earthly glories. Mañara wisely entrusted to Murillo the scenes of charity to the destitute, and left to Valdés Leal the more dramatic subjects of death and the misery of human vanity.

The beautiful church of the Hospital (fig. 31), decorated with Murillo's paintings until the majority of them were taken by Marshal Soult at the time of the Napoleonic invasion, is a large single-nave structure with an impressive *Entombment* on the high altar by Pedro Roldán, the best Sevillian sculptor of his day. Mañara chose the *Entombment of Christ* as the subject of this altar because the Brotherhood of Charity had originally been founded to bury executed criminals. Burying the dead was also one of the Works of Mercy that Mañara wanted to emphasize to the members of the Brotherhood and visitors to the church.

The remaining six Works of Mercy were painted by Murillo, who took his subjects from both the Old and New Testaments. Beneath the cupola were placed two enormous paintings representing the giving of drink to the thirsty and food to the hungry. For the former the artist chose the story of *Moses Striking the Rock* and for the latter, the episode of *The Miracle of the Loaves and Fishes* (figs. 18 and 19). The Old Testament passage reads:

And the people chode with Moses, and spake, saying, Would God that we had died when our brethren died before the Lord! . . . And Moses and Aaron went from the presence of the assembly unto the door of the tabernacle of the congregation, and the glory of the Lord appeared unto them. And the Lord spake unto Moses, saying, Take the rod, and gather thou the assembly together, thou, and Aaron thy brother, and speak ye unto the rock before their eyes; and it shall give forth his water, and thou shalt bring forth to them water out of the rock: so thou shalt give the congregation and their beasts drink. . . . And Moses lifted up his hand, and with his rod he smote the rock twice: and the water came out abundantly, and the congregation drank, and their beasts also.

Numbers, XX, 3, 6–8, 11

Murillo created a scene with numerous figures masterfully organized, contrasting the divine inspiration of the group around Moses and Aaron with the human sensations of those suffering from thirst. Their happiness is expressed by the child on horseback at the upper left who points to the miraculous rock. On either side men and women hurry to assuage their thirst, forming two groups of unequal size. At the extreme left a mother impatiently drinks from a jug, momentarily neglecting her child whose gesture suggests that perhaps thirst overcomes even maternal instincts, while the father pours a crystalline jet of water from his jar into the small jug held aloft by his son. The most dramatic illustration of the quenching of thirst is the group of a young man who turns his back towards us and a woman, her figure heavily foreshortened, framing two children. The expressions on the faces of the children are admirable, particularly that of the boy totally absorbed in drinking from a bowl, unmindful of all those around him, and the other one behind him who still feels the pangs of thirst.

It has long been known that Murillo knew a painting of this subject by the Genoese artist Asseretto (now in the Prado; fig. 17), which inspired some of the secondary figures. A

fig. 17 Giovachino Asseretto *Moses Striking the Rock* (Museo del Prado, Madrid)

fig. 18 Murillo *Moses Striking the Rock* (Church of the Hospital de la Caridad)

fig. 19 Murillo *The Miracle of the Loaves and Fishes* (Church of the Hospital de la Caridad, Seville)

comparison between these two works serves only to underline the mastery of Murillo.

The other pictures in the Church are smaller in scale. *Abraham Visited by the Three Angels*, the *Liberation of St. Peter*, the *Healing of the Paralytic at the Pool of Bethesda* (Cat. 45) and the *Return of the Prodigal Son* (Cat. 46) allude to other Works of Mercy: sheltering the homeless, consoling the imprisoned, visiting the sick and clothing the naked. The *Return of the Prodigal Son* had been painted by Murillo a number of years before in a series of pictures now in the Beit Collection (Cat. 47–52). When he was commissioned to paint this subject again by Mañara, far from repeating or paraphrasing his early work, he created entirely new compositions. The principal difference in Murillo's manner of treating the subject in this new version is the emphasis on the act of clothing the naked figure as a work of charity. This new focus derives from the emphasis in St. Luke's text which reads: 'Bring forth the best robe, and put it on him, and put a ring on his finger and shoes on his feet'. (*Luke*, XV, 22). Murillo carefully follows the words of the Evangelist and places the servants bringing the tunic, sandals and ring in the foreground of the picture.

The *Healing of the Paralytic* illustrates the text of St. John:

Now there is at Jerusalem by the sheep market a pool which is called in the Hebrew tongue Bethesda, having five porches. In these lay a great multitude of impotent folk, of blind, halt, withered, waiting for the moving of the water. For an angel went down at a certain season into the pool, and troubled the water: whosoever then first after the troubling of the water stepped in was made whole of whatsoever disease he had. And a certain man was there, which had an infirmity thirty and eight years. When Jesus saw him lie, and knew that he had been now a long time in that case, he saith unto him, Wilt thou be made whole? The impotent man answered him. Sir, I have no man, when the water is troubled, to put me into the pool: but while I am coming, another steppeth down before me. Jesus saith unto him, Rise, take up thy bed, and walk.

John, V, 2–8

fig. 20 Murillo *St. John of God*
(Church of the Hospital de la Caridad, Seville)

fig. 21 Murillo *St. Elizabeth of Hungary*
(Church of the Hospital de la Caridad, Seville)

The porticos referred to in the biblical story gave Murillo the opportunity to create one of the most fully developed architectonic settings in any of his paintings; the gradation of the zones and the light effects lend great depth to the painting.

Besides emphasizing the Works of Mercy in the paintings for the church, Miguel de Mañara also wished to remind the brothers of their duties as hospitalers. They were to gather the sick and abandoned from the streets and care for them. To this end he commissioned Murillo to execute two other large altarpieces of *St. John of God* (fig. 20) and *St. Elizabeth of Hungary* (fig. 21).

Although the presence of an image of St. John of God, the apostle of charity from Granada, needs no justification in the context of a beneficent institution, we might remember that Mañara's young wife, a woman from Granada, had recently died, and that the passage of the life of the saint which was illustrated by Murillo is echoed in the Book of Rules that governed the Brotherhood of Charity:

The indigent poor who fall ill often remain on the streets until they die. We charge that when any of our brothers sees such a case . . . he should, with a fatherly heart, help him in his misery and seek to bring him into our house: and he should remember that beneath those rags is the poor Christ Himself, his Lord and God, and picking him up by his shoulders, he should bring him into this house; and happy is he to whom this occurs.

Another rule adds: 'Bring him to the infirmary and before putting him to bed, wash his feet and kiss them.' The painting is now very dark for lack of cleaning, even though it is a night scene.

For the altar facing that of *St. John of God*, Murillo painted *St. Elizabeth of Hungary*, a noble queen in the midst of the sick and diseased to whom she ministers. Murillo's realistic depiction of the wounds of the afflicted persons may seem shocking, but it was in keeping with another of the Rules of Mañara in which the brothers were admonished, when caring for the sick, that 'no matter how disgusting their sores, do not turn your head away, but offer this mortification to God with fortitude.' It is interesting to note that when this painting was taken to Paris at the height of neoclassical fervour in the early nineteenth century, the artist's manner of treating this subject led critics to accuse Spanish painters of dirtying their brushes by depicting such themes. Yet years later during the romantic period, when the painting had already been returned to Spain, its mere memory provoked the admiration of the French who held this work up as an example of the co-existence of the sublime and the mundane. We know that Murillo owned a print by the sixteenth-century Flemish Mannerist Sadeler (fig. 22). He took from it the general idea of the saint curing the wounds of a person afflicted with scabs, but he changed the position of the sick man and transformed a dull, somewhat contrived group into a composition of almost Renaissance equilibrium.

After the paintings for Hospital de la Caridad, Murillo

fig. 22 Raphael Sadeler *St. Elizabeth of Hungary* (engraving)

undertook one more large-scale project before his death. This was the paintings for the high altarpiece of the Capuchin church in Cádiz. It was here that he met his death as the result of a fall from the scaffold on which he was working. He had only sketched his overall ideas for the project and had just begun work on the large central canvas depicting *The Mystic Marriage of St. Catherine* (fig. 23), which was finished, as was the rest of the altar, by his disciple Meneses Osorio. The Mystic Marriage is painted in the grand manner employed in the *St. Elizabeth of Hungary* and the *Return of the Prodigal Son* in the Hospital de la Caridad. The balance of this pyramidal composition seems almost as if it were the end product of superimposing the two compositions of the Caridad pictures; the distribution of light and shadow on the background architecture is also similar to that in the *St. Elizabeth*. Yet in the Cádiz picture, Murillo introduces an imposing heavenly glory that is not found in the Caridad paintings. This element, with its strongly oblique lines, counter-balances the equilibrium of the composition.

Naturally, Murillo painted many other works throughout his life besides these great cycles of paintings. One of the themes that did most to spread his fame was that of the Immaculate Conception. The immaculatist fervour of the Spanish was extraordinary in the seventeenth century, and the papal injunction against those who questioned the belief had consequences for the artistic interpretation of the theme. Immaculate Conceptions painted in Spain during the first half of the seventeenth century retained much of the quietude and solemnity of those of the last third of the sixteenth century, yet after *c.* 1650 the Virgin is shown with more movement and there is a greater baroque dynamism in her drapery and in her retinue of angels.

It is important to observe how Murillo's sensitivity to this theme evolves. *The Immaculate Conception* (Cat. 13), which was painted for the principal Franciscan monastery in Seville, is a simple and grandiose composition. The Virgin is accompanied by only three rather large angels; her mantle gently flows in the breeze. If we remember that the Franciscans had been the principal defenders of the belief in the Immaculate Conception of Mary against the Dominicans, we might say that this image has the connotations of a triumphal banner. In later versions this grandeur disappears, the Virgin is smaller in scale and the angels become ever younger and more numerous, invading the whole picture space. A comparison between *The Immaculate Conception* painted for the Venerable Fathers (Cat. 75) and that done for the Franciscans (Cat. 13) shows how Murillo's

fig. 23 Murillo and Francisco Meneses Osorio
The Mystic Marriage of St. Catherine (Museo de Bellas Artes, Cádiz)

fig. 24 Murillo *The Infant St. John* (Museo del Prado, Madrid)

artistic sensibility had been transformed. If in the scale and movement of the Franciscan picture there still remains much of the taste of the earlier part of the century, the feeling of *The Immaculate Conception* made for the Venerable Fathers is virtually rococo.

Murillo was, in addition, also the foremost Spanish artist of the theme of the Virgin and Child. Some of his versions of this theme are objects of devotion for Catholics throughout the world, a token of their success in capturing the religious sensibility of their time. But apart from their religious content they are also masterful depictions of childhood grace and pictorial masterpieces in their own right.

Although the general format of these images persisted throughout his career, Murillo continuously revised the composition and expressive tone. In the earliest examples the Virgin is on a large scale, her expression is usually slightly melancholy and the Christ Child is dressed; in later versions Mary became more elegant and the beauty of the naked Infant was displayed. Compare the Eden Collection Virgin (Angulo no. 156) with the later Madonna in the Pitti (Cat. 11). Around 1660, while the pictures still follow his early scheme, there are signs of change. In the *Virgin and Child with Angels* (Cat. 26) the composition is more complex; we are presented with an image of humanity and maternal affection.

The evolution of the Catholic sensibility in baroque painting led Murillo to paint scenes of the infancy of Jesus and St. John the Baptist. He painted two beautiful versions of the traditional subject of the Good Shepherd, substituting the Christ Child for the usual representation of a grown man. In the first example (Cat. 27) the Child is seated, he has a grave expression and a somewhat tense yet commanding pose. In accordance with the evangelical text, the stray lamb is the focus of the love of Jesus and is placed in the foreground of the picture. In the Lane Collection version (fig. 88) painted years later, the Christ Child's expression overflows with fervour as he communes with God the Father and the pastoral elements are emphasized; we see the Good Shepherd in a verdant landscape accompanied by his flock. While the first painting is typical of seventeenth-century sensibility, the second heralds the following century. And it was undoubtedly this prefiguration of eighteenth-century taste that aroused such interest in London where a copy of the composition was known in the second half of that century.

A similar progression can be seen in Murillo's paintings of the Infant St. John the Baptist, culminating in the *Infant St. John* in the Prado (fig. 24), one of the masterpieces of this genre, and a painting in which all traces of rigid formality have disappeared; the child and the lamb are fused in both form and spirit. The lamb looks at the young St. John, while the child, with his hand on his breast, his half open mouth and an upwardly directed gaze, expresses the totality of his mystical aspirations. This is a worthy companion piece to the Lane Collection *Good Shepherd* (fig. 88) and one in which the artist anticipates eighteenth-century sentiments. But the profound fervour of expression, typical of the seventeenth century, is still retained. Although the composition of the *Children with the Shell* (*Ninos de la Concha*; Prado) is a product of the seventeenth century, its general impression also anticipates the next century.

Murillo's secular painting consists almost entirely of themes involving young children, yet it is not exclusively devoted to this subject. At times he painted scenes of family life with their own particular characteristics. Murillo's taste for subjects drawn from childhood is deeply rooted; the frequent introduction of purely anecdotal topics in his religious pictures bears witness to this. He began to paint secular scenes of children early in his career; it was at that time an unprecedented genre of painting in Spain and was taken up again only in the eighteenth century, particularly by Goya. The Danish painter Eberhardt Keil, who arrived in Rome in 1656, painted peasants, old woman and children, but in his pictures the figures dominate the background; his style is somewhat stilted and the poses of his figures rather artificial. He was interested in the picturesque and his subjects lack the light heartedness and apparent spontaneity of the characters created by Murillo. Murillo, in fact, created his own genre, deriving from the paintings of the naturalistic school of Seville in which he had developed, and from his innate love of childhood, the subjects that we have observed in his religious paintings. In the early eighteenth century there is no record of Murillo's genre paintings in Seville, although they appear shortly afterwards in Antwerp and London, so it is possible that they were painted specifically for visiting northern merchants.

The Street Urchin (Cat. 6), with its intense chiaroscuro and distinctive handling of paint typical of the young Murillo, is the earliest example of the genre. Murillo seems to commiserate with the boy. But his approach to the theme of childhood soon changed and in *Grandmother Delousing her Grandson* in the Alte Pinakothek, Munich, the note of sadness and abandon has disappeared despite the poverty of the setting. This picture is a scene of domestic hygiene; the diligent grandmother has just put aside her sewing to attend to her grandchild. It reflects the optimism of the then popular refrain 'Child with lice, healthy and happy' (an optimism which seems strange to us today) and that of another saying, 'Sick child will breed no lice'. The boy is not infirm and abandoned, but cared for and content; as his grandmother tends to his head, he eats a bit of bread and plays with a dog at his feet. The painter was attracted by the soul of the happy, playful child and it is effectively the real theme of the painting.

Happiness, at times tinged with a light note of pessimism, was the subject of most of Murillo's paintings in this genre. He depicted the joys of the most optimistic period of life, the joys which come from things that are important to a child such as a toy or food. The simple happiness of a child poking his head out of the window of his house and laughing at something we do not see, is the subject of one of his paintings (Cat. 71). At other times he deals with children playing dice, or eating pastry, a melon or a bunch of grapes. Beautifully composed, these pictures of children or the *Fruit Vendor* (Pushkin Museum) would not be out of place in the range of subjects of an eighteenth-century rococo porcelain factory.

In fact Murillo not only foreshadowed eighteenth century taste in the formal composition of some of his religious paintings; he also created a secular pictorial genre which seems to belong more to the Rococo than to the seventeenth century.

As far as we know Murillo painted few portraits, but those which have come down to us are surprising in their variety. That of *Don Justino de Neve*, (fig. 44) a great friend of the painter and founder of the Hospital de los Venerables, is of a traditional type with the subject seated in a chair. Nonetheless, his pose and expression are surprisingly spontaneous. The *Portrait of Don Antonio Hurtado*, (Cat. 34) shows him in hunting dress. Although the sitter may have requested the costume himself and Velázquez's hunting portraits may have been an additional inspiration, the inclusion of the pack of hounds and the attendant gives the work an original air. Although the portrait of the Fleming *Nicolás de Omazur* (Cat. 63), with its *vanitas* reference in the skull held by the sitter, was painted in Seville during the age of Mañara, it nonetheless follows the tradition of mid-sixteenth century northern portraiture.

Murillo was an artist who enjoyed great fame in Seville during his lifetime, yet his paintings did not enter the Spanish royal collections until the early eighteenth century, when the court moved to Seville and Isabel Farnese acquired a considerable number of the pictures which are today in the Prado.

Even before 1700, paintings by Murillo were in Antwerp, Rotterdam and London, evidently due to the active commerce of the port of Seville. The king of France bought the two works now in the Louvre; the *Good Shepherd* was copied by Gainsborough in London, and Queen Catherine of Russia acquired the *Flight into Egypt* (Hermitage) on the recommendation of Diderot. Murillo's name was better known than that of Velázquez in Europe and in the mid-nineteenth century his *Immaculate Conception of Los Venerables* (Cat. 75) fetched the highest price ever paid for a painting at that date. Yet some years later, around 1900, Murillo's fame began to decline with changes in taste and he was esteemed only as a colourist. For some time now a reaction in Murillo's favour has begun to gain ground, and it is hoped that this exhibition celebrating the tercentenary of his death will contribute to the recognition of the high place he should rightfully hold in the history of painting.

Murillo was an excellent colourist and a good draughtsman who knew how to create fine compositions. He was undoubtedly one of the greatest religious painters of the baroque era and probably the best interpreter of Catholic sensibility of his time. In biblical scenes his religious fervour is restrained, and far removed from the dynamism of Rubens or the theatricality of some Italian painters. Although he painted themes of the Passion, these were not his favourite subjects, nor did he cultivate a taste for martyrdoms. His expressive tone, like the other aspects of his art, evolved over the course of his career, and if some of the characters of his early subjects remind us of Zurbarán, in his maturity and old age they lose this dramatic sense and become softer and milder, while keeping all their devotional content. *Mutatis mutandis*, if we consider one of his figures of children – the spiritual abandon of the *Infant St. John* in the Prado is no less profound than Zurbarán's Carthusian monks. One must also keep in mind, when evaluating the artistic personality of Murillo, that he not only looks forward to the aesthetic taste of the eighteenth century in the formal interpretation of some of his pictures, but is also capable of creating paintings of contemporary daily life, above all with his children who laugh, play and eat, and who might appear to be more appropriate for the decoration of a rococo salon than a seventeenth-century house in Seville.

If the many facets of Murillo's art are justly valued, Murillo emerges as one of the greatest seventeenth-century Spanish painters, who was surpassed only by Velázquez.

fig. 25 Alonso Sánchez Coello *View of the Port and the City of Seville* (Museo del Prado, Madrid; on deposit at the Museo de America, Madrid)

fig. 26 Braun *Civitatis orbis terrarum*, view of Seville (Biblioteca Nacional, Madrid)

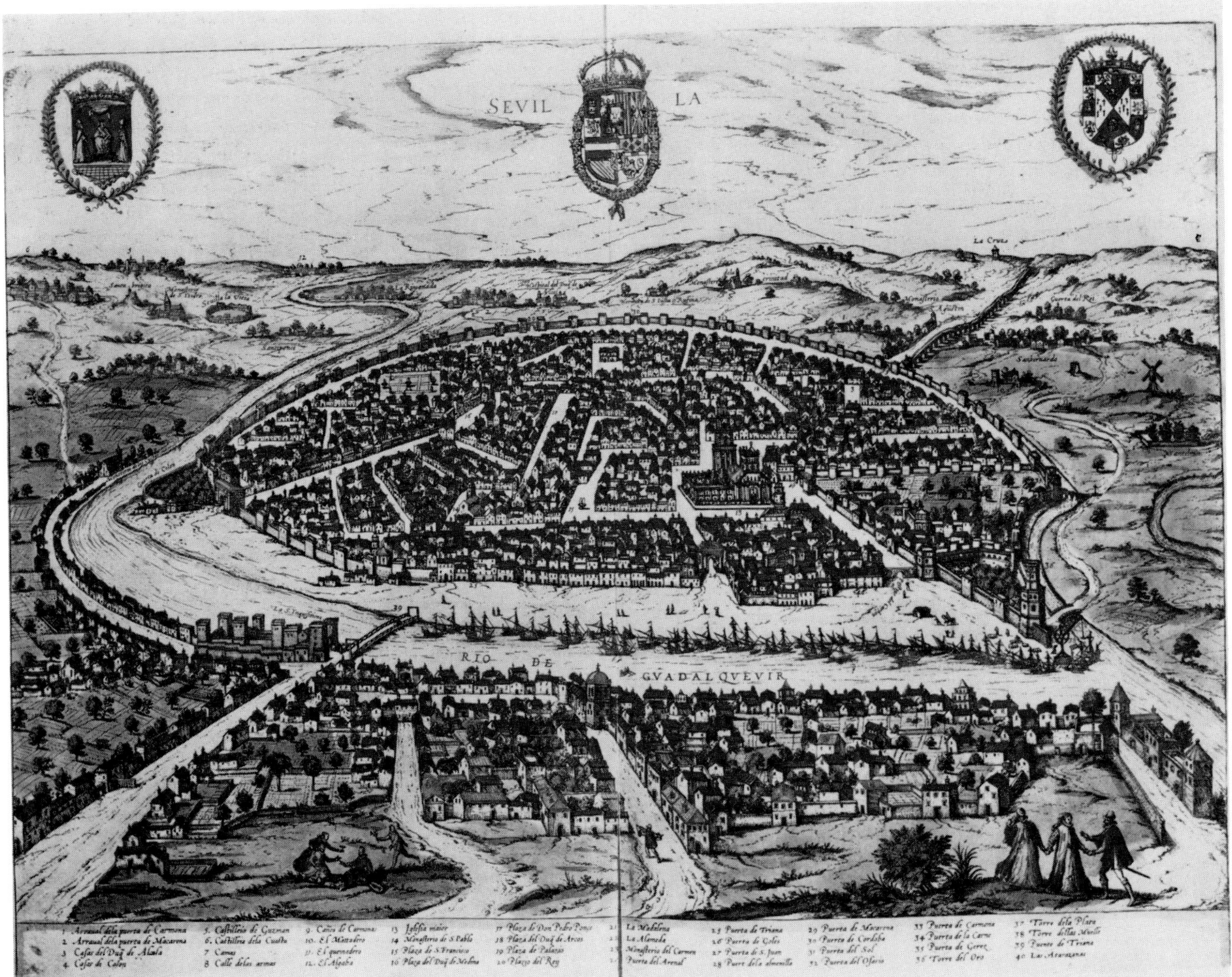

Murillo's Seville

Antonio Dominguez Ortiz

There are cosmopolitan artists, perpetual travellers, who break all ties with their place of birth. There are others so identified with their native city that we cannot fully understand their art without knowing their place of origin. Without any doubt, Murillo has to be included in this second group; closely identified with Seville (fig. 25), he left it rarely and then only briefly. To a certain extent – I would say to a great extent – Seville modelled the artist and, at the same time, it allowed itself to be modelled by him. Generations of critics, writers and travellers have pictured Seville as it was painted by Murillo; they have formed an idea of its devotion to the Virgin Mary from his Immaculate Conceptions, of its poverty from his street urchins, and – by a stretch of the imagination – they have been able to visualize his paintings in the aristocratic houses and convent churches to which they originally belonged, paintings that have since been dispersed among the world's museums and private collections.

Given this mutual identification of city and artist, it might be useful to sketch a general view of the Seville in which the painter lived. Bartolomé Esteban Murillo lived from 1618 to 1682, an adverse and troubled period for both Seville and the whole Hispanic world; the destinies of the two ran parallel – perhaps it would be better to say they were identical. Spain declined, and Seville – its noblest city, its most brilliant jewel, thanks to the immense wealth that was accumulated there – also declined. To study Murillo's Seville would require nothing less than to study the whole process of Spain's decline. But even to witness the history of the city through the eyes of its artists will give us some understanding of the changes that occurred in Seville during these years: Roelas and Pacheco witnessed Seville's hours of splendour; Martínez Montañés, thanks to his long life, knew the ups and downs of the Andalusian city; Velázquez, when he departed, left a metropolis in which the symptoms of decline were already incipient; but Murillo experienced its race to the abyss, saw it roll down the incline which led it from the twilight years of Philip III's reign to the black days of 1682, one of the most disastrous years for Seville and for all Andalusia. But it is the privilege of genius to sublimate pain, and the Seville artists of the seventeenth century idealized hunger, pain and death, conferring upon them simultaneously Christian resignation and human dignity; they even added notes of optimism and joy to their works, as if mirroring their compatriots' will to surmount their difficulties and to look ahead to happier times.

It is not hard to show that certain experiences affected Murillo's early years; there are many reports and they have the simple eloquence of first-hand accounts:[1] to take just one example, 'A hand's height of snow lasted two days', a reference to the snowfall of 3 January 1622, a rare spectacle in Seville.

In 1624 the town was dressed in festive mood because Philip IV, recently proclaimed king, was about to arrive with a large retinue of ministers and servants. Amongst the group of ministers was Philip's favourite, Don Gaspar de Guzmán, Count of Olivares and later Duke of Sanlúcar la Mayor. Although born in Rome, his family was from Seville and he proclaimed his affection for the town while at the same time trying to wrap his tentacles around it, putting men he could rely upon in key positions and extending his lordly sway at the expense of Seville's independence. Religious and civic festivities, receptions, masques and excursions along the river in flower-bedecked boats filled the days and emptied the municipal coffers and citizens' pockets. Doubtless Murillo saw these spectacles or at least heard of them. And perhaps he was present at another event that greatly impressed the people of Seville in that year of 1624: the Inquisition held proceedings there on 30 November, and several well-known and important persons were brought before the Inquisition for their involvement with a heretical sect called the *alumbrados*, 'the exalted'. It would not be hard to imagine Martínez Montañés, for example, mixed up in this investigation; he was a conspicuous member of the Granada congregation and, because of his mystical and esoteric inclinations, some wished to have him brought before the Inquisition. This *Auto de fe*, which was exceptionally notorious, took place in the Plaza de San Francisco but many others were conducted in a church near the house in which Murillo was born (and near the house where Martínez Montañés was living), the Convent of San Pablo – today, the Magdalena parish church. It was used for several reasons; its spaciousness, its proximity to the Triana Castle used by the Inquisition and the long standing connection between the Inquisition and the Dominicans.

In 1625 the English appeared off Cádiz. There was a general alarm; troops were immediately despatched and repelled the invaders. The following year, when Murillo was eight years old, the most famous of the floods from which Seville periodically suffered occurred. The whole town was flooded except for the high-lying districts, and boats operated in many of the streets, rescuing those who were in danger and carrying provisions to those who sought refuge on the roofs of their houses. I do not know Murillo's work sufficiently well to say whether these scenes left some trace in his pictures.

In 1630 festivities held in honour of the canonization of San Fernando[2] were celebrated with the lavish pageantry that was customary for these occasions: temporary triumphal arches, illuminations, liturgical celebrations and theatrically staged ceremonies very similar to those which occurred during the feast of Corpus Christi, which were studied by Sentaurens as part of Seville's theatrical life.[3] It is worth remembering that artistic spectacles were not confined to theatres or galleries as they are today. The city was

fig. 27 Anonymous artist of the 16th century *Hospital del Pozo Santo during the Plague of 1649* (Hospital del Pozo Santo, Seville)

literally immersed in a tide of cultural events that were accessible to everyone and dependent on wide popular participation. When some celebration was being prepared, private individuals vied with each other to decorate their houses as richly as they could afford, and the guilds erected temporary constructions and organized processions in which sacred, historical and mythological characters were all mixed up together. The people regarded these free spectacles as a service from and to the community; they acted as a catharsis in that rigid hierarchical society, momentarily suppressing or disguising differences and uniting all in communal celebrations. The violent reaction caused by Archbishop Palafox's attempt to suppress the dances during the festival of Corpus Christi can therefore be understood.[4]

Fiestas never disappeared from Seville; even today some, such as the *Cruces de Mayo* (May Crosses), survive. But their greater or lesser brilliance reflected the ups and downs of Seville life. Murillo's childhood years belonged to the period when Seville was, beyond dispute, the foremost city of Spain. Madrid's rising star had been halted by the Court's transfer to Valladolid, and it was some time after its return in 1606 before everyone was convinced there would be no more changes. Other cities, possible competitors, remained far behind. Thirty years later the 130,000 inhabitants of Seville at the end of the sixteenth century were somewhat reduced by the epidemic of 1599, by the expulsion of the *moriscos* (Moslem converts to Christianity), and above all, by the first symptoms of economic decline, which become very noticeable from 1635 onwards: taxes on wages and prices, anti-inflationary measures, a decrease in trade with the Indies and a series of bad harvests. Even so, Seville was still famous as a wealthy metropolis and, among Western cities, only Paris, London and Naples surpassed it in size of population; Madrid, Lisbon, Venice and Amsterdam were more or less equal in scale.

The seven years from 1633 to 1640 which coincided with Murillo's early youth and adolescence, while not a time of insuperable difficulty for Seville, certainly witnessed increasing troubles. Seville was subject to repercussions from the many conflicts in which the monarchy was involved, particularly the war with France from 1635 onwards, the interminable hostilities in Flanders and the Thirty Years War. In Seville, a large commercial centre, the repercussions – increasing taxation, recruitment, the raising of levies from property holders, the confiscation of the goods of the French colony – were particularly hard hitting.

From 1640 disaster followed disaster: the uprising in Catalonia; the separation of Portugal from Spain which started a new war close to Seville; growing insecurity on the shipping lanes; intolerable taxation; levies and conscription; fluctuating currency values; growing social tension and unrest; and the dismissal of the Count-Duke Olivares, which solved nothing. There were two other events peculiar to the region that strongly affected the inhabitants of Seville: the plague of 1649 and the popular uprising of 1652. The revolt was short-lived, but it finally showed that the people's capacity for tolerating their lot had reached a limit. It was a cry of protest that sounded in other Andalusian towns, also to little effect.[5] The plague of 1649 was a devastating event with long-term repercussions (fig. 27). We are fairly well informed about it; Chaunu, an expert on the subject, considered that after this catastrophe Seville ceased to be Seville; another city that had the same name, but lacked the universal dimensions of the earlier one, took its place.

Yet the plague, with its terrible holocaust (some 60,000 dead, in other words half the population), was in reality only the final detonator of a change that had already silently taken place. Seville had already lost its primacy in trade with the Indies (merchants preferred the ports of the Gulf of Cádiz) and this, together with other adversities, had so undermined the Andalusian city's prosperity that, after 1649, the population started to decline. People still arrived from all over the peninsula and Seville continued to be a cosmopolitan and colourful city, but the number of inhabitants did not exceed 80,000 until nearly two centures later.

In terms of population, it was still Spain's second largest city but the atmosphere was very different. The living standard of all civilians was very much lower, but the ecclesiastics were still able to defend their interests thanks to tithes, the inalienable possessions of the church and the donations that continued to flow in. Amongst laymen, collective misfortune intensified piety and encouraged the rejection of worldly goods, the vanity of which was becoming evident; at the same time the ravages of the epidemic reinforced the Spanish inclination to meditate upon death and survival, and increased the desire to intercede for souls in purgatory and store up merit for the life to come. This mental climate was not new; this climate, in which Heaven and Hell with their attendant hopes and fears were intimately bound up with daily life, removed rather than emphasized the frontiers between life and death. In our secular society, we are intent on separating suffering and

fig. 29 Convento de los Padres Capuchinos, Seville

death from the living by relegating it to separate places and surrounding it with scientific 'care', while at the same time trying to make man forget that his destiny is death and that continuity and a community of ideas, feelings and interests must exist between the living and the dead. In those centuries, a corpse was not a disagreeable sight that had to be kept apart, but a being who continued living his own life and who, in exchange for prayers, offerings and remembrance, afforded his family protection and intercession. None of this was new, these ideas were forcibly expressed in the Middle Ages; but they were reinforced by the experience of the seventeenth century, particularly in towns afflicted by frightful holocausts, such as Seville. It was at this period that devotion to souls in purgatory was intensified: fraternities whose aim was to procure intercession and decent burial for its brothers were formed. Their names are expressive: the orders of *Los Agonizantes* (Order of the Dying), *Cristo del Buen Fin* (Christ of the Good End), *Cristo de la Buena Muerta* (Christ of the Good Death), and paintings representing the Death of the Just and other related subjects were widespread. The Church won material benefit from its burial rights and from the establishment of chaplaincies and anniversaries; the Society of the Dead had its own income and was administered by the Church.

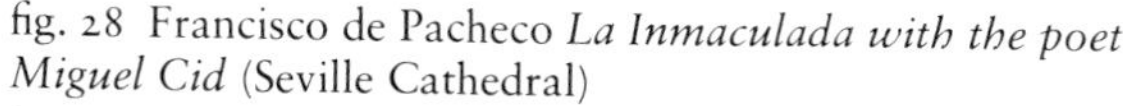

fig. 28 Francisco de Pacheco *La Inmaculada with the poet Miguel Cid* (Seville Cathedral)

Nevertheless, the intensity of the crisis was underlined by the drop in the number of monastic foundations. In the year of Murillo's birth, there were 33 monasteries and 27 convents; another ten institutions (nine for men and one for women) were founded before 1649. From then on, foundations were virtually suspended; there were only two or three more up to the time of the disentailment of church property in 1836.

But these figures should not be interpreted as a decline in the piety of the people of Seville, or in the Church's artistic patronage. No more convents were founded because those that existed were already excessive for an impoverished city. Yet work in the existing establishments was continued; old images and altars were replaced by others in keeping with new artistic styles, and parish churches and convents gave way to chapels, hospitals and houses for lay sisters. There was terrible inequality in the division of income; cathedral canons were very rich, while the canons of El Salvador were hardly able to support themselves; the Charterhouse was wealthy, but Miguel Cid, who was the poet of the Immaculate Conception (fig. 28), left a thousand masses to the Convent of San Francisco de Paula 'because it is very poor'[7]. The Capuchin friars who took possession of their convent and church opposite the Córdoba gate in 1627 (fig. 29) were doubtless also very poor; they were able to embellish their buildings with Murillo's paintings because this great artist venerated them and freely offered his extraordinary talents – and because they received donations.

The case of the Hospital de la Caridad (figs. 30, 31) was different again. Although it was of ancient origin, it did not become famous and active until a rich merchant, Don Juan de Mañara, had a spiritual crisis in 1661 and dedicated himself, body and soul, to aiding the helpless sick and to burying the dead whose corpses were unclaimed; the executed felons, for example. Mañara carried with him many members of the Seville upper middle-class, who devoted a good part of their profits to charity. It is known, for example, that Bucarelli gave more than 20,000 ducats, and that Don Francisco Gómez de Castro, one of the wealthiest *Indianos* (Spaniards who had returned rich from the Americas), appointed the Hospital heir to his immense fortune. It can be calculated that from 1661 to 1679, the years during which Mañara directed the Fraternity, a million ducats was spent on works and on help for the poor.[8]

fig. 30 Hospital de la Caridad, Seville; patio

These figures prompt various lines of thought. One concerns the continuing importance of mercantile activity in Seville; there was still trade with the Indies (despite the fact that by this time a large part had already moved to Cádiz) and also with other countries of Europe. As the rolls of its various boards show, the merchant groups in the *Consulado* (a mixture of guild and mercantile court) were numerous; the *Casa de Contratación* (House of Trade) stayed in Seville and half a century would elapse before it was moved to Cádiz. There were less *flotas* (shipping convoys), but they were probably as rich as, or even richer than, earlier ones.

The *compradores de plata* (silver buyers) who took charge of the ingots, refined them and then transferred them to be worked at the Mint, formed part of a profession that was exclusive to Seville. We know their names and their activities; one of them, Bernardo de Valdés, aged 24, was famous for his generosity. As the convoys were no longer annual – they sailed at two or three-yearly intervals – the Mint's activity was intermittent. Despite directives that unworked silver should be shared out for minting among several cities, almost all of it was minted in Seville, both to avoid transport costs and to placate the impatience of treasure owners who needed a fast turn-over in order to pay their debts and to re-invest it in the purchase of merchandise for the next convoy. In the intervals, the Mint workers were unemployed unless the Government gave them the job of minting and restamping *vellón* money (copper coinage). But other Castilian mints had taken over this poorly rewarded task from Seville.

Trade with the Indies was mostly in agricultural products (wine and oil); there was little industrial investment although Seville continued to send quantities of textiles, books and artistic objects, but the commission and dues earned in Seville still mounted to a significant sum. Although Camoen's words written in the preceding century certainly no longer held true:

The two extremities of the terrestrial globe
depend on Seville and on Lisbon

Seville still counted in the world, and if its material riches declined, its artistic wealth continued to accumulate. In those days, social welfare and cultural advancement were not funded through state channels but by private intitiative, no doubt less comprehensive and less systematic, but perhaps tinged with more generosity and human warmth. A good example of both charity and patronage is furnished by the foundation Mañara sponsored, into which aristocrats and merchants poured the treasure of a Seville that was declining but still held true to its traditions.

fig. 31 Hospital de la Caridad, Seville; church façade

fig. 32 Archbishop's Palace, Seville; main entrance

The accounts of the Caridad Fraternity prompt another thought: given its wealth, it could pay well for its commissions. In the prevailing scale of values, Murillo was handsomely rewarded for his pictures for the Hospital de la Caridad. For *St. Elizabeth of Hungary* and *St. John of God* (figs. 21 and 20), he received 8,240 *reales* each (the *reale* was equivalent to 150 *pesetas*, or 80 pence today). It was considerably more than Valdés Leal was paid for his altarpiece; and much more than the 1,000 reales Juan de Mesa asked for his *Cristo del Amor*, even taking into account that prices had doubled in the half-century or more that had elapsed. In any event, the modest prices Murillo asked for his work are surprising, particularly if we compare them with the hurry of many of today's professionals to amass a large fortune.

Murillo invested in property in Seville and in Pilas where his wife came from. Velázquez, in spite of being a confidant and friend of the world's most powerful monarch, had to add the heavy duties of quartermaster-general of the king's household to his post of court painter in order to augment his scanty income. Murillo and Valdés Leal were exceptions; they had work and their pay was reasonable yet not excessive. But at the end of the seventeenth century, the guild system as a whole was in a difficult position: not only were many of its members in permanent or semi-permanent unemployment but, in spite of the excellence of their work, they continued to find themselves looked on with the suspicion that all activity calling for manual labour aroused in that punctilious society. The more fortunate painters were able to pay for a clerk or an apprentice to prepare canvases, grind colours and do the other 'mean and mechanical' jobs that were incompatible with the 'purity of function', an obsession that came to be nearly as strong as the 'purity of blood'.

Thus, we see the painter's guild joined in a battle already more than a century old, one going back to the lawsuit El Greco fought to avoid having to pay *alcabala* (sales tax) on his paintings. The frontier between artisan and artist continued to be blurred, and each time a sumptuary law was promulgated, negotiations to have painting recognized as a liberal art were renewed. In 1692, when Murillo was already dead, this aspiration was revived yet again by Seville's painters: they wanted to be excluded from the prohibition forbidding the wearing of silk by artisans. Up to a point, the Council of Castile gave them satisfaction, ruling that

'professors and master-craftsmen of the Art of Painting in the city of Seville should not apply the prohibition to themselves but only to apprentices and those who work in the masters' studios and workshops for a daily wage.'[10]

Did the acute social and economic crisis of the second half of the seventeenth century play a part in the decline of standards in the Seville school of painting? If there was a correlation between Seville's boom and the summit of its artistic achievements, there must also have been an all-time trough for both as well. Acknowledged masters, such as Murillo and Valdés Leal, still got important commissions but their followers had difficulty in finding work. They did not have the means to travel from their studios and foreign artists no longer arrived in numbers, as they had in the sixteenth century. Something of that lack of communication which was to damage the development of Spanish science so badly, also occurred in the artistic field. The inherent abilities of the people of Seville in 1700 would not have been inferior to those of their fathers and grandfathers, and they were able to benefit from the accumulated experience of a century, but they lived in a more difficult and less stimulating climate, in which the fight for daily bread was hard, leaving less margin for artistic endeavour and for luxuries. How many lost vocations! How many wasted talents!

And that was in a city where there was still wealth, even if very unevenly distributed. In other cities the picture is more obscure. Recent historians have questioned the decline of Spain under Charles II and have claimed there was a recovery in the last years of that century. My personal opinion, stated elsewhere,[11] is that this recovery, although in no way spectacular, did occur in some provinces but not in lower Andalusia, excepting Cádiz and the surrounding area. Historical accounts and documents are clear enough; Murillo's mature years coincided with a series of disasters interspersed with a few better years.

Some preachers, possessed by an extreme fervour typical of a religiosity that saw sin in every manifestation of profane joy, manipulated and exacerbated a depressing state of affairs. Fra Tirso González, a famous missionary who became the Jesuits' Vicar General, had acquired a great name in Seville after he converted a number of Moorish slaves during one of his overseas missions. In 1677, the city was terrified by an epidemic which engulfed a large part of Andalusia, and a repetition of the plague of 1649 was feared. He promised the city that if the theatre was shut, it would remain free from infection; the civil and religious authorities acted accordingly, in spite of the fact that the plays performed were completely harmless from the moral point of view. Thus, dramatic art in Seville ended, and was not restored for more than a century.

However, the closure of the theatre did not produce many material advantages; crops were bad for several years. The famine in 1678 was frightful; a loaf of bread cost 5 *reales*, a farm-labourer's wage. An earthquake in 1680 left the city's old buildings so weakened that coaches were prohibited from driving around the city in order to prevent the collapse of buildings. In the same year the value of *vellón* money,

fig. 33 Santa María la Blanca, Seville; interior

which had been artificially raised to fund the Royal Exchequer, was depreciated; this measure was intended to cut inflation and to abolish the *premio* or subsidy on silver. This step did not affect the wealthy landowners or those who hoarded gold and silver coin, but it left merchants and the general public ruined; this, and the persistence of adverse weather conditions – years of drought alternating with others of excessive rainfall – eventually plunged Seville and the whole region into a severe crisis. Thousands had recourse to the charity that the Archbishop Ambrosio de Spínola shared out, as did the Cartuja de las Cuevas (the Charterhouse), the Caridad Fraternity and other charitable institutions and persons, 'so that although want was widespread, nobody died of hunger' as one historian, who witnessed these events, asserted.[12]

Such was the situation in Seville during the last years of Murillo's life. In the Caridad's archives, there is a list of the poor, parish by parish, which serves to show the extent of beggary. But it is not possible to measure it exclusively in terms of the thousands who milled around the gateway of the bishop's palace, waiting to receive the loaves distributed by the Archbishop; many others, some from well-known families, who did not dare ask for alms in public, stayed at home in the hope of receiving some discreet charity that would not offend their dignity. In the parish of Feria alone, there were 163 of these 'ashamed' poor.[13]

It is well known that times of crisis deepen class divisions. Seville society was far more integrated at the end than at the beginning of the seventeenth century: the Moors had been expelled and almost all the slaves, who up to 1640 had formed an important proportion of the urban population, had disappeared. The Inquisition continued to persecute Jews but almost all the Jews involved were of Portuguese origin; the majority of *conversos* (Spanish Jews converted to Christianity) had been assimilated into the population. The foreign colony had also decreased; less foreigners arrived because the opportunities for gain had lessened. Surnames of trans-Pyrenean origin continued to be numerous but, in the main, these families had been fully integrated with local society. For professional reasons, Murillo had contact with several of them: Miguel Mañara, son of Tomas Mañara from the island of Corsica, who was fabulously rich, like the Lecas and the Corzos families (fig. 15). The Bucarellis came from Italy; Justino de Neve, patron of the parish of Santa María la Blanca (fig. 33) and founder of the Hospital de los Venerables Sacerdotes (fig. 34) belonged to one of the Flemish families who had made their fortune in trade with the Indies. Archbishop Ambrosio de Spínola was of Genoese descent. The list could be lengthened, but in each case, we reach the same conclusion: these men, whatever their origin, had been transformed into genuine Seville citizens, passionate converts in many cases.

On the other hand, class differences had widened because, even though many in the upper and middle classes had suffered from the consequences of the devaluation of National Debt annuities (*juros*) and from other financial burdens engendered by interminable wars, and although a considerable number of merchants had been bankrupted, the privileged classes in general had been better able to resist the blows of adverse fortune, aided by the institution of primogeniture, which assured the continuance of the family inheritance. Several families increased the size of their estates, and one of the characteristics of the period was the concentration of rural property. Seville, like all the cities of the *ancien régime*, lived primarily off agrarian rents.

The people, on the other hand, had suffered more intensely from the effects of crises, wars and taxes. They had had a moment of outrage in 1652, and then returned to their habitual acceptance of things. It was a situation of injustice alleviated by charity, and of latent protest offset by age-old resignation in the face of a way of life that was considered inevitable and to which alternatives were not perceived. With the same matter-of-factness they accepted that class differences should be reflected by external signs: food, clothing, housing. Properly speaking, there were no residential quarters in seventeenth-century Seville, no rich districts, although some were more plebeian and others more distinguished, but in all there were palaces, ancestral seats that formed a contrast with the modest housing of artisans and with the picturesque tenements, home of the disinherited classes.[14]

We can imagine Murillo's Seville, but only imagine it, for Seville, homeland of several great painters, did not have a Guardi or a Canaletto to leave us a visual record of its urban landscape. Antonio Sancho Corbacho's carefully compiled *Iconografía sevillana* testifies to this gap; there are very few pictorial reproductions of seventeenth-century Seville. There are some fairly accurate overall views and engravings of its main monuments, but the appearance of its streets and alleyways, its houses and the life that animated them eludes us. Certainly, an expert on that period could reconstruct the city by using Olavide's plan (essentially Seville had not changed for a century), and this could be supplemented by using both existing and demolished buildings of which pictures have survived and by referring to municipal documents and literary descriptions. In spite of the demolition carried out in the last decades, small corners and sometimes even entire streets have survived to preserve the image of a city of great contrasts, where a religious building is found every few metres, where opulence and poverty rub shoulders, where next to a sumptuous palace stands a poor dwelling, disguising its poverty with flowers and the whitewashed walls as has always been done in Andalusia.

Large areas of Seville remained semi-deserted after 1649,

fig. 34 Hospital de los Venerables Sacerdotes, Seville; church interior

fig. 35 Seville Cathedral; sacristy

especially in the northern parishes and in the popular parts where the plague had hit most severely; in San Gil, San Román, Santa Lucía and elsewhere, many houses were replaced by orchards or allotments. There was no accommodation problem in Seville; the only problem was for proprietors, who had to let their houses for peppercorn rents because empty property deteriorated rapidly. At least half the urban property in Seville belonged to the Town Council (the *Cabildo*), religious and lay communities and fraternities. The drop in rents, ground rents and National Debt annuities (*juros*) following the successive cuts imposed by a government permanently on the brink of bankruptcy, explain the poor state of housing, the crisis in the industries associated with building and the lack of resources of the many persons and institutions that had entrusted their savings to investments that they had considered steady and safe. This, for example, was what happened to the Casa Cuna (an orphanage studied in an exemplary monograph by Alvarez Santaló[15]) which, together with its unfortunate pupils, was bankrupted when its resources failed. There remained alms, but in those days, so many were asking!

Hundreds of coaches, a rich man's privilege, ran through those narrow, winding streets, the authorities limiting these on many occasions because of the problems that they caused. The desire for a coach was not simply a matter of prestige; it was also related to the inconvenience of going on foot along extremely badly paved streets, dusty in summer, muddy in winter, and almost all of them prodigiously dirty. In the street plan compiled by S. Montoto, there are seven which have the name 'dirty', not because other streets were clean but because these were particularly dirty. The least populated areas in the north of the city were especially rich in dunghills and rubbish tips (rubbish heaped against the city walls reached up to the battlements): the nobleman or burgher, leaving his comfortable house, had to confront a network of thoroughfares that were infected, evil-smelling, ill-lit and dangerous; this was why he wanted to have a coach and an escort of lackeys. Service was one of the few cheap and plentiful commodities available.

An imaginary walk through the Seville of those days would be pleasant as well as instructive. Limited by space, I shall restrict myself to saying that at every step the traveller would be halted by something exceptional or picturesque, distasteful or attractive, but in each case very different from the dull housing estates and the look-alike crowds of today. He would see gentlemen wearing swords rubbing shoulders with beggars, porters, petty crooks and vagrant children, with the carefree gaiety of the age in spite of their hunger and near-nakedness. He would see, as Labat saw in 1706, monks seated on mules 'with large hats and enormous glasses', slaves branded on the forehead or cheek, high society ladies accompanied by their *duennas*, village women and street vendors (small-time hagglers of ill-repute but indispensable because there was no central market and retailers were needed in the outlying districts). If he had the right instinct, he would also discover prostitutes and pimps, for as Cervantes wrote, this was a profession that no well-ordered commonwealth could do without. But following the moralizing wave that spilled over into the 1623 law ordering the closure of brothels, prostitution was illegal. Inmates, under the care of the brothel's 'father', no longer waited for clients in the Compás de la Laguna. Prostitution still existed of course, but it was hidden and, therefore, uncontrolled and more dangerous, as was proved by the crowd of patients in the bubo hospital devoted to the cure of syphilitics.

The religiosity, although in some ways excessive, was sincere. It is necessary to emphasize this because it is sometimes written that such a spiritual state could only be the result of hypocrisy, social pressure or fear of the Inquisition. So it was in specific cases, but not in general because pious manifestations arose spontaneously. The overwhelming predominance of religious painting in the Seville school did not stem from Church patronage alone; private buyers also wanted to have religious pictures and there was not a family, however poor, that did not have some image in its home. A similar feeling multiplied the number of images and small altars in the city streets. The motives for crosses were more varied: some commemorated miraculous or unlucky events, such as a violent death; others signalled the site of a cemetery, the Plaza del Salvador for example (the little squares opposite parish churches used to serve as cemeteries); and not a few times crosses were put or painted on walls in the hope of keeping away those who approached them intent on satisfying the call of nature.

fig. 36 Murillo *The Immaculate Conception of the Capuchins* (Museo de Bellas Artes, Seville)

Within this framework of religious exaltation there were several persistent themes, and they inspired sculptors and painters. Local sainthood was one such theme: Santa Justa and Santa Rufina, San Isidoro and San Leandro, and, among those newly canonized during the seventeenth century, San Hermengildo and San Ferdinando, two kings (a curious union of monarchic and religious sentiments) who, although not born in Seville, were closely linked to the city on the banks of the Guadalquivir. Devotion to the Eucharist in all its forms, especially everything related to Maundy Thursday and Corpus Christi, was another theme. We have already referred to the wave of pro-Marian feeling in 1616–17. There was a second upsurge but it lacked the intensity of the first because, without proclaiming the dogma, the Holy See had already inclined towards 'pious opinion'. In 1654, the Octave of the Immaculate Conception was celebrated for the first time in Seville Cathedral. In 1662, following Alexander VII's papal brief in favour of the Immaculate Conception, solemn festivities were enacted. In 1663, the Town Council commissioned a sermon from the Carmelite friar, Brother José de Valasco; although he did not pronounce against devout opinion, certain reservations were detected in his sermon and this was sufficient for him to be denounced to the Conception Committee in Rome. The Roman authorities absolved him from the faults imputed against him; nevertheless, when his co-religionists elected him Provincial for Andalusia, an outcry, serious enough to claim the attention of the Council of Castile, resulted. Even in 1670, passions were inflamed by such an issue.

It is very difficult to evoke the atmosphere in which Murillo lived in a few pages. I hope, however, that these notes may be useful for those who are interested in the work of the great Seville master, who is now, after a long and unmerited eclipse, re-emerging to claim the attention of both public and critics.

NOTES

1. A compilation of several of the most vivid accounts has been published by F. Morales Padrón: *Memorias de Sevilla (Noticias sobre el siglo* XVII*)*, Córdoba, 1981.
2. Historians do not always express themselves clearly on this matter. What was celebrated in September 1630, was 'the function of bringing the *remissoriales* for the canonization of the holy King Ferdinand'. The actual canonization was celebrated in the year 1671 (also with important festivities – and Murillo was involved in creating the 'triumphal machine' stationed in the cathedral sacristy).
3. In his unpublished doctoral thesis *El Teatro en Sevilla*, (University of Bordeaux-Talence).
4. These well-known incidents took place in the last decade of the century. (See, for example, *Los Seises de la Catedral de Sevilla*, by Don Simón de la Rosa).
5. A. Domínguez Ortiz: *Alteraciones andaluzas*, Madrid, Narcea, 1973.
6. To the earlier works of Caldera de Heredia, Velázquez y Sanchez (*Anales epidémicos de Sevilla*) and others, we shall add only two modern studies: that already cited in Note 1, rich in first-hand accounts, and the unpublished paper, *La población de Sevilla en las series parroquiales de los siglos* XVI-XIX, by L.C. Alvarez Santaló, in the conference on The Modern History of Andalusia, which took place in Córdoba; it cites figures that confirm the magnitude of the catastrophe.
7. His testament, revealing about the mentality of the average man in Seville, was published by Rodríguez Jurado in the *Boletín de la Academia Sevillana de Buenas Letras*, September 1919.
8. Jesús María Granero, S. J.: *D. Miguel de Mañara. Un caballero sevillano del siglo* XVII, Seville, 1963.
9. This point is not entirely clear in spite of the investigation of writers such as Lutgardo García and Michel Morineau. But this is not an opportune place to deal with this problem.
10. National Historical Archive, Councils, 51.436–6, consultation of 10 May 1692.
11. See, for example, 'La crisis de Castilla en 1677–1687' in *Crisis y decadencia en la España de los Austrias*.
12. Morales Padrón, op cit., p. 142.
13. Granero, op cit. This document has been used by M.E. Perry in an unpublished thesis (H. Kamen, *La España de Carlos* II, ch. XI, note 4).
14. Morales Padrón: *Los corrales de Sevilla*.
15. *Marginación social y mentalidad en Andalucía Occidental: Espósitos en Sevilla*, Seville, 1980
16. There is documentation on this episode in the A.H.N. (National Historical Archive) in Madrid (Councils, file 7, 180, no. 25) and in some pamphlets in the university library of Granada (A–31–131, nos 5 and 6).

Art and Decline in Seventeenth-Century Spain

John H. Elliott

In the winter of 1683–84 Samuel Pepys seized the opportunity afforded by a visit on government business to Tangier to cross over into Spain and do some sight-seeing in Andalusia. This at least was the intention, but during his six weeks in Seville it poured with rain. Neither prayers in the city's churches, nor solemn processions through its streets, succeeded in halting the torrential downpour, which put a sad damper on Pepys's sight-seeing, and – to his intense disappointment – prevented him from making a trip to Málaga. But nothing – not even the rain in Spain – could dampen Pepys's habitual curiosity. Although he did not keep a diary during those weeks in Spain, he did jot down notes on points that attracted his attention, or 'contraries' and 'extraordinaries' as he called them: 'no chimneys in Spain'; 'rare to see a Spaniard drunk'; 'fleas are a mighty plague in houses'; 'no chamber-pots in all the country.'[1]

For all the sharpness of observation, it is sad that we do not have the more considered reflections of this most qualified of English tourists on the country which was still, at the time of his birth in 1633, the greatest power in Europe. How much one would have given to have heard the views of this robust representative of a rising Britain on a declining Spain! But his one summary judgement is predictably harsh:

> *Men of the Toga who have never been in the World do govern all in Spain, and men of the Spada [the sword] are put into most employments at sea without knowing anything of their business, and so their state is governed and will be lost. In a word, never were a people so overrun with fools in all states as they are.*[2]

If this should seem the characteristically arrogant remark of a supercilious foreigner, it is worth noting the comment of a Spaniard who complained to Pepys about 'how their country is under a fatality in all their businesses of state.' This despairing observation reflects a mood of fatalism which had become fashionable in seventeenth-century Spain. As early as 1600, twelve years after the defeat of the Invincible Armada, an acute observer of the economic and social problems of his native Castile used the word *declinación* – 'decline' – in relation to its condition.[3] The notion of decline – a decline of power, a decline of prosperity, a decline of national greatness – was often evoked in the following decades by ministers and government officials, and by the numerous commentators and analysts who anxiously diagnosed the state of the Spanish body politic and prescribed a wide variety of differing and often contradictory remedies to effect a cure.[4] The image seemed especially appropriate because of its associations with the fate of another great empire, that of ancient Rome.

The analogies between the Roman and Spanish experience had always been regarded as close, and now, in the seventeenth century, became painfully closer. Sixteenth-century Spain, under the government successively of Ferdinand and Isabella, of the Emperor Charles V, and then of Philip II, had conquered and colonized a world-wide empire, even greater than that of Rome. The language of Castile, its laws, its arms, were supreme over wide portions of the globe. Here was an empire on which, as Ariosto had said, the sun never set.

Or so at least it was thought. But then, after a series of shocks and setbacks, the mood began to change. The crisis of confidence can be traced back to the last few years of the sixteenth century. The defeat of the Armada came as a severe psychological shock to a Castile which had come to think of itself as the chosen nation of the Lord. The death of the old king, Philip II, in 1598, meant change after decades of firm and well-tried government – change to a young and manifestly ineffectual new king, Philip III, who abandoned his father's practice of poring far into the night over state papers, and entrusted the business of government to the hands of favourites. Then, in 1599–1600, Castile and Andalusia were hit by famine and plague, which claimed perhaps half a million victims in a population of some six million. On top of this, acute financial troubles, culminating in state bankruptcies, forced Spain into peace – with the French in 1598, the English in 1604, and into a humiliating twelve-year truce with the rebellious Dutch in 1609. The Spain of these years was the Spain of Don Quixote, of which the first part appeared in 1605 and the second in 1615 – a Spain which, like a bemused knight errant, showed signs of having lost its bearings in a changing world. 'It seems', wrote a Castilian commentator as he surveyed the parasitic rentier society with its extravagant dreams and conspicuous consumption and neglect of economic realities, 'it seems as if one had wished to reduce these kingdoms to a republic of enchanted beings, living outside the natural order of things.'[5]

There were many moralists in the Spain of Philip III who felt that something had happened to Castile's moral fibre, and again they recalled the Roman analogy. One of them quoted Sallust to the effect that 'when a kingdom reaches such a point of moral corruption that men dress like women,... that the most exquisite delicacies are imported for its tables, and men go to sleep before they are tired..., then it can be regarded as lost, and its empire at an end.'[6] It is not surprising, then, to find that in 1621, on the death of Philip III, a new regime comes to power on a wave of popular acclaim – a regime committed to an austere programme of economic and moral reform. The new king, the 16-year old Philip IV, chose as his principal minister a man of very different stamp from his predecessors: Don Gaspar de Guzmán, known to history as the Count-Duke of Olivares (fig. 37). He was a ruthlessly energetic and authoritarian figure, who was determined to save his country from disaster and bring about a great national revival. For two decades, the

1620s and 1630s, Spain felt the smack of stern and purposeful government.

Olivares sought on the one hand to restore Spain's former imperial grandeur, reviving its military virtues and leading it back to war. On the other, he embarked on a programme for national recovery, grappling with the problem of inflation and planning a whole series of measures to increase productivity. But the two decades of the Count-Duke's government ended in disaster. Reform had to be sacrificed to war, and the crippling burden of war taxation imposed intolerable strains on Spain's political and social fabric. In 1640 both Catalonia and Portugal revolted against the government of Philip IV, and although Catalonia later returned to allegiance, Portugal was lost for ever.

Sir Arthur Hopton, the British ambassador in Madrid during these years of disaster, wrote to London in 1641: 'I am induced to think that the greatness of this monarchy is near to an end.'[7] Two years later, in 1643, Olivares fell from power.

Hopton's judgment was right. Under Olivares, the Spain of the House of Austria had shot its final bolt. The second half of the reign of Philip IV was at best a holding operation, as a disillusioned and world-weary monarch struggled to maintain what he could of Spain's former power and primacy. On Philip's death in 1665, only the fragile life of his pathetic son, Charles II, stood in the way of the extinction of the male line of the dynasty.

The history of Spain during the last 35 years of the seventeenth century is often equated with the moribund existence of the last of the Spanish Habsburgs. This is not entirely fair. From around 1680 there are in fact some flickering signs of renewal, even in Castile, the depressed central region of the Iberian peninsula, which had borne the heaviest fiscal burdens. But the long-expected and long-delayed death of Charles II in 1700 effectively marks the end of an era.

Looking back over those hundred years between the death of Philip II in 1598 and of his great-grandson in 1700, there seems no good reason to contest the established view that this was the century of Spain's decline – a decline partially concealed from the world during the first decades of the century by the lingering survival of fading imperial glories and the short-lived burst of energy during the regime of Olivares. But the disasters of the 1640s stripped off the mask to reveal the hollowness within. The Spain of Murillo – the Spain visited by Samuel Pepys in 1683, the year following the artist's death – was a once-great imperial power reduced to second-class status, an object of European derision.

Yet when we speak of a country in decline, what do we really mean? To some extent the indicators of decline change with the perspective of different ages, but some of the characteristics of the Spanish condition appear instantly recognizable: a marked reduction in military and diplomatic effectiveness; an inability to generate new sources of wealth and to cope with the causes and consequences of inflation; a failure of leadership and a paralysis of the political will; the fossilizing of traditional institutions; a narrow, inward-looking frame of mind, given to excessive self-examination, and always prone to relapse into fatalism. These characteristics are all to be found in seventeenth-century Castile – a society with a vast, top-heavy bureaucracy, and an entrenched and privileged elite in church and state, a society of rentiers and parasites, clinging to its ancient ways and setting an exaggerated store by outward appearances.[8]

fig. 37 Velázquez *Portrait of the Count-Duke of Olivares* (Museo del Prado, Madrid)

But there is another possible angle of vision. Spain's century of decline, the seventeenth century, is also known as the Golden Age of its arts. In literature, it is the century of Cervantes, of Góngora and Quevedo; in the theatre, of Lope de Vega and Calderón and Tirso de Molina; and in painting, of El Greco, Ribera, Zurbarán, Velázquez and Murillo. The great creative impetus admittedly seems to belong to the first, rather than the second, half of the century. Calderón and Murillo, who died in 1681 and 1682 respectively, are generally represented as the last surviving giants in a land increasingly peopled by pygmies. But at least where painting is concerned, the verdict may have been prematurely returned. Inside Spain, and, still more, outside it, far too little

fig. 38 Velázquez *Portrait of Philip IV* (Museo del Prado, Madrid)

fig. 39 Alonso Sánchez Coello *Portrait of Philip II* (Museo del Prado, Madrid)

is known of the artists at work in the second half of the century; the Golden Age of Spanish painting may well have been too abruptly terminated by historians and art-historians anxious to ring down the curtain.

But whether or not Spain's Golden Age is prolonged beyond the death of Velázquez in 1660, the fact remains that a remarkable age of literary and artistic creativity coincided with an age of political and economic decline. This apparent paradox raises some difficult questions. Is there, or need there be, any correlation between a nation's cultural vitality and its economic performance? Is it possible that national misfortune actually serves as a stimulus to cultural achievement, whether by promoting an escapist search for alternative fields of endeavour, still unmarked by failure, or by giving artists and men of letters that extra dimension of awareness which enables them to see the realities beneath the glittering surface?

It is easier to find support for this last hypothesis in the realm of literature than of painting. *Don Quixote* is, after all, a brilliant disquisition on the complex relationship of illusion and reality. But how far can even Don Quixote be convincingly related to a crisis of confidence in a society which has begun to see itself as afflicted by the symptoms of decline?

When it comes to painting, the problem is still more difficult, for reasons suggested by a consideration of Velázquez's remarkable portrait of the aging Philip IV (fig. 38). At first glance it would seem that Velázquez had stripped away all the majesty of kingship to reveal the pathetic figure behind the mask – a weak, defeated and disillusioned man. But this is to ignore the Spanish tradition of royal portraiture to which Velázquez faithfully adhered. The Kings of Spain are normally depicted with great simplicity, and with none of the traditional appurtenances of royalty (fig. 39). This iconographical tradition, which persists to the end of the seventeenth century, reflects certain assumptions about Spanish kingship that tend to be overlooked. The Kings of Spain were the greatest monarchs in the world, and their greatness was taken for granted. Therefore there was no need to insist on the trappings of power, as the painters of lesser European monarchs tended to insist on them. The very austerity and simplicity of the king's image in Spanish painting was itself an indication of his overwhelming majesty. It may well be that Velázquez, as a supremely great artist, could not but reveal the human frailties of the king he served. But there seems no reason to doubt that the intention, at least, was to produce an official royal image, and it would be surprising if any contemporary read this portrait as a symbol either of the weakness of Spain's king or of the waning of its power.

The attempt to find hidden correspondences between the psychological or economic health of a society and its cultural creations is a hazardous enterprise, as the example of Velázquez's portrait of Philip IV suggests. In some instances at least, such correspondences may indeed exist, although perhaps at such a deep and subtle level that the writer or artist is himself unaware of them. In other instances, there seems to be no sign of correlation. It would be hard to deduce from the paintings of Murillo that he spent his working life in a country experiencing the traumas of economic crisis and military defeat, and in a city that suffered a catastrophic loss of population as the result of a devastating plague, and saw its prosperity ebbing away.

The example of Murillo suggests a need to move away from the more speculative aspects of the relationship between creativity and decline, and to examine the kind of circumstances that may have favoured artistic endeavour in seventeenth-century Spain, in spite of Castile's acute economic troubles. Some clues to the character of this society and the ways in which its organization, interests and aspirations helped to shape the work of the creative artist, can be gleaned from a survey of its three leading cities: Toledo, the spiritual capital of Habsburg Spain; Seville, its effective economic capital; and Madrid, its political capital. Certain recurring themes in the social and cultural history of Spanish urban society suggest a common underlying pattern, which makes more understandable the achievement of Murillo and his fellow artists.

It was in Toledo that El Greco settled in 1577, and here that he lived and worked until his death in 1614.[9] Toledo liked to think of itself as a second Rome. Its archbishop was a primate of Spain, and the archbishopric possessed vast revenues and enjoyed enormous influence. Periodically Toledo also served as the seat of the court until the decision of Philip II in 1561 to make Madrid his capital.

The fortunes of Toledo might almost be taken as symptomatic of the fortunes of Spain as a whole. In the mid-sixteenth century it was a flourishing city of some 60,000 inhabitants. It had a fine cathedral, an impressive clerical establishment, a resident local nobility and a small but respectable university. It also had an important merchant community, which derived its wealth from the sale and export of local manufactures – textiles, especially fine silks, and the famous Toledan steel blades.

But during the nearly 40 years of El Greco's residence in Toledo, its fortunes took a turn for the worse. Harvest failure made his first two years in the city, 1577 and 1578, two of the hungriest years in Toledo's history. While harvest failures were a normal hazard of the times, the late sixteenth century and the first two decades of the seventeenth saw a progressive weakening of the Toledan economy, for reasons not yet fully clear. The removal of the court to Madrid led to the departure of some of the local nobility, along with their spending power. But above all, there were growing difficulties in the textile industry, on which Toledo's prosperity depended, partly because of competition from cheaper foreign textiles, and partly because of the high level of taxation and the lack of incentives to invest. The resulting lack of work and opportunities precipitated a migration to Madrid, and by 1646 the city's population was down to 25,000 – less than half its size at the time of El Greco's arrival.

El Greco's Toledo, then, was a city beginning its slide into decline, although the situation seems only to have become acute in the years after his death in 1614. By that time the city authorities were expressing grave concern; but a royal official who was sent to examine the situation in 1619, and expected to find a desert, was still agreeably surprised: 'Although', he wrote, 'it enjoyed greater prosperity in the past, Toledo is less affected than anywhere else by the common decline from which these kingdoms are suffering.' The streets, he explained, were crowded, the houses occupied, the buildings well maintained.[10]

Consequently, at least into the reign of Philip IV, Toledo represents a case of very relative decline in comparison with many of the other cities of Castile. In El Greco's time it still boasted an extremely wealthy church and a civic elite of substantial families that had made their money in trade. It was among the members of this elite that El Greco found his patrons. Members of the great Toledan families – many of them educated in Toledo University – dominated municipal life and the cathedral chapter. They possessed an intense civic pride; a genuine interest in scholarship and learning; and a strong concern with religion.

It is not surprising that El Greco, who liked to think of himself as an intellectual artist, should have felt at home in this late Renaissance city. He may have been attracted to it in the first instance by Luis de Castilla, a Toledan cleric and classical scholar, who first made El Greco's acquaintance in Cardinal Farnese's household in Rome. Luis de Castilla was the illegitimate son of Diego de Castilla, dean of the Toledo cathedral chapter, and it was probably he who arranged for El Greco to be commissioned to paint *The Disrobing of Christ*, for the vestuary of the cathedral sanctuary (fig. 40).

fig. 40 El Greco *The Disrobing of Christ* (Toledo Cathedral)

El Greco was not the easiest or most obliging of artists as far as patrons were concerned. He came from Italy with an elevated image of the standing of the artist, to find that the artist in Spain was regarded as no more than an artisan, and paid an artisan's wages. But his contacts and friendships with leading members of Toledo's lay and clerical establishment proved to be his salvation. In times of trouble his friends would rally round, either because they enjoyed his company or recognized his genius, which stood out all the more strongly against the prevailing mediocrity of painting in Toledo at the time of his arrival. The workshop of El Greco was able to survive because the canons of Toledo, the scholars, the merchants, continued to come forward with requests for their portraits, and to commission altarpieces for their family chapels, or persuade convents and parish priests to follow suit.

Toledo, therefore, was still a relatively prosperous city with an affluent and enlightened civic elite; a city proud of its great traditions, but, at least in El Greco's day, in touch with the outside world. The enclosed and mystical character of religion in the Toledo of El Greco has been exaggerated in an attempt to explain the idiosyncracy of his paintings. The city was very much in the mainstream of orthodox Counter-Reformation spirituality, with its emphasis on the sacraments and the saints, and on pious and charitable works. But those decades saw a particularly strong movement for spiritual and ecclesiastical reform, under the direction of successive archbishops; and the intellectual life of the Toledan elite combined with the highly-charged religious atmosphere to create an ideal environment for El Greco – one in which he could develop to the full his virtuoso Mannerist style, so well adapted to capturing the kind of Counter-Reformation spirituality practiced in the city he had made his home.

In the second great city, Seville, where Velázquez was born in 1599, a similar pattern emerges.[11] Sixteenth-century Seville was the great metropolis of the western world, a city whose streets, at least in the popular imagination, were paved with the gold and silver of the Indies. By 1600, it was one of the largest cities in Europe, with a population of around 150,000. The life of this teeming port town was geared, like that of Spain, and indeed of all Europe, to the regular annual arrival of the New World treasure fleets. Trade with the New World was nearing its peak at the time of Velázquez's birth; but for the first two decades of the seventeenth century vast quantities of silver were still being shipped to Seville from the mines of Mexico and Peru. Although some of this silver belonged to the king, much of it was sent back on account to private individuals. The settler community in the Spanish Indies provided an expanding market for European goods, and especially for luxury items, which were purchased with American silver. Works of art were also in demand, and during the seventeenth century Seville studios turned out standard works for the American export trade: run-of-the-mill religious paintings for remote convents in Mexico or the Andes, or still-lifes for the houses of gentry and merchants in Cartagena, Lima and Mexico City.

But by 1640, under the impact of war and financial difficulties, the fleets were arriving with increasing irregularity, and Seville's American trade was clearly in deep trouble. Then, at the end of Spain's fateful decade of the 1640s, the city suffered a devastating plague, which wiped out half its population. Recovery was painfully slow, and the Seville visited by Pepys in 1683 was a much diminished city, living in the last sunset rays of the wealth of the Indies, as its primacy passed to Cádiz.

But the Seville of Velázquez and Zurbarán, and even the later seventeenth-century Seville of Murillo, remained

fig. 41 Murillo *Peasant Woman and Boy* (National Trust, Dyrham Park)

immensely wealthy in spite of its vicissitudes. Its wealth was inevitably distributed with extreme inequality – nowhere in Spain were the social contrasts starker. An affluent elite, reinforced by returning *indianos* (men who had made their fortunes in the Indies) indulged spectacularly in conspicuous consumption. But there was also a vast, poverty-stricken sub-world of unemployed and underemployed – vagabonds, rogues, street-urchins, casual labourers, dock-workers, hawkers, pedlars, water-sellers, all of them anxiously wondering where and how to get a square meal. According to Sancho Panza's grandmother, 'there are only two races in the world, the haves and the have-nots',[12] and the distinguishing criterion was food. Seventeenth-century Spanish society was obsessed with food. The contrasts are nowhere more neatly pointed than in two of Murillo's paintings: *The Prodigal Son Feasting* (Cat. 49; repr. on p. 126), which can be regarded as a seventeenth-century version of conspicuous consumption; and his *Peasant Woman and Boy* (fig. 41) with its depiction of life on the poverty line.

Seville, like Toledo, was dominated by a network of families, many of which had originally made their money in

fig. 42 Velázquez *Kitchen Scene with Christ in the House of Mary and Martha* (National Gallery, London)

trade, and then invested it in houses and land, in government bonds, in silver and precious objects. Like Toledo, it contained aristocratic families, like the Dukes of Alcalá and the Counts of Olivares, who played their part in municipal life and lived on fairly easy terms with the civic elite. It was a city, too, with strong civic pride, but because of its character as an emporium of trade, it was much more open than inland Toledo to external influences. It maintained close commercial ties not only with the New World, but also with Italy and the Netherlands. It is not therefore surprising that the young Velázquez, as apprentice, and then son-in-law, to the Sevillian artist Francisco Pacheco, should have had access to northern engravings, like Peter Aertsen's engraving of a *Woman Cleaning Fish, with the Supper at Emmaus*, which may have served as an inspiration for his kitchen scene in the National Gallery in London, with Christ in the house of Mary and Martha (fig. 42).

The Sevillian elite, like that of Toledo, was a cultivated elite, combining strong humanist interests with the doctrinal and practical concerns of Counter-Reformation Catholicism. Again, as in Toledo, the cathedral canons, drawn from the great city families, played an important part in the city's cultural life. They were prominent in the informal literary academies which sprang into existence in the sixteenth century, like that of Canon Pacheco, which on his death was taken over by his nephew, Francisco Pacheco.[13] Here the young Velázquez, who entered Pacheco's household as an apprentice in 1611, would have heard discussions on literary themes, artistic theory (fig. 43), and the great doctrinal issues of the day. One of the most intensely debated of these issues was the Immaculate Conception, which became a favourite subject for seventeenth-century Spanish artists, and especially those of Seville.

Seville was the most theatrical of Spanish cities. It conducted its civic and religious life in a splendid blaze of drama, with the whole city participating in the processions for the great religious occasions, organized by the church and the confraternities. In a city dedicated to display, those who had money were expected to spend it lavishly for the enjoyment of the community. The result was a high degree of private and corporate patronage, which naturally spilt over into commissions to local artists. A good proportion of this patronage, especially in the second half of the century after the plague of 1649, was directed towards religious and charitable foundations. It is therefore natural that much of the work of Murillo and his Sevillian contemporaries should have been commissioned by churches, confraternities and convents, like his *Return of the Prodigal Son* (Cat. 46; repr. on p. 119), commissioned by the confraternity of the Caridad – a brotherhood devoted to charitable works for the poor – for the church of their hospital.

Murillo himself was a member of this confraternity, and was in touch with many of the leading figures in the religious life of the city. One of these, and one of his closest friends, was a canon of Seville cathedral, Don Justino de Neve, of whom he produced a brilliant portrait (fig. 44). Neve was a characteristic Sevillian patron. He came of a family of rich Flemish merchants established in Seville; he became a canon in 1658, and devoted his wealth and energies to founding a hospital for elderly priests, the Hospital de los Venerables, to which he bequeathed his portrait on his death in 1685. The inventory of his possessions shows that he owned four large and four small clocks, one of which sits on the table beside him.[14]

It is significant that the Count-Duke of Olivares, the favourite and first minister of Philip IV, was a native of Seville – though of an earlier generation than Neve – and spent his formative years in the city, between 1607 and 1615. He was in touch with the city's leading scholars and writers. He was a well-known figure at meetings of the academies, including that of Pacheco, and he spent lavishly on cultural

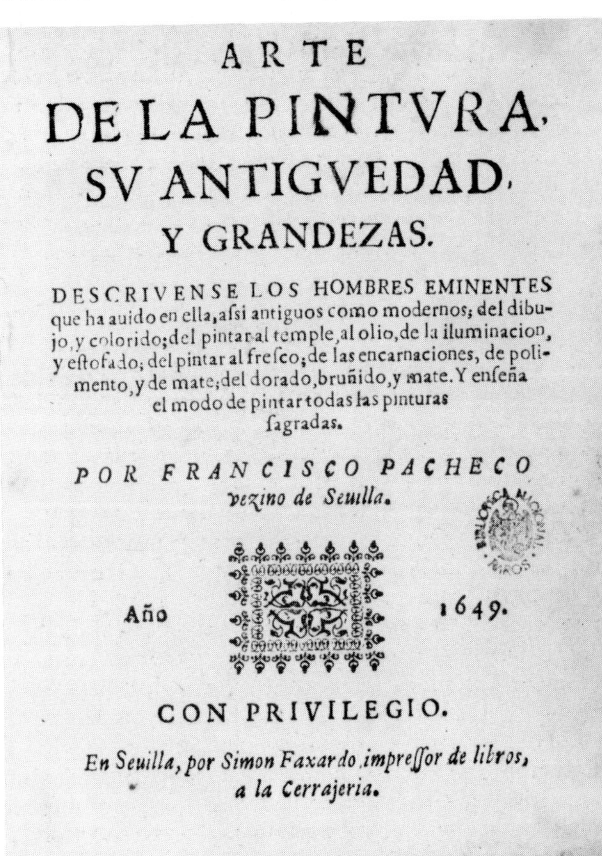

ARTE
DE LA PINTVRA,
SV ANTIGVEDAD,
Y GRANDEZAS.

DESCRIVENSE LOS HOMBRES EMINENTES que ha auido en ella, asſi antiguos como modernos; del dibujo, y colorido; del pintar al temple, al olio, de la iluminacion, y eſtofado; del pintar al freſco; de las encarnaciones, de polimento, y de mate; del dorado, bruñido, y mate. Y enſeña el modo de pintar todas las pinturas ſagradas.

POR FRANCISCO PACHECO
vezino de Seuilla.

Año 1649.

CON PRIVILEGIO.

En Seuilla, por Simon Faxardo, impreſſor de libros, a la Cerrajeria.

fig. 43 Title page of Francisco de Pacheco's *Tratado del Arte de la Pintura*, 1649

fig. 44 Murillo *Portrait of Don Justino de Neve* (National Gallery, London)

patronage. His own tastes ran more to books than paintings – he built up one of the great libraries of the seventeenth century – but his Seville years seem to have imbued him with a strong sense of the profound importance of patronizing and cultivating the arts and letters.

This attitude was to be of enormous importance when he acquired power at court in Madrid in 1621. Madrid – the late-comer in this trio of cities – was a boom town. In 1561, when Philip II chose it as his capital, it was little more than an overgrown village. By 1621 it had a population approaching 150,000, almost as large as that of Seville. It was a parasitic city, an artificial capital which lived for and off the court, and sucked in the wealth, not only of the surrounding region, including Toledo, but also of Spain's European and American possessions. For Madrid was the capital of a world-wide empire.

Madrid, therefore, like Toledo and Seville, boasted a wealthy, leisured elite – an elite, in this instance, of the high aristocracy who rented or built houses in Madrid to be near the king, and of government officials, who waxed fat on the legal and illegal perquisites of office. Already under Philip III (1598–1621) writers and artists were gravitating to Madrid in the search for patrons, and little coteries were forming around nobles with cultural interests; but the court of Philip III, whose interests did not extend beyond hunting, card-playing and church-going, set no very distinctive stamp on Madrid's cultural life. All this changed with the accession of Philip IV in 1621 and the advent of Olivares.

Olivares came to power with a clear sense of his mission – not only to revive the fortunes of a declining Spain, but also to make his royal master supreme in the arts both of war and peace. He wanted to make the court a brilliant centre of patronage, and he brought with him from Seville the traditions of his native city – splendour, stage-management, and generosity. And he also brought Sevillians. It was natural that he should give a welcome to writers and artists from his native city, not least among them the young Velázquez, who moved to Madrid in 1623 and became painter to the king. Under the inspired direction of Olivares the court of Philip IV blended the rather showy tastes and styles of Andalusia with the more sober traditions of the Spanish Habsburgs, whose official architecture continued to follow the austere lines of the Escorial.

Olivares set out to groom the 16-year old Philip for his destined role as the 'Planet King', the first luminary in the hierarchy of power and patronage. Philip embarked on an intensive reading course to supplement his very inadequate education; he was an enthusiastic theatre-goer; and he soon showed that he had a very discriminating eye for painting, like so many of his family. There seem to have been two critical events in the 1620s for his development as a patron and connoisseur. One was the extraordinary visit to Madrid in 1623 of Charles, Prince of Wales. For the first time, Philip found himself face to face with a prince of his own generation, who was far more refined than himself and had an insatiable thirst for pictures. He was quick to learn the lesson. The other great event of the 1620s was the visit in 1628–29 of Rubens. Philip spent long hours in his company, as also did Velázquez, discussing paintings in the royal collection with him, and watching him at work. Rubens's visit was decisive both for the king and Velázquez, opening up new vistas and giving them a genuinely European vision of contemporary trends in art. In 1629 Philip gave Velázquez

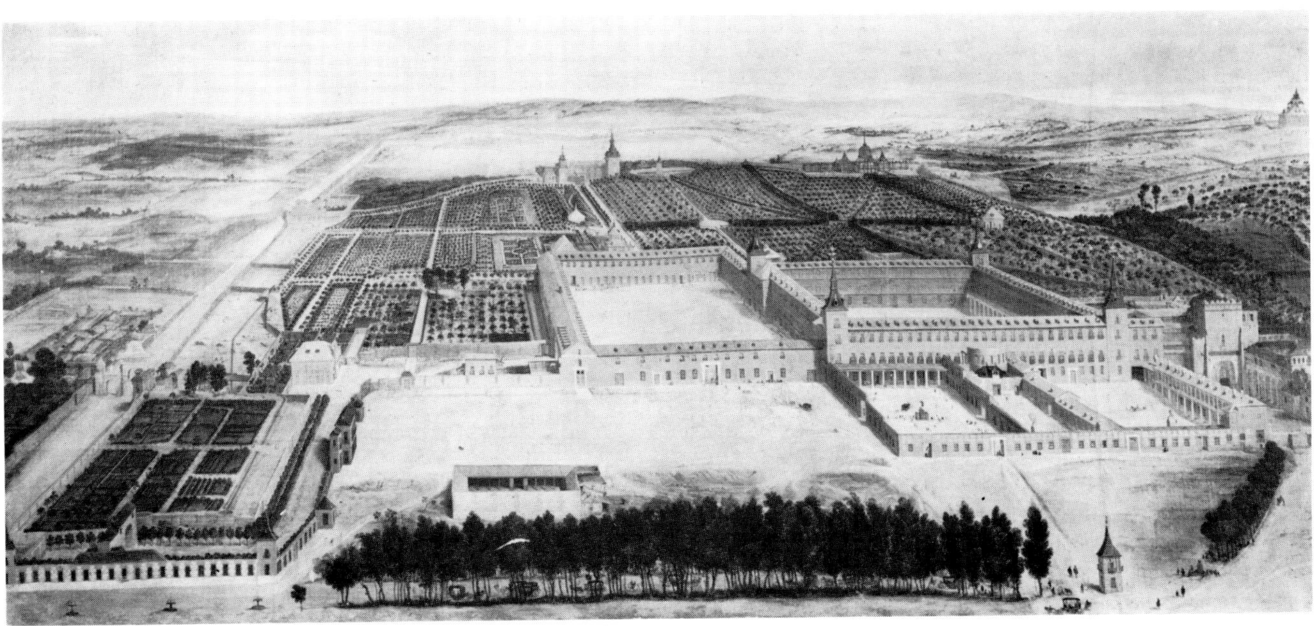

fig. 45 Jusepe Leonardo *View of the Buen Retiro Palace* (Palacio Real, Madrid)

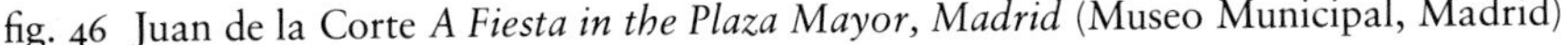

fig. 46 Juan de la Corte *A Fiesta in the Plaza Mayor, Madrid* (Museo Municipal, Madrid)

permission to visit Italy, in order to extend his knowledge of the great masters and get abreast of the most recent artistic developments. The opportunity had come at last for Spanish painting to break free from the rather archaic provincialism which until now had been one of its most distinctive features.

By the early 1630s, then, Philip IV had become exactly what Olivares had planned: the model of princely refinement, a discriminating connoisseur, a patron of arts and letters. All he lacked was a suitable setting in which to pursue his interests in the theatre and the arts. But Olivares provided him with this, too, by constructing for him the pleasure palace of the Buen Retiro, on the eastern outskirts of Madrid (fig. 45). The Buen Retiro was run up at enormous speed – most of it in the three years 1630–33, under the frenetic personal direction of Olivares – and it showed. The palace was criticized by contemporaries as being unworthy of so magnificent a king; but at the same time Olivares came under attack for spending money on a pleasure palace in times of war, high taxation, and economic recession. Over ten years the costs probably came to about three million ducats – equivalent to one year's expenditure on Spain's army in the Netherlands.[15]

While it was true that the exterior of the Buen Retiro was undistinguished, the interior made up for this. 'The house', reported Hopton, 'is very richly furnished and almost all by presents, for the Count of Olivares hath made the work his own, by which means it hath not wanted friends.'[16] In practice he dragooned his unfortunate relatives, along with the entire Spanish establishment, into providing furniture, tapestries and paintings, and had Spain's viceroys scouring the earth for pictures to cover its walls.

Some paintings were specially commissioned for the Retiro, notably those which were to decorate its great ceremonial hall, the Hall of Realms, inaugurated in 1635. The Retiro, then, provided a splendid opportunity for the patronage of native artists like Velázquez and Zurbarán, but they could not be expected to cover all the walls in the short time available, and so it also became a great repository of paintings collected from all over Europe.

All told, about 800 paintings were acquired for the Buen Retiro, the great majority of them in that spectacular decade, the 1630s. This meant a vast increase in the size and range of the Spanish royal collection. When Philip IV came to the throne in 1621, there were around 1,200 paintings in the various royal palaces. In the 44 years of his reign, he added at least 2,000 paintings to the collection, which is approximately the number of paintings in the Prado Museum today. Nor was it simply a question of quantity. Philip had a very good eye, and his tastes ran especially towards Rubens and the great Venetian masters. He would go to any length to add a masterpiece to his collection; his ambassadors were primed to be on the lookout for any important works coming on to the market; and when Charles I's collection was dispersed, the Spanish ambassador in London, acting under strict instructions from the king, picked up everything he could.

This royal obsession with picture-collecting was of momentous importance for the development of art and taste in seventeenth-century Spain. It had a major impact both on the tastes and interests of the Spanish ruling class, and on the artists themselves.

The social impact of the king's activities is pithily summed up in a letter of 1638 from Sir Arthur Hopton to Lord Cottington:

> *They are now become more judicious in and more affectioned unto the art of painting, than they have been, or than the world imagines. And the king within this 12 month hath gotten an incredible number of ancient and of the best modern hands, and over with the Count of Monterrey came the best of Italy, particularly the Baccanalian of Titian, and in this town is not a piece worth anything but the king takes and pays very well for them, and in his imitation the Admiral of Castile, Don Luis de Haro and many others are making collections.*[17]

Picture-collecting, in fact, became the fashion in the Madrid of the 1630s, especially in the circle of Olivares's relatives, friends and dependents, all of them anxious to imitate their royal master. Olivares's brother-in-law, the Count of Monterrey, who was immensely wealthy, returned in 1638 from Naples, where he had been serving as viceroy, with a very choice collection, including seven paintings attributed to Titian and 13 to Ribera, and built a picture gallery to house them in the garden of his Madrid palace.[18] His cousin, the Marquis of Leganés, a general who served in the Netherlands and Italy, had a collection of some 1,300 paintings by the time of his death in 1655 – one that was particularly strong in Flemish paintings.[19] His nephew and successor as Philip's principal minister, Don Luis de Haro, also had a splendid collection, part of which came through his wife; and Haro's son, the Marquis of Carpio, who died in 1687, while viceroy of Naples, was one of the greatest collectors of the age.[20]

The Olivares clan among the high nobility, which dominated Spain's political life between the 1620s and the 1680s, dominated its cultural life, too, as patrons and collectors. The habit of collecting extended, moreover, to government ministers and officials. Olivares's lawyer, José González, who ended his career as one of the principal ministers of the Spanish crown, had a collection of around 750 paintings at the time of his death in 1668. His widow's inventory shows that the principal room of his Madrid house was decorated with ten panels of a Brussels tapestry of the life of Jacob, along with 50 paintings, including several portraits. There were 20 more paintings in the dining-room,

fig. 47 Murillo *The Virgin and Child in Glory* ('*La Vierge Coupée*; Walker Art Gallery, Liverpool)

including portraits of himself and his wife; another 30 in the main first-floor room – two of them portraits of Olivares – and 100 paintings, including two originals by Teniers, in his summer quarters.[21] But the general effect may have been slightly marred by the framing. Pepys remarks in his notes on Spain: 'Tawdry frames in their best pictures of great masters and solemn things.'

By the time of Philip IV's death in 1665, then, the taste for picture-collecting was well established in court circles in Madrid; and the very fact that it was so fashionable must have had its impact on taste and patronage in the country at large, and not least in Seville. Here Cardinal Ambrosio Spínola, archbishop from 1669, set a magnificent example, commissioning works by Valdés Leal and Murillo for his palace, including the latter's famous *Virgin and Child in Glory* (fig. 47). As the son of the Marquis of Leganés, that great collector of the reign of Philip IV, Spínola had presumably spent his early years in houses full of paintings.

For all the economic troubles of the later seventeenth century, the demand for paintings seems to have kept up – for religious paintings, in particular, to decorate family chapels and convents, and pious foundations; but also for still-lifes or *bodegones*; for the new genre developed by Murillo of cheerful scenes of street urchins, which were presumably produced in the first instance for a Seville clientele (Cat. 66; repr. on p. 137); and for portraits, although many of these have disappeared with the dispersal or extinction of so many of Spain's great families.

Although some of this activity took place in provincial capitals, especially Seville, the court retained its pre-eminence as the centre and focus of artistic activity, in spite of the death in 1665 of Philip IV, one of the greatest royal collectors and patrons in seventeenth-century Europe. His son, Charles II, seems to have added only a few works to the royal collection, but the habit of patronage had taken hold. And Philip, in addition to helping form the artistic taste of a whole generation of nobility, left another major legacy in the royal collection itself.

When Murillo, following in the steps of his fellow artist from Seville, Francisco de Herrera the Younger, paid his visit to Madrid in 1658, the royal and private collections in the capital contained a splendid sample of the works not only of Titian and his fellow Italians but also of the great northern masters of the seventeenth century, and especially Rubens and Van Dyck. The high baroque style that was now introduced into Seville by Murillo and his colleagues, and was adopted by the leading painters of the post-Velázquez generation in Madrid, among them Carreño de Miranda and Claudio Coello, directly reflects the influence of these Italian and northern masters. By making their work accessible to Spanish artists, the great collectors of the seventeenth century, beginning with the king himself, had helped to shape the vision of a whole generation of painters.

Artistic activity, drawing fresh inspiration from these foreign masterpieces, was sustained, both in Seville and Madrid, until the last years of the century. It is only then that the barren age of Spanish painting begins, to end nearly a hundred years later with the emergence of Goya. But the seventeenth century – this century of falling economic productivity, and of a dramatic decline in Spain's political influence and military power – had by any measure been a scintillating century for painting in Spain.

It may now be possible to get a little closer to the heart of this apparent paradox of a golden age of the arts coinciding with an iron age of political and economic disaster. No social or economic interpretation can explain genius – the genius of a Velázquez or a Murillo. But even genius needs a conducive climate in order to reach fulfilment, and it is clear that seventeenth-century Spain, for all its troubles, did manage to create a reasonably favourable climate, at least for writers and painters, although not, it seems, for architects.

The relative poverty of seventeenth-century Spanish architecture may provide a clue to the patronage of painters. Architecture requires a a considerable – and, above all, a continuing – outlay of cash; and at every level of society in seventeenth-century Spain, from the king downwards, potential patrons were inhibited by acute problems of cash flow. It is therefore not surprising that great building enterprises are few, and rather undistinguished; and that even well-endowed religious orders take decades over the completion of their churches and convents.[22]

The patronage of writers and artists, on the other hand, can be managed more cheaply and on a more sporadic basis, without doing irreparable damage to artistic and literary enterprise, although there may be sad instances of individual casualties – men whose artistic careers are blighted by the ruin or death of their patrons, as happened with Antonio de Pereda.[23] And it is here, in the exercise of patronage, that a key is to be found to the problem of artistic activity in an age of decline.

For effective patronage there must exist a group in society with both the means, and the desire, to support artistic enterprise. As this tale of three cities has suggested, the structure of Spanish society in the seventeenth century was such that there did indeed exist, in church and state, an affluent elite with sufficient reserves of wealth to escape the worst vicissitudes of the times. Indeed, those very vicissitudes may actually have encouraged the tendency to conspicuous consumption, precisely because, in an age of sudden inflation and no less sudden deflation, there was no inducement to save, and there were few economically productive outlets for the use of capital.

But, along with the means, there must also be the desire. In a hierarchical society like that of Spain, royal and aristocratic example was paramount; and here the natural taste of Philip IV and the impetus given to royal patronage of the arts by Olivares at the start of the reign, were of crucial importance. In a fragment of autobiography, Philip wrote that it was important not only to honour the profession of arms, but also 'those who have learned to improve themselves in letters, scholarship and the arts. For these two', he continued – arms and letters – 'are the two poles which govern the movement of monarchies, and are the foundations on which they rest, because together they form a perfect harmony, each supporting the other.'[24] This is as good an exposition as any of the underlying philosophy of his policy of patronage.

In 1621, at the beginning of Philip's reign, a commentator wrote enthusiastically that a *siglo de oro* – a Golden Century – was dawning in Spain.[25] As far as Spanish power, and the Spanish economy were concerned, his prophecy proved wildly inaccurate. Spain's ruling class, and, with it, Spain itself, failed drastically to adapt to the requirements of a changing world, and paid the resulting price. But in the arts it was a different matter. Here a governing class which was fast losing the political and military touch that had given Spain its empire, turned, almost as if in compensation, to enlightened patronage. And so it became possible – not perhaps for the last time in the history of European civilization – for economic decline and cultural achievement to walk hand in hand.

NOTES

1. *The Tangier Papers of Samuel Pepys*, ed. Edwin Chappell (London, 1935), pp. 254–63.
2. *Ibid.*, p. 168.
3. Martín González de Cellorigo, *Memorial de la política necesaria y útil restauración a la república de España* (Valladolid, 1600), fo. 1.
4. See J.H.Elliott, 'Self-perception and decline in early seventeenth-century Spain', *Past and Present*, no. 74 (1977), pp. 41–61.
5. González de Cellorigo, *Memorial*, fo. 25v.
6. Fray Juan de Santa María, *República y policía christiana* (Lisbon, 1621), p. 200.
7. Public Record Office, SP.94.42, fo. 192, Hopton to Vane, 26 July/4 August 1641.
8. For the history of Spain in the seventeenth century, see the following: Antonio Domínguez Ortiz, *The Golden Age of Spain, 1516–1659* (London, 1971); J.H.Elliott, *Imperial Spain, 1469–1716* (London, 1963); Henry Kamen, *Spain in the later Seventeenth Century, 1665–1700* (London, 1980); John Lynch, *Spain under the Habsburgs*, vol. II (2nd. ed., Oxford, 1981).
9. The discussion of Toledo and El Greco which follows draws on the introductory essays to the catalogue of the 1982 exhibition of El Greco, *El Greco of Toledo* (Boston, 1982), and especially those of Richard Kagan and Jonathan Brown. I am especially indebted to the latter for his help and advice on many points on the history of art in seventeenth-century Spain discussed in the pages that follow.
10. Cited in Elliott, 'Self-perception and decline', p. 54.
11. For the history of Seville in the seventeenth century, the best studies are those of Antonio Domínguez Ortiz, *Orto y Ocaso de Sevilla* (2nd. ed., Madrid, 1974) and *Historia de Sevilla*, vol. IV (Seville, 1976).
12. *Don Quixote*, part II, ch. XX.
13. Seville's academies are discussed in Jonathan Brown, *Images and Ideas in Seventeenth-Century Spanish Painting* (Princeton, 1978).
14. Diego Angulo Iñiguez, *Murillo* (Madrid, 1981), vol. I, pp. 463–65; vol. II, pp. 325–56.
15. For the Buen Retiro and the court of Philip IV, see Jonathan Brown and J.H.Elliott, *A Palace for a King* (New Haven and London, 1980).
16. *Ibid.*, p. 88.
17. *Ibid.*, p. 115.
18. Alfonso E. Pérez Sánchez, 'Las colecciones de pintura del conde de Monterrey (1653)', *Boletín de la Real Academia de la Historia*, 174 (1977), pp. 417–59.
19. José López Navío, 'La gran colección de pinturas del Marqués de Leganés', *Analecta Calasanctiana*, no. 8 (1962), pp. 259–330; Mary Crawford Volk, 'New Light on a Seventeenth-Century Collector: The Marquis of Leganés', *The Art Bulletin*, vol. 72 (1980), pp. 256–68.
20. Gregorio de Andrés, *El Marqués de Liche, bibliófilo y coleccionista de arte* (Madrid, 1975). See also José M. Pita Andrade, 'Los cuadros de Velázquez y Mazo que poseyó el séptimo Marqués del Carpio', *Archivo Español de Arte*, vol. 25 (1952), pp. 223–36, and Enriqueta Harris, 'El Marqués del Carpio y sus cuadros de Velázquez', *Archivo Español de Arte*, vol. 30 (1957), pp. 136–39.
21. See Janine Fayard, 'José González (1583?–1668), "créature" du comte-duc d'Olivares et conseiller de Philippe IV', in *Hommage à Roland Mousnier* (Paris, 1980), pp. 351–68. For another official engaged in collecting, see José Luis Barrio Moya, 'La colección de pinturas de don Francisco de Oviedo, secretario del rey Felipe IV', *Revista de Archivos, Bibliotecas y Museos*, lxxxii (1979), pp. 163–71.
22. See Virgina Tovar Martín, *Arquitectos madrileños de la segunda mitad del siglo* XVII (Madrid, 1975).
23. Pereda's career is discussed by Alfonso E.Pérez Sánchez in the exhibition catalogue, *D.Antonio de Pereda (1611–1678) y la pintura madrileña de su tiempo* (Madrid, 1978).
24. Quoted by Brown and Elliott, *A Palace for a King*, p. 42.
25. *Cartas de Andrés de Almansa y Mendoza* (Madrid, 1886), p. 53.

fig. 48 Murillo *SS Justa and Rufina* (Musée Bonnat, Bayonne)

Murillo as a Draughtsman

Manuela Mena Marques

Murillo is one of the few great Spanish artists of the seventeenth century whose graphic work has survived to this day; his drawings vary considerably in character, as indeed do those of Ribera and Alonso Cano. An analysis of the drawings that can be considered autograph reveals the role played by draughtsmanship in the genesis of his paintings and illustrates the various techniques he employed.

The first systematic study of Murillo's drawings dates from the middle of the nineteenth century. In 1848, in his *Annals of Artists in Spain*, Sir William Stirling-Maxwell listed 29 drawings; a few more came to light in later publications. Then, in 1930, the five volumes of Sánchez Cantón's *Dibujos españoles* were published; he attributed 12 drawings to Murillo, but recent critics consider only three of these to be autograph. Diego Angulo reassessed these attributions – at times over-optimistically – in a series of articles published between 1960 and 1974 in *Archivo Español de Arte*, and identified new drawings, thereby expanding our knowledge of Murillo's style. In 1976, Jonathan Brown published what can be considered a 'corpus' of Murillo's graphic work to coincide with an exhibition of the artist's drawings in Princeton.[1] It assembled a total of 95 drawings, many hitherto unpublished or recently attributed, which Brown presented as unquestionably autograph Murillos. But two subsequent appraisals of his work by Diego Angulo and A. Hyatt Major[2] have cast serious doubts on a considerable number of them. Their inclusion in a Murillo catalogue could cause confusion about aspects of his technique and style, particularly if those doubtful works were used as a basis for new attributions. Brown also produced an extensive essay in which he analyzed the antecedents of Murillo's drawings, the evolution of his style, his different techniques and the place drawings occupied in the artist's work; it is the most complete and informative study so far and constitutes the basis for any future research.

The relative scarcity of Murillo's drawings, despite his being one of Spain's best known artists, graphically speaking, can be ascribed to the general lack of interest in this medium among Spanish collectors. They saw drawing more in its purely functional aspect – a tool to be used inside the painter's studio – than in its own artistic right. As Pérez Sánchez has pointed out in his study of Spanish drawing: 'Spanish artists drew as much as their European contemporaries, and a close reading of essayists and biographers, and a study of the inventories of artists' studios that have been preserved by legal documents dealing with wills, depositions and lawsuits, leaves no room for doubt and entirely discredits the legend still alive among certain critics that "the Spanish seem to have felt a certain repugnance for the abstraction that a chalk mark on a sheet of paper represents".'[3]

As in other European countries in the seventeenth century, the teaching of drawing was the basis of painters' and sculptors' training; their apprenticeship consisted of copying engravings or their masters' sketches, or drawing from nature. Artists executed their works with the aid of numerous preparatory studies. It was possibly the importance attached to the use of drawings in the studio that caused their disappearance; it is also the reason why, in general, they have come down to us in a regrettable state of preservation, torn and stained by oils and pigments, indicative of their constant use in the workshops. As Palomino has pointed out, collections of Spanish drawings in the seventeenth century were primarily made by artists; and even Ceán Bermúdez, at the beginning of the nineteenth century, implied that they were more frequently acquired by 'practitioners', precisely because of their functional interest and possible use for compositions and figure studies in other painters' works.

However, at the end of the seventeenth and during the eighteenth century, some interesting collections began to be formed by both private individuals and artists themselves. Two such collections are particularly relevant to Murillo: that of Nicolás de Omazur, a friend and admirer of the painter, which must have been made in Seville and included drawings by Murillo, Valdés Leal and Cornelius Schut;[4] and the collection assembled in the eighteenth century by the Conde del Aguila, whose books, manuscripts and drawings were acquired on his death in 1809 by the Chapter of Seville Cathedral for its library.

At the end of the eighteenth century and the beginning of the nineteenth, Murillo's drawings began to be known and appreciated by foreign collectors, especially the English, and it is from this date that the drawings began to leave Spain. Frank Hall Standish, the English collector, acquired from the Conde del Aguila's collection 22 drawings attributed to Murillo, according to Curtis. He removed them from Spain at the beginning of the nineteenth century and in 1841 sold them to Louis Philippe of Orléans; some of them were subsequently bought by the Louvre. Jonathan Williams, the English vice-consul in Seville at the end of the eighteenth century and a connoisseur of Spanish art in general, became interested in Murillo's graphic work, including his drawings; he acquired amongst others, the study for *The Crucifixion* (Cat. D13), which he later gave to the English painter Richard Ford. Alleyne Fitzherbert, Baron St. Helens, the English ambassador in Spain in the 1790s, also assembled an extensive collection of over 70 Murillo drawings, which, in the catalogue of the sale of his collection in London in 1840, were said to have been bought from the library of Seville Cathedral. Another 28 drawings attributed to Murillo appeared in the collection of the Mexican painter, José Atanasio Echevarría; today in the Kunsthalle, Hamburg.

But if all the drawings attributed to Murillo in early sources are added together, and even overlooking the fact that some were not his, there are still less than 150 in all, which must represent a very small percentage of the painter's graphic output. For one thing, the incredible mastery and virtuosity of the originals, in varying techniques and styles, are proof of a constant use of this medium, a medium in which Murillo equalled the achievements of other contemporary masters both inside and outside Spain. In fact, the study of the different types of drawing that have survived suggests that the corpus of his graphic work must have been substantial; there are quick sketches, preliminary ideas for compositions, more finished studies with both figures and light and shade defined, and, finally, drawings with fully elaborated figures, some of which correspond exactly to his paintings, leading us to suppose that a similar process was employed in the preparation of the rest of his known works; all this accords with the purest academic tradition.

fig. 49 Murillo *San Junípero and the Beggar* (Ecole des Beaux-Arts, Paris)

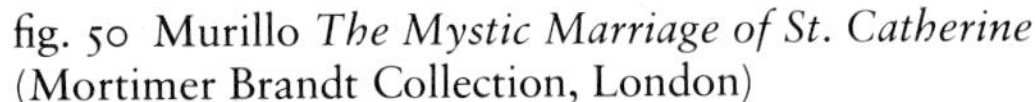

fig. 50 Murillo *The Mystic Marriage of St. Catherine* (Mortimer Brandt Collection, London)

This method of work, which laid the foundations for Murillo's extraordinary drawing skills, is borne out by the organization of the Academy of Drawing founded by Murillo, Francisco de Herrera the Younger and other Seville painters in 1660;[5] drawing of the live model was stressed among its precepts for the teaching of art, as it was in the Italian academies. Brown describes the Academy's methods of work and mentions the existence of a volume containing many drawings, possibly from Seville; the poor quality of some and the erasures and corrections of others suggest that the book may be a selection of examples of work done in the Academy.

Between the first datable Murillo drawing, *San Junípero and the Beggar* (fig. 49), a preparatory sketch for one of the paintings for the small cloister of the Monastery of San Francisco, Seville, and the last, a sketch for the *Mystic Marriage of St. Catherine* in Cádiz Cathedral, which was begun around 1680 and left unfinished by the artist on his death (fig. 50), there are no more than 70 drawings that can be considered autograph. With a few exceptions, nearly all are compositional studies, some highly finished; the rest are studies of individual figures, preparatory drawings for characters that appear in his paintings. The numerical disparity between these two types of drawing does not mean, as some art historians have claimed, that Murillo preferred to make a quick sketch of the whole scene to a detailed study of a figure or part of a figure; the fact that examples of the latter type of drawing have not survived may be due to the choice of collectors who preferred compositional drawings to studies of details of figures, draperies or accessories. There probably were many such studies in Murillo's graphic output. In a collection of letters edited by Bottari, there are some recommendations for the acquisition of drawings which show that collectors were inclined to favour finished compositional drawings, and although the letters refer almost exclusively to Italian collecting habits, they give a good idea of what interested connoisseurs. Thus, a letter from Giuseppe Pinacci to the Florentine painter, Francesco Gaburri, dated 1713, says in this respect:

> *... the drawings that are esteemed are those that offer finished and well preserved work. As for the studies of drapery, feet, hands and other things lightly sketched, even if they are by great artists, they interest only painters and not people of quality.*[6]

The majority of drawings considered to be autograph Murillos are executed in a simple technique: pen, or pen with wash applied by brush; in each case the artist first drew a very faint sketch in black or red chalk of the chief features of a scene or figures and then the outlines were gone over in pen and brush. Between the artist's early and late drawings there was no fundamental change in technique and so, as Angulo points out, in Murillo's earliest drawings there already 'exists something of the summary, quick style of the later period' and in the later period he continued to use the precise, meticulous shading characteristic of his early phase. Murillo's style was fundamentally tied to traditional methods of Seville drawing, very different from the working methods of contemporary artists in Madrid or Valencia. The preference for pen drawings with parallel and cross-hatching, which was in general use in European drawing, was particularly evident in Seville. Francisco de Herrera was already using it in the early seventeenth century (fig. 51); he had learned this basically Italian technique through his association with the Italian artists working at the Escorial. The Bolognese Giacomo Passarotti had made it a fashionable style about this time, and it produced solid drawings of great vigour and expressive force. Herrera the Elder was the source of another style – pen and wash drawings with strong, contrasting shadows (fig. 52), which Murillo also learnt to use to great effect.

There are no drawings that can definitely be attributed to Juan del Castillo, Murillo's master,[8] and, since it seems likely that they would have been similar to those of Herrera or other Seville masters, it is impossible to trace the influence of Castillo's graphic style on his young follower. If the numerous drawings by his nephew, Antonio del Castillo, are taken as an example, the tradition established by Herrera the Elder – the forceful technique using parallel and cross-hatched pen strokes – is evident (fig. 53). Both Angulo and Brown mention the influence of Alonso Cano in the formation of Murillo's graphic style and, although he left Seville in 1638, never to return, his drawings must have been appreciated by the young painter. Cano was a prolific draughtsman and used a technique with abbreviated and zig-zag pen strokes (fig. 54), which Murillo adopted most noticeably in his early drawings.

It is natural that Murillo would have been influenced by earlier Seville masters, but this does not mean that he did not have his own drawing technique. Perhaps the most innovatory quality of his drawings was his creation of a delicate style, which, as in his paintings, at times obtained effects that have been called *vaporoso* (soft and sweet). The

fig. 51 Francesco de Herrera the Elder *St. Andrew* (Biblioteca Nacional, Madrid)

fig. 53 Antonio del Castillo *Pastoral Scene*
(Real Academia de Bellas Artes de San Fernando, Madrid)

fig. 52 (*left*) Francesco de Herrera the Elder *The Marys at the Tomb*
(Museo del Prado, Madrid)

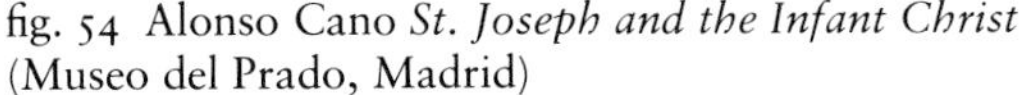

fig. 54 Alonso Cano *St. Joseph and the Infant Christ*
(Museo del Prado, Madrid)

feeling of freedom in his drawings is doubtless aided by the loose and rapid – yet precise – pen strokes; at the same time, his zag-zag lines accentuate the surface movement. The abbreviated flourishes, at times carried to the point of near abstraction, and the interrupted forms and outlines obtained by means of wavy or broken lines produce a masterly effect of movement, by which figures merge into the space that surrounds them, and add an atmospheric quality to the drawings. His feeling for colour, so obvious in his paintings, is also evident in his graphic work and in this respect his drawings far surpass those of his contemporaries.

Unless new drawings come to light, the pen or brush and wash technique must, for the present, be considered Murillo's most characteristic style; but he did use other techniques with equal mastery. There are some black chalk drawings: *San Diego of Alcalá* of around 1645, the 1656 *St. Antony* for the great painting in the Cathedral (fig. 5), the group of drawings of angels in the Louvre (Cat. D10–12) and *St. Francis Embracing the Crucified Christ* (Cat. D6) of around 1668 or 1669 for the painting in the Capuchin Church in Seville (Cat. 43). In all these drawings Murillo employed a soft technique, faint and smudged at times, with little definition either of outline or of anatomical details or drapery. Murillo also used red and dark red chalk, the best known example being the *Mystic Marriage of St. Catherine* (Hamburg Kunsthalle), which is dated, perhaps by Murillo himself, 1655 (fig. 57). This work is exceptional within his graphic *oeuvre* on account of its highly finished state; it is related to a painting in the Museo de Arte Antiga, Lisbon, which is attributed to Murillo and with which it has very close similarities.[9] Mayer suggested that the drawing was a copy of the painting by Murillo himself, made as a record of work in the manner of a *Liber veritatis*.

Murillo also employed a more complicated technique; a combination of red and black chalk, sometimes with touches of white chalk. This technique first appeared in the sixteenth century and was more generally employed at the beginning of the seventeenth century in Italy, from where it travelled to Spain and gained widespread acceptance among Spanish masters. Murillo employed it to great effect in, for example, the *Christ Child Sleeping on the Cross* (fig. 56); the artist highlights the figure – drawn in red chalk – with some faint touches of black chalk, which is also used in the soft, dense shading surrounding the Child. A fine example of this technique is the *Crucifixion* (Cat. D13) in the collection of Brinsley Ford. The body of Christ, drawn with thin fine lines in red chalk, revealing the underlying anatomy, is emphasized by black chalk, which the painter also uses for shading the hair, loin cloth, and Cross; it is one of the supreme examples of Murillo's achievement as a draughtsman.

Murillo employed yet another technique for two draw-

fig. 55 Murillo *St. Antony of Padua* (private collection)

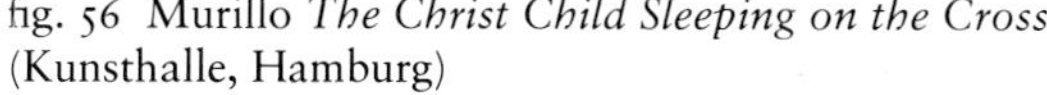
fig. 56 Murillo *The Christ Child Sleeping on the Cross* (Kunsthalle, Hamburg)

fig. 57 Murillo *The Mystic Marriage of St. Catherine* (Kunsthalle, Hamburg)

ings, unanimously accepted as autograph works; *The Virgin and Child with Joseph and Two Angels* (Cat. D14) in the British Museum, and the *Vision of St. Antony of Padua* (Cat. D15) in the Louvre. In these, Murillo used red and black chalk for the outlines and for sketching in the shadows, and delicate brush strokes to give substance to the outlines, shadows and modelling; finally he used white lead to highlight the luminous areas. The paper was lightly tinted with brown wash, which increases the composition's atmospheric and spatial effects. These two drawings are highly pictorial in character and completely original in the context of seventeenth-century Spanish graphic art.[10]

If the technical aspects of Murillo's work seem to pose few problems – apart from the scarcity of examples in each technique – the dating and stylistic evolution is much more complicated: few drawings can be precisely dated apart from those that are preparatory studies for documented paintings. A further difficulty is the fact that his drawing style did not change greatly during his working life; the abstraction of line and the areas of shading with zig-zag or cross-hatched lines are always present. In addition, there is some difficulty in dating Murillo's paintings themselves. Angulo, in his study of Murillo's drawings, tried to establish a chronology based on general characteristics, while Brown, following this approach, has attempted to group the drawings in several periods that parallel those of his paintings. According to Angulo and Brown, Murillo began as a realist painter using dark colours and dramatic lighting effects; from the early 1660s he developed brighter lighting although his compositions were still restrained; gradually he evolved a style full of movement and increasingly bright in colour, until in his last phase, between 1670 and 1682, he achieved extraordinary atmospheric effects through his soft dissolving technique.

The earliest surviving Murillo drawings are preparatory studies for some of the paintings decorating the small cloister of the Convento de San Francisco, dating from between 1645 and 1646. Both *San Junípero and the Beggar* (fig. 49) and *A Scene from the Life of St. Francis Solano* (Cat. D1) show that the artist had been well trained as a draughtsman. In the first he used pen only, producing a strong and forceful line in the style of Herrera the Elder and a form of shading – slightly intricate in some areas – that heralds his late style. In the second, wash is applied by brush to indicate wide areas of shadow, which create both volume and modelling. In both drawings the outlines are perfectly defined, as are the areas of light and shade, giving effects similar to the chiaroscuro in the paintings of the period. Brown calls this Murillo style 'virile' because of the strong and vigorous feeling of these compositions. Several more drawings, such as the *San Diego Supporting the Cross* (Kunsthalle, Hamburg) and *A Miracle of St. Antony of Padua* (Cat. D2) belong to this early group of drawings dating from before 1650, given their similarity to the two works mentioned above.

The Adoration of the Kings (fig. 85), in a French private collection, is a preparatory sketch for the painting of the same subject (Cat. 28), a work dated around 1652, and it marks a moment of change in Murillo's pen and wash style. Because of the complexity of the composition, which had to include a large cast of characters, Murillo was forced to adapt his technique; along with the delicate outlines, he used a richer wash, which fluctuates in intensity from the more opaque areas in deep shadow to the clearest and most transparent surfaces. Two of the preparatory drawings for the *San Isidoro* and *San Leandro* (Cat. 16 and 17), dated 1655, follow this technique.

The *San Isidoro* in the British Museum is the first example of a Murillo drawing done entirely in brush over faint traces of black chalk, a technique that created an effect of great delicacy and softness, particularly in its treatment of drapery. One of Murillo's masterpieces, the Louvre's *San Isidoro* (Cat. D3) was a preparatory drawing for the same series; it is an essential work for understanding the evolution of the painter's graphic style. The extraordinary virtuosity with which Murillo realised the scene – using a variety of parallel, zig-zag and cross-hatched lines with forceful, decisive strokes – makes it almost certain that earlier drawings in the same style (essentially a Seville style) must have existed from which these sketches evolved. Of this type and possibly from the same period, is a *St. John the Baptist* in a Munich private collection, although in both there is a greater tendency towards movement in the scene than in the *San Isidoro*. Another *St. John* (fig. 58) and the *Study of Angels and the Head of the Virgin* (Cat. D5) may be slightly later.

In 1655 and 1656 Murillo did several paintings for the altarpiece of the Capuchin church in Seville; a drawing for

fig. 58 Murillo *Studies of St. John the Baptist* (British Museum, London)

fig. 59 Murillo *Boy with a Dog* (Staedelisches Kunstinstitut, Frankfurt)

fig. 60 Murillo *St. Joseph and the Christ Child* (Biblioteca Nacional, Madrid)

one of them, *SS Justa and Rufina*, is in the Bonnat Museum in Bayonne (fig. 48). Light wash is used to define the shapes, and this technique seems to be characteristic of the works of this date. In this period, Brown places *The Agony in the Garden* (Cat. D8), the *St. Joseph and the Christ Child* (fig. 60; Biblioteca Nacional, Madrid), *The Assumption of the Virgin* (Cat. D7) – one of the best known works of this time – and *St. Joseph and the Christ Child* (Cat. D9). The Louvre's Angel series (Cat. D10–12) together with the *Vision of St. Clare* in the same collection probably also belong to this period, although some of these seem to follow models used by Murillo in his earlier pictures.

The sketch in the Pierpont Morgan Library, New York, for *St. Félix of Cantalicio* (fig. 61), a preparatory study for the picture painted in 1668 for the Capuchins of Seville, is obviously autograph. However, some of the drawings Brown attributes to this period cannot be accepted as the work of Murillo; these include the *Penitent St. Dominic* (Vienna) and *Christ Carrying the Cross* in the Hamburg Kunsthalle. The delicate atmospheric effects that Murillo introduced at this time culminate in two drawings already mentioned, the *Virgin and Child with Joseph and Two Angels* in the British Museum (Cat. D14) and the Louvre's *Vision of St. Antony of Padua* (Cat. D15), to which can be added the *Mystic Marriage of St. Catherine* (fig. 62) in which Murillo employed the same brush technique used for *San Leandro* in the Louvre.

Examples of Murillo's drawings in the last decade of his life are *Roman Charity* (Cat. D18), the *Virgin and Child* (Cat. D19), *The Immaculate Conception* (Cat. D24) and the *Mystic Marriage of St. Catherine* for the painting in Cádiz Cathedral (fig. 50). Others accepted by Brown for this date do not display sufficient technical and stylistic skill to be placed with absolute certainty in this period. The chief characteristics of his late style are wavy outlines, extreme abstraction of forms, zig-zag strokes and abrupt changes in the breadth of the lines, which are extremely fine at times and broad and smudged at others. These traits are apparent in *The Immaculate Conception* (Cat. D21) and the *Penitent St. Peter* (Cat. D22), the *Virgin Annunciate* in the Biblioteca Nacional, Madrid, and the *Assumption of the Virgin* (fig. 65; English private collection). It is less certain that the *Flying Angels* in the Courtauld Institute and the series of studies of the Good Shepherd (figs. 63, 64) are of this period; they date more probably from the previous decade.

The chronology of Murillo's chalk drawings is less problematic than that of the pen and wash sketches, since the few that have survived can be related to paintings. However, their scarcity means the role played by these drawings in the evolution of a composition cannot be understood fully. It seems that like many other artists, both Spanish and foreign, Murillo used this medium for his studies of figures that

fig. 61 Murillo *St. Félix of Cantalicio* (Pierpont Morgan Library, New York)

fig. 62 Murillo *The Mystic Marriage of St. Catherine* (British Museum, London)

fig. 63 Murillo *The Good Shepherd* (Musée du Louvre, Paris)

fig. 64 Murillo *The Good Shepherd* (Musée du Louvre, Paris)

needed to be completely resolved before being transferred to canvas. The quickly sketched compositions which seem to be preliminary ideas for paintings do not vary stylistically between those done in his early years, such as the *verso* of the drawings for San Francisco's small cloister (Cat. D1) of 1645, and those of much later date, such as the *St. Francis Embracing the Crucified Christ* and the *Adoration of the Shepherds* (Cat. D6 *recto* and *verso*), both of 1688, for the Seville Capuchins, and the *Inmaculada* (fig. 65) drawn with a few, barely visible smudged lines.

Murillo's figure studies are sometimes loosely drawn, as in the *St. Antony* (fig. 55) for the *Vision of St. Antony* (fig. 5) of 1656; at other times, they are more detailed as in the *Penitent Magdalen* (fig. 66), the *St. Francis Receiving the Stigmata*, the *Christ Child Sleeping on the Cross* (fig. 56), or the study of the *Crucifixion* (Cat. D13), which is the latest of this group, perhaps drawn at the beginning of the 1670s. Among the black or red chalk drawings attributed to Murillo are some figure studies and compositions, all very finished,[12] which have to be rejected as autograph Murillos on account of their poor quality. However, as they are closely related to works known to be by the artist and because they have stylistic resemblance to genuine Murillos, they may be copies of lost drawings. It should be remembered that Murillo prepared his works meticulously, using figure studies, and that later he produced very finished drawings in order to have a record of his paintings, as in the magnificent autograph *Mystic Marriage of St. Catherine* (fig. 57).

Although the number of drawings chosen for this exhibition is small, they are intended to demonstrate the remarkably high quality of Murillo's work as a draughtsman, certainly of the same calibre as his painting; it is also hoped that the sketches and studies in different techniques give some idea of the range and variety of Murillo's graphic art.

NOTES

1. J.Brown, *Murillo and His Drawings*, Princeton, 1976.
2. D.Angulo Iñiguez, review of the 'Exposición de Dibujos de Murillo en Princeton' *Archivo Español de Arte*, 1977, p. 337 et seq. and A.Hyatt Major, Review of J.Brown, *Murillo & His Drawings*, *Master Drawings*, II, 1977, pp. 184–85.
3. A.E.Pérez Sánchez, *El Dibujo Español de los Siglos de Oro*, Madrid, 1980, p. 9.
4. J.Brown, op. cit., 1976, p. 51.
5. J.Brown, op. cit., p. 44–46 and Diego Angulo Iñiguez, *Murillo*, 1981, I, pp. 54–64.
6. Bottari, *Raccolta di Lettere sulla Pittura, Scultura ed Architettura scritti da' piu celebri personaggi dei secoli* XV, XVI *e* XVII ... Milan, 1822, II, p. 121.
7. D. Angulo Iñiguez, op. cit., 1981, p. 337.
8. It is hard to accept that the two drawings attributed to Juan del Castillo by J.Brown (op. cit. 1976, p. 25, fig. 3–4) are autograph, and both Angulo and A.Pérez Sánchez (*Corpus of Spanish Drawings 1400–1600*, 1975, nos. 109–112) consider them to be connected with Italian artists working at the Escorial; stylistically, they are more related to the latter than to the Seville artist.
9. J.Brown, op. cit. 1976, fig. 47.
10. In his catalogue (op. cit., nos. 64–65), Brown accepts the attribution to Murillo for the two drawings in the Louvre (inv. no. 18426–18427). Although on the Saint Joseph and the Child Jesus theme and executed in a rich and varied technique on toned paper, with preparatory work in black chalk, wash and white lead, Angulo rejects them as autograph Murillos in his critique – rightly, in my opinion: we are dealing with Italian drawings, very probably by the Roman painter Lazzaro Baldi.
11. J.Brown, op. cit. nos. 52–53; they are probably copies of lost drawings by Murillo, since the style is similar to his, although badly drawn.
12. The rest of the figure studies or compositional sketches in red and black chalk which Brown attributed to Murillo in his catalogue, have been rightly rejected by D.Angulo; it is hard to accept works of such second rate quality as originals; they have all the characteristics of copies by followers or imitators; they follow, too faithfully, famous compositions of the painter. I think that the following numbers in Brown's catalogue have to be rejected: 4, 14, 24, 25, 26, 28, 30, 31, 32, 67.

fig. 65 Murillo *La Inmaculada* (private collection, London)

fig. 66 Murillo *The Penitent Magdalen* (private collection)

The Influence of Murillo on Painting in Seville

ENRIQUE VALDIVIESO

It has come to be accepted that when Murillo died, the Seville school of painting died with him. Any possibility of new and inventive creative work, it was thought, was exhausted by the imposition of his style on succeeding generations of artists content to repeat his formulas. But it must be pointed out that, even if Murillo's influence was very strong, painters in Seville learnt how to adapt to other artistic tendencies, allowing the emergence of an art that had a character of its own and held a prominent place in Spanish art of the eighteenth century.

Murillo's influence on the Seville school of painting was noticeable from 1650 onwards; the presence of elements of his style in the work of Zurbarán is the most frequently cited example, but this needs qualification. Zurbarán's evolution towards a gentler style cannot be explained solely by the advent of Murillo and his influence on the taste of the Seville clientele; it can also be accounted for by the movement of Spanish religious and social ideology towards more humane standards, away from the rigours and severity which had been a consequence of the Council of Trent. This acceptance of more open criteria is noticeable in Spanish painting from the middle of the seventeenth century and Zurbarán was also affected by this change, independent of the fact that Murillo intuitively found a pictorial style that accorded with the spirit of the new age.

fig. 67 Francisco Polanco *St. John the Baptist* (Seville Cathedral)

And if Zurbarán was obliged to accommodate his style to the new aesthetic demands, it is logical that the many lesser painters who lived in Seville and imitated him, should have done likewise. The consequence was that Zurbarán's former disciples soon became followers of Murillo, producing paintings that were in tune with the demands of the market. This process of stylistic transition is poorly understood today, owing to the lack of signed and dated paintings by these lesser masters. Francisco Polanco (d. 1651) is one of the rare examples whose work enables us to form certain opinions of this phenomenon. A *St. John the Baptist* (fig. 67) in Seville Cathedral, which bears his signature, clearly shows an amalgam of Zurbarán's traditional language and the expressive qualities introduced by Murillo from 1645 onwards. Another artist who began by imitating Zurbarán, and was subsequently inspired by Murillo, was Ignacio de Ries (d. 1661). His signed works in the Capitán Contreras chapel of Segovia Cathedral, executed in 1653, show the influence both of Zurbarán and of Flemish effects derived from Rubens. But in one of his signed pictures,the *Assumption of the Virgin* in San Bartolomé, Seville, undated but obviously much later, the inspiration of Murillo is already evident. Murillo's influence is also apparent in the *La Inmaculada* in San Ildefonso, Seville (fig. 68); there is a similar version of this subject in the church of Las Teresas, Seville.

Matías de Areteaga (d. 1703) was a contemporary of Murillo who came under his influence (fig. 69); Ceán Bermúdez suggested that he was a follower of Valdés Leal, but the influence of Murillo is obvious in his work. This is evident in the series he painted for the Hermandad Sacramental del Sagrario de la Catedral de Sevilla (a fraternity of Seville Cathedral); in the picture depicting *Elijah in the Desert*, he reproduced the composition of the *Liberation of St. Peter* painted by Murillo for the Hospital de la Caridad, now in the Hermitage, Leningrad. Similarly, many of the figures in the series of the *Life of St. Lawrence*, painted by Arteaga around 1700 for the chapel dedicated to the saint in Seville Cathedral, show Murillo's influence.

We still do not have enough signed and dated paintings to know much about the artistic personality of Cornelius Schut,

fig. 68 Ignacio de Ries *La Inmaculada* (San Ildefonso, Seville)

fig. 69 Matiás de Arteaga *Santa Rosa of Viterbo with the Virgin and Child* (private collection, Seville)

an artist of Flemish origin who lived in Seville for a long time and who became president of its Academy of painters in 1670. However, despite the fact that the number of his indisputably autograph paintings is very small, it is evident that he tended to follow Murillo's artistic directives.

The biographical details of Francisco Martínez Gradilla (d. 1682), characterized by Ceán Bermúdez as a Zurbaránesque painter, have still to be discovered. We know that he was one of the founders of the Seville Academy and therefore he must have been in contact with both Murillo and Valdés Leal. His painting, at least during his late period, is that of an eclectic artist continually adapting himself to the art market's prevailing taste. In *The Holy Eucharist and SS Roch and Sebastian* in the parish church of Alcalá del Río, signed and dated 1682, he synthesized the styles of Murillo and Valdés Leal. There is another work which may be by this painter: the *Holy Family with SS Joachim and Anne* (MacCrohen Coll., Madrid), catalogued by Angulo (1981, no. 1265) among the anonymous works of Murillo's followers.

Of Murillo's contemporaries his most faithful follower was Francisco Meneses Osorio (d. 1721; fig. 70); he finished the paintings for the Capuchin Church in Cádiz, left uncompleted by Murillo on his death. His fidelity to Murillo's style has meant that his work has often been attributed to the master himself. Nevertheless, his paintings definitely have the stamp of a personal style, which enables us to identify his work. This is true of *The Virgin Appearing to St. Peter Nolasco*, (Museo de Bellas Artes, Seville), which was believed to be by Murillo until Angulo (1981, no. 2343) catalogued it as a school work. In the present writer's opinion, it is the work of Meneses Osorio, as it was listed in the inventory of the paintings deposited in the Alcázar by the French in 1810.

In the second half of the seventeenth century, there were very few artists who could free themselves from Murillo's influence. One painter who did was Juan de Valdés Leal (d. 1690); he created an art totally opposed to that of Murillo, one which was genuinely original. Another independent painter was Francisco Herrera the Younger (d. 1685) who, during the short time he lived in Seville, painted in a brilliant, dynamic style far removed from the Murillo imprint. Among the minor artists who resisted Murillo's impact, Sebastián de Llanos Valdés should be mentioned; his eclecticism produced some genuinely original works.

Apart from a few second rank artists, such as Juan José Carpio and Juan Carlos Gijón, who followed Valdés Leal or Herrera the Younger, most artists in Seville fell under Murillo's influence, sometimes in an excessively servile way. A survey of Murillo's imitators reveals such a monotony of style that it is difficult to distinguish between the work of one

fig. 70 Francisco Meneses Osorio *The Archangel Michael* (Hospital de la Caridad, Seville)

artist and another when the paintings are unsigned, which is frequently the case. In addition it is necessary to remember that the city's economy at the end of the seventeenth century and beginning of the eighteenth century continued to decline. This meant that ambitious artistic projects were not undertaken and that artists, lacking commissions, had to be content with executing lesser works in which they could not exercise their creative capacity to the full.

The foremost painter during the transition from the seventeenth century to the eighteenth century, and a faithful exponent of Murillo's style, was Juan Simón Gutiérrez (d. 1724). In his *The Death of St. Dominic* in the Museo de Bellas Artes, Seville, and *The Virgin and Child with Augustinian Saints* in the convent of the Trinidad de Carmona (his only two surviving paintings), he displays a personal style while working within the Murillo tradition, particularly in the shaping of his figures' faces. These two works enable us to identify other paintings by him with some degree of certainty.

Other painters of Murillo's school pose problems because of the scarcity of signed work. This is the case with Sebastián Gómez el Granadino, an artist who served his apprenticeship in his home town, Granada, where he assimilated the style of Alonso Cano. But when he settled in Seville in 1690 his art was influenced by that of Murillo and he evolved a personal style that, in his only signed work – *Santa Rosalia* (Salamanca Museum) – appears to be definitive, but which poses problems when we come to attributing works to him on stylistic grounds.

Even more confusing is the case of Sebastián Gómez el Mulato (d. 1730), an artist sometimes confused with Sebastián Gómez el Granadino. No signed works by him are known, so his *œuvre* has to be reconstructed through paintings attributed to him in historical records. El Mulato was a slave belonging to Murillo and was obviously likely to imitate his master's style faithfully, which makes the investigation of his work still more problematical.

Among Murillo's followers, Esteban Márquez (d. 1720) was one of the better painters. He is known through a small body of work which enables us to identify his style with some precision; although only two signed paintings by Márquez are known – *Jesus and Children* in Seville University and *The Vision of St. Dominic* (fig. 71) in the Fuentes de Andalucía parish church – other attributions can confidently be made. These include paintings from the Trinidad Convent, Seville, now dispersed among private collections and art galleries. Two episodes from the life of St. Augustine in the Museo de Bellas Artes, Seville are also by Márquez and the present writer considers that he also painted the large *Coronation of St. Augustine* in the church of San Juan de Aznalfarache.

A late imitator of Murillo was Andrés Pérez (d. 1727). He was a painter of little creative talent whose work was peopled with diminutive figures of gentle appearance. His only signed work is in the Museo de Bellas Artes, Seville; it depicts *The Last Judgement* and is a copy of an engraving by Jean Cousin. Other works in the same gallery attributed to him also show a lack of energy and inspiration.

Another artist who remained faithful to Murillo's style was Alonso Miguel de Tovar (d. 1758). His only signed religious work is the *Virgin of Consolation* in Seville Cathedral, dated 1720; like the other religious works attributed to him it bears the imprint of Murillo's influence.

However, contact with the Italian and French artists of his time is evident in his portraits, and these paintings are very different in spirit.

Bernardo Llorente Germán (d. 1759) also continued to practise Murillo's pictorial style throughout the first half of the eighteenth century. In the early part of his career, until approximately 1730, he was a modest imitator of Murillo. From then, however, his contact with the French and Italian painters who were in Seville at the court of Philip V encouraged him to adopt a more cosmopolitan style; his paintings acquired more technical skill and greater expressive power.

While some artists managed to resist Murillo's influence, there were less gifted painters in Seville who continued to work in the master's style. One of these was Juan Ruiz Soriano (d. 1763), who devoted himself to producing large paintings for the decoration of convent cloisters. We know that he worked for the convents of Los Terceros, San Agustín and San Francisco; sadly his style is repetitive and unoriginal.

A similar judgement can be made about Pedro Tortolero (d. 1766), an artist who was more interesting as an engraver than as a painter. We know that he worked for the cloisters of the Carmelite and Augustinian monasteries, but these works have not been identified. His only known autograph works are those which, according to Ceán Bermúdez, he made for San Nicolas de Bari, Seville: *The Betrothal of the Virgin and St. Joseph* and *The Death of St. Joseph*. Murillo's influence is evident in these works, but their technique is extremely poor.

Domingo Martínez (d. 1749) was the dominant figure in Seville painting in the first half of the eighteenth century. He was trained in Murillo's style and worked in this way until the Spanish court arrived in Seville in 1729. Then he came into contact with the French and Italian painters working for Philip V and Isabel de Farnese. Martínez is associated in particular with Jean Ranc, who became a close friend. It was a singularly beneficial contact for Martínez since it enabled him to incorporate the innovations of the French school into his style, which gave his painting a formal and spiritual elegance. Martínez worked mainly for Archbishop Luis Salcedo y Azcona, executing a large body of work under his patronage (fig. 72).

Andrés Rubira was another artist who discarded Murillo's influence as a result of his contact with French painting. After serving his apprenticeship in Seville alongside Domingo Martínez, with whom he later collaborated, he lived in Lisbon between 1740 and 1745 and absorbed the cosmopolitan spirit of the city. His work is not well known because of the scarcity of signed pictures, both religious works and portraits, but according to Ceán Bermúdez he was a consummate portrait painter.

The cultural effects of the age of enlightenment began to be felt in Seville from the middle of the eighteenth century. A desire for reform was felt in the city, and there was an attempt to improve the standard of living and to reverse the process of decline that had been dragging on for over a hundred years. The lively presence of Pablo de Olavide and Francisco de Bruna at the centre of city affairs activated various administrative and cultural reforms that made a notable difference to the general quality of life. Culturally Seville began to turn towards the rest of Europe, opening itself to the spirit of rococo and later of neo-classicism, both of which, particularly the rococo, left their mark on local art. Nevertheless, the imitation and copying of Murillo continued, partly as a result of the high esteem in which his work was held by foreign collectors and also because of the admiration his work still aroused among local painters.

fig. 71 Esteban Márquez *The Vision of St. Dominic* (parish church of Sta. Maria, Fuentes de Andalucía)

The spirit of the enlightenment revitalized artistic activity in the second half of the eighteenth century; in 1759 the artists of Seville established an artistic Academy, a revival of the one that had existed in Murillo's time. At first the Academy existed as a private enterprise, but, thanks to the intervention of Francisco de Bruna, in 1770 Charles III conceded an annual subsidy that guaranteed the continuing

fig. 72 Domingo Martínez *St. Barbara* (parish church of Hombrete, Seville)

fig. 73 Juan de Espinal *La Inmaculada of the Zodiac* (Museo Lázaro Galdiano, Madrid)

function of what then became known as the Real Escuela de la Tres Nobles Artes (Royal School of the Three Noble Arts). It was in this academy that the cult of Murillo was revived, imposing on young artists the routine exercise of copying the master's works which inevitably led to an impoverishment of local talent.

The most outstanding painter in Seville in the second half of the eighteenth century was Juan de Espinal (d. 1783) (fig. 73) who married one of Domingo Martínez's daughters and inherited his studio. Espinal absorbed the style of his father-in-law and grafted the language of French paintings on to the tradition of Murillo. In addition to these influences, Espinal incorporated rococo elements; this combination made him one of the most interesting painters of his time in Spain. Espinal, without being a slavish imitator of Murillo, was able to utilise aspects of Murillo's work which, when clothed in a new narrative technique, enabled him to achieve excellent results.

Another late devotee of Murillo was José Joaquín Cano (d. 1784), mentioned by Ceán Bermúdez as a good copyist. However, his personal work shows that he was an accomplished disciple of Espinal, immersed in the rococo. Juan de Dios Fernández (d. 1801) belonged to the last generation of eighteenth-century painters. He was an artist who copied Murillo and also used elements of his style in his own paintings with disappointing results.

Throughout the first half of the nineteenth century Murillo's style continued to dominate Seville's painters, and its School of Fine Arts was a sanctuary devoted to preserving his art. The desire to emulate his style was furthered by the international appreciation of his painting and the general demand for his work. At the very beginning of the century

Charles IV proposed replacing most of Murillo's paintings housed in Seville's religious buildings by copies. Luckily this project did not materialize, but a few years later Marshal Soult sacked the city's artistic riches and carried off all the Murillos he could find. Finally, from 1812 onwards Spanish and foreign collectors and antiquarians literally swept the city clean of Murillo's works; at this point he was Europe's most fashionable painter.

The passion for Murillo resulted in the endless imitation of his style in Seville from the beginning of the nineteenth century; his autograph works were tirelessly copied and sold as substitutes. This mass imitation of Murillo obviously impoverished the Seville school of painting.

Joaquín María Cortés (d. 1835) stands out among the painters who, from the beginning of the nineteenth century, dedicated themselves to emulating the master. He was known in his time as the second Murillo, and was the artist commissioned by Charles IV to make copies of all the Murillos in the Hopital de la Caridad in Seville (they were to be substituted for the originals that the king was considering removing to his projected Royal Museum in Madrid).

During the romantic period, most Seville artists served an apprenticeship based on Murillo's work. Although a number of landscapes began to be produced in this period, religious painting did not disappear. Certainly, many religious establishments were suppressed after the disentailment of Church property in 1836, and therefore ceased to patronize painters, so that artistic work of a decorative nature for altarpieces, cloisters and church interiors went out of fashion almost completely. Nevertheless, a fresh clientele who demanded works with religious themes designed for private devotion, to hang in bedrooms or in small chapels and domestic oratories, emerged among the pious new bourgeoisie. The religious paintings engendered by this demand – a flourishing business in which nearly all local painters were engaged – were mostly painted in a style derived directly from Murillo.

Antonio Cabral Bejarano (d. 1861) is typical of such a painter. He produced many copies of Murillo, as well as compositions in which he imitated his style. The series of paintings Cabral did to decorate the Palace of San Telmo, then the residence of the Duke and Duchess of Montpensier, is one of the best proofs of the devotion to Murillo in Seville throughout the nineteenth century. His sons, Francisco and Manuel, also produced religious paintings in the style of Murillo.

At this date artists also imitated Murillo's paintings of scenes from popular life. The subject of child beggars or street urchins was romanticized by artists such as José María Escacena (d. 1858) and Andrés Cortés (d. 1879) in pictures that were given nineteenth-century settings but kept an expressive and compositional formula based on Murillo's famous child paintings.

Other artists, such as Antonio María Esquivel (d. 1857), were trained in Murillo's style and assimilated it so thoroughly that they never rid themselves of the influence. José Gutiérrez de la Vega (d. 1865), both in his early portraits and more particularly in his religious paintings, displayed a special enthusiasm for Murillo's work. Another Seville artist with the same predilection was José María Romero (d. 1880), whose religious work shows this long lasting devotion to Murillo in the local school of painting.

In the last third of the nineteenth century, Seville painters turned to historical subjects or realism and there was a rapid decline in Murillo's influence on local artists. From this time on prints and engravings, and later printing itself, began to reproduce Murillo's work in vast quantities. Public taste was finally saturated and this resulted in a tendency to reject Murillo. At the beginning of the twentieth century, this was endorsed by art critics who identified Murillo's painting with sickly sweetness and an odious, affected prettiness. It was thus, that at the end of the nineteenth century, the influence of Murillo disappeared from Seville painting.

Murillo and Eighteenth-Century Painting Outside Spain

Ellis Waterhouse

Until the Napoleonic invasion of Spain in 1808 the works of Spanish painters were surprisingly little known in the rest of Europe – except for the work of Ribera, who was almost universally known as *Spagnoletto*, as if the spirit of Spanish art was concentrated in him. He was indeed a Spaniard, but he had lived all his life in Naples and a great many of his paintings had been exported to other European countries. This had not happened with the work of other Spanish painters, and certainly not with Murillo, who had spent nearly all his life in Seville, and whose work was only sparsely represented, even in Madrid collections, in his own lifetime. Yet his was the only native Spanish name known to the German Sandrart, who gave a brief (and wonderfully inaccurate) biography of him in the Latin version (*Academia Picturae Eruditae*) of his 1675 history of the fine arts in Europe, published in 1683. Sandrart invented for Murillo a visit of some years study in Italy and important commissions from a number of Cardinals in Rome, presumably because he could not imagine that a painter whose *Self Portrait* had been engraved in Brussels with such distinction in the year of his death (1682) by Richard Collin (page 152) had not benefited from these advantages! And Sandrart repeated the Collin engraving in his own book, so that the name of Murillo remained not unfamiliar, before the end of the seventeenth century, to cultivated persons who were interested in painting and were not Spaniards.

fig. 74 Joshua Reynolds *Young Shepherd Boy* (Collection The Earl of Halifax)

Knowledge of Murillo outside Spain was, however, gradually spread by the occasional acquisition of pictures by him by merchants and diplomats during the later seventeenth and the eighteenth centuries. Spaniards were naturally unbusinesslike and the economy of the country in the seventeenth century was increasingly in the hands of Genoese merchants. One of these, of the Bielato family, in 1674 bequeathed to the Capuchins of Genoa half a dozen religious paintings by Murillo,[1] which were on view in their church of the SS Concezione until they were bought for England in 1806 at the time of the Napoleonic invasion of Italy. Merchants from the Low Countries were also in close contact with Seville. Josua van Belle from Rotterdam in 1670 and Nicolás Omazur, a silk merchant of Antwerp, in 1672 had their portraits painted by Murillo (Cat. 62 and 63), and a member of the Antwerp family of De Fraula (probably merchants, but ennobled in 1736 as 'Counts') had a sale in Brussels on 21 July 1738,[2] which contained four religious works by Murillo, two of them certainly important, and one of them probably the *Marriage at Cana* which later belonged to Jean de Julienne in Paris (Cat. 57) and may have been studied with attention by Watteau. But for Murillo's *fortuna* in England the most important person was a rather mysterious character, a merchant and perhaps a banker named Sir Daniel Arthur,[3] who had been knighted in Dublin in 1690 by James II (then already in 'exile') and whose widow, by 1729,[4] had brought to England an important group of old masters which included the Murillo *Self Portrait* (Cat. 61) and the Woburn and Boughton pictures (Cat. 74 and 59).

Other Murillos were imported into England, apparently before 1760 by John Blackwood of Soho Square, some of which were sold to Sir Lawrence Dundas, while others passed by descent to the Cartwrights of Aynho, where one at least was copied by Thomas Gainsborough. Others were also imported by diplomats, Sir William Stanhope (later Lord Harrington), the ambassador in Madrid in 1729, and Sir Benjamin Keene, who provided one of the Murillos which entered the collection of the Prime Minister, Sir Robert Walpole, at Houghton. By the middle of the eighteenth century, Murillo's work was not at all badly represented in British collections and both Reynolds and Gainsborough were familiar with some of his works and gave evidence of that knowledge. Several of Reynolds's 'fancy pictures' (notably the *Shepherd Boy* in the collection of the Earl of Halifax; fig. 74) are deliberately modelled on Murillo, and Gainsborough admired Murillo's handling of paint sufficiently to have acquired one of his pictures – the *St. John the Baptist* now in

fig. 75 Thomas Gainsborough *Girl with a Dog* (Sir Alfred Beit Collection)

the National Gallery, where it is considered a studio work. One of the most important Murillos in England was *The Flight into Egypt* (Cat. 7) bought at auction in London in 1756 by Sir Samson Gideon.

The earliest record of a Murillo in England is of the sale of a picture of 'Boys' bought in 1693 for the sum of 80 guineas, which Evelyn, who saw it, thought was expensive: but there is some reason to think this may not have been an original. The same uncertainty also rests over the only Murillo recorded in France in the seventeenth century – a picture of 'St. James' (a saint curiously absent from Murillo's certain *oeuvre*), which was said to have been in the chapel at Bussy Rabutin. But there is fairly good reason to believe that there may have been good examples of Murillo present in the collection of the Comtesse de Verrue at Paris, although they do not appear in the surviving catalogues of the sale in 1737.[5] One of these was the *Laughing Boy* in the National Gallery (Cat. 71), and another may well have been *The Good Shepherd* (fig. 88), which was copied in Paris by Grimou, probably in the 1730s. This Grimou copy, which later passed in England as the original (and was engraved as a famous Murillo), seems also to have been looked at with interest by both Reynolds and Gainsborough.

It was certainly the disruption of the European scene by Napoleon's invasions which made it possible for the real Murillo, the Spanish devotional painter, to become one of the most famous of European artists: but it remains unclear whether, before 1800, Murillo's reputation outside Spain rested very largely on his secular pictures of Spanish peasant children. Angulo (nos. 378 to 404) lists only about 25 such pictures among Murillo's enormous output: the earliest record of all but about two of these is outside Spain. Two of those now at Munich (Cat. 65 and 66), which were perhaps Murillo's best known works outside Spain before 1800, seem to have been bought on the Antwerp market before the end of the seventeenth century. It seems to me quite likely that such pictures were specifically designed for the Flemish market, and the idea of painting them may even have been suggested to Murillo by Antwerp merchants who frequented Seville and perhaps did a little art dealing on the side. Certainly the impact of Murillo's art outside Spain before the nineteenth century is limited to such pictures. There is a case to be made for the view that Murillo was one of the most positive influences on certain of the 'fancy pictures' which were among the most popular and original inventions of both Reynolds and Gainsborough.

NOTES

1. See Angulo no. 93 for the bibliography of the Genoese bequest. Several of the pictures are now in the Wallace Collection.
2. The sale catalogue is reprinted in Gerard Hoet, *Catalogus of Naamlyst van Schilderyen . . .*, 1752, I, pp. 518–44.
3. His name figures in the Secret Service Expenses of James II (*Camden Society*, 1851) as a channel through whom James subsidized his illegitimate children abroad. He seems to have left a family in Spain (one of whom was presumably the 'D. Francesco Artier' recorded by Palomino as owning certain pictures by Murillo) and the death of a Mr Arthur, 'a Spanish merchant', is recorded in the *Gentlemen's Magazine* for 1764.
4. His widow married Mr Bagnall (Bagnols) and brought the pictures to England, where they were shown to Lord Egmont (when he was Viscount Percival) 3 Feb. 1728/29. The extract from his Diary is reprinted (with the correction of Moriglio for 'Monglio'!) in *The Burlington Magazine* LXXXIX, 1947, p. 78.
5. For the tangled story of the MS copies of the Verrue sale catalogue, see Allan Braham, *The Spanish School* (National Gallery Catalogues), 1970, pp. 64–65, note 3.

1 *The Virgin Presenting the Rosary to St. Dominic*

2 *The Vision of Friar Lauterio*

3 *The Two Trinities*

4 *San Diego Giving Food to the Poor*

5 *St. Francis Comforted by an Angel*

7 *The Flight into Egypt*

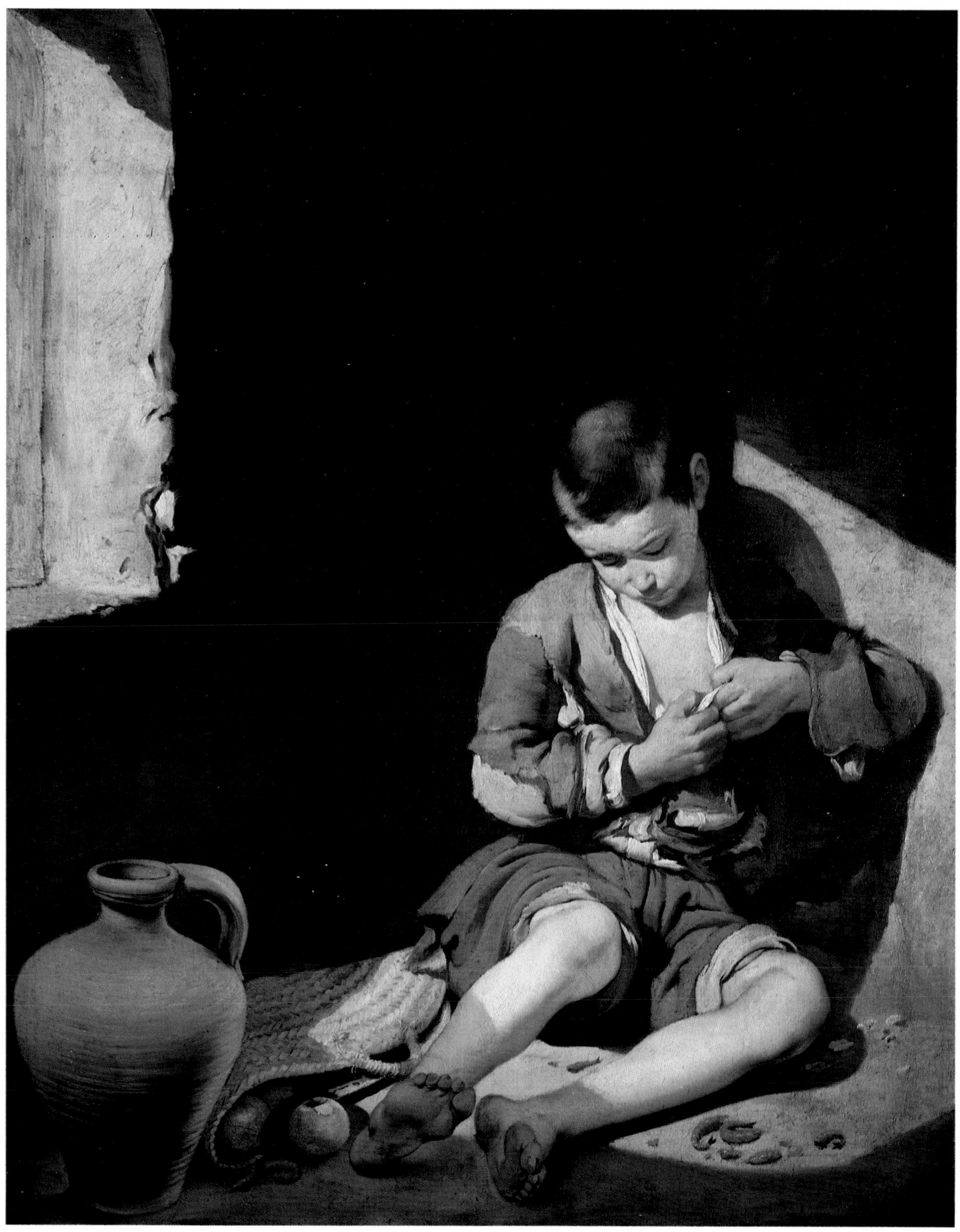

6 *The Street Urchin*

18 *Adoration of the Shepherds*

8 *The Holy Family with the Little Bird*

9 *Virgin of the Rosary*

12 *The Penitent Magdalen*

10 *Virgin of the Rosary*

11 *Virgin and Child*

14 *The Immaculate Conception with Friar Juan de Quirós*

13 *The Immaculate Conception*

16 *San Isidoro*

17 *San Leandro*

21 *The Resurrection of Christ*

15 *San Rodrigo*

20 *St. Ildefonso Receiving the Chasuble from the Virgin*

19 *The Vision of St. Bernard*

24 *St. John the Baptist and the Pharisees*

22 *St. John the Baptist Pointing to Christ*

23 *The Baptism of Christ*

25 *Virgin and Child*

28 *Adoration of the Kings*

26 *Virgin and Child with Angels*

27 *The Good Shepherd*

35 *The Infant St. John the Baptist and the Lamb*

29 *Santa Justa*

30 *Santa Rufina*

31 *Immaculate Conception of the Escorial*

34 *The Hunter: Portrait of Don Antonio Hurtado de Salcedo*

32 *Jacob Setting the Peeled Rods before the Flocks of Laban*

33 *Laban Searching for his Stolen Household Gods in Rachel's Tent*

41 *Santa Justa and Santa Rufina*

40 *San Leandro and San Buenaventura*

39 *The Triumph of the Eucharist*

38 *The Immaculate Conception*

36 *The Dream of the Patrician*

37 *The Patrician John and his Wife before Pope Liberius*

SANCTÆ MARIÆ MAJORIS ICHNOGRAPHIA.
MDCCCXIII.

45 *The Healing of the Paralytic at the Pool of Bethesda*

46 *The Return of the Prodigal Son*

44 *Adoration of the Shepherds*

42 *St. Thomas of Villanueva*

43 *St. Francis Embracing the Crucified Christ*

53 *The Prodigal Son Receiving his Portion*

54 *The Prodigal Son Leaving his Father's House*

55 *The Prodigal Son Feasting*

56 *The Prodigal Son Feeding Swine*

47 *The Prodigal Son Receiving his Portion*

48 *The Prodigal Son Leaving his Father's House*

49 *The Prodigal Son Feasting*

50 *The Prodigal Son Driven Out*

51 *The Prodigal Son Feeding the Swine*

52 *The Return of the Prodigal Son*

57 *The Marriage of Cana*

60 *The Christ Child Asleep on the Cross*

59 *The Infant St. John*

58 *The Holy Family*

64 *St. Thomas of Villanueva as a Child Dividing his Clothes Among Beggar Boys*

65 *Two Boys Eating a Pie*

66 *Children Playing Dice*

67 *Invitation to the Game of Pelota*

68 *Three Boys*

71 *Laughing Boy*

69 *The Flower Girl*

72 *The Virgin and the Child with Santa Rosalia*

70 *Santa Rosa of Lima*

73 *The Martyrdom of St. Andrew*

76 *The Presentation of the Virgin in the Temple*

74 *Cherubs Scattering Flowers*

75 *Immaculate Conception of Los Venerables*

61 *Self Portrait*

63 *Portrait of Nicolás de Omazur*

77 *Portrait of Don Juan Antonio de Miranda y Ramírez de Vergara*

62 *Portrait of Josua van Belle*

Engraving after Murillo's *Self Portrait* by Richard Collin, Brussels, 1682

Catalogue of the Paintings

1

2

1

The Virgin Presenting the Rosary to St. Dominic

207 × 162 cm
Signed: *Ba*[meus] *Murillo fc*
c. 1638–40
Archbishop's Palace, Seville
[*repr. on p.* 73]

This picture, which comes from the Dominican Monastery of Santo Tomás, Seville, has always been considered to be Murillo's first known work, painted around 1638–40. Both composition and style obviously derive from the work of earlier Seville masters. This is evident in the figure drawing, particularly in the facial expressions of the characters, which show the influence of Murillo's master, Juan del Castillo, who used fine, delicate strokes in the depiction of faces that almost invariably were characterized with a faint smile (fig. 76).

fig. 76 Juan del Castillo *The Virgin of the Rosary* (private collection, Carmona)

Murillo has also introduced a celestial apparition; flooded by golden light, music-making angels appear with cherubim who are throwing flowers at St. Dominic. This type of celestial *gloria* was first used in Seville painting by Juan de Roelas, a master who died when Murillo was very young, but whose pictures he doubtless saw in Seville's churches and convents. This picture furnishes evidence that Murillo learnt from older masters at the beginning of his career, before establishing his definitive style; the clothing, with strongly modelled, but broken folds, reveals the influence of Zurbarán. The absence of characteristics typical of Murillo's work has caused some authors to deny – unjustifiably – that the work is his.

There is a version of this painting very close to the original in the Toreno Collection, Madrid.

PROVENANCE
Santo Tomás Monastery, Seville; 1810 removed by the French to the Alcázar, Seville; 1835 Archbishop's Palace, Seville

EXHIBITIONS
Seville 1896, no. 34; Seville 1982, no. 42

REFERENCES
Angulo 1971, p. 344; Angulo 1981, I, p. 240; II, p. 270, no. 185; Braham 1965, p. 445; Carriazo 1929, p. 796; Ceán Bermúdez 1800, II, pp. 49, 58; Gaya Nuño 1978, no. 2; Gestoso y Pérez 1896, p. 14; Gómez Imaz 1896, no. 112; Montoto 1923, p. 20; Valdivieso and Serrera 1979, p. 73

2

The Vision of Friar Lauterio

216 × 170 cm
c. 1638–40
Fitzwilliam Museum, Cambridge
[*repr. on p.* 74]

In the bottom right-hand corner of the painting there is a long inscription explaining the subject: once, when Friar Lauterio was studying theology, he encountered serious difficulties with problems of interpretation and he therefore prayed to St. Francis, asking him to reveal the solution to his problems; at that moment, the Virgin, St. Thomas Aquinas and St. Francis appeared to him. St. Francis, addressing himself to Friar Lauterio, recommended him to consult St. Thomas's *Summa Theologica*, which the friar had hitherto disdained to read; when the friar turned to St. Thomas's text after this apparition he discovered the explanation to the problems he had raised on the very pages at which he opened the book.

The style and technique of this painting show that it belongs to Murillo's early period. It can be placed between 1638 and 1640; very close, therefore, to *The Virgin Presenting the Rosary to St. Dominic* (Cat. 1). In this

3

picture Murillo reveals his early training; the faces in particular reflect the style of his master, Juan del Castillo, while the severe poses remind us of Zurbarán's style. The influence of Roelas is also evident in the bright background with its golden light and in the group of angels.

PROVENANCE
Painted for the Dominican Convento de Regina Angelorum, Seville; 1810 removed by the French to the Alcázar, Seville; 1883 Canon Pereira; Joaquín Reinoso; sold to William George Clarke; passed to Joseph Prior, who donated it to the Museum

REFERENCES
Angulo 1981, I, p. 241; II, p. 131, no. 124; Arana de Varflora 1789, I, p. 48; Braham 1965, p. 445; Ceán Bermúdez 1800, II, p. 49; Ceán Bermúdez 1806, p. 35; Curtis 1883, no. 117; Gaya Nuño 1978, no. 1; Gómez Imaz 1896, no. 111; Mayer 1923[1], p. 3; Montoto 1923, p. 20; Ponz 1947 ed., p. 786; Standish 1840, p. 314

ADDITIONAL REFERENCES
J. W. Goodison and D. Sutton in Fitzwilliam Museum *Catalogue of Paintings*, I, Cambridge, 1960, no. 100, pl. 109

3

The Two Trinities

222 × 162 cm
c. 1640
Nationalmuseum, Stockholm
[repr. on p. 75]

This is a very early work of Murillo's, just post-dating *The Virgin Presenting the Rosary to St. Dominic* (Cat. 1) and *The Vision of Friar Lauterio* (Cat. 2); it can be dated around 1640–42. Despite the painting's large dimensions, Murillo confidently created a complex composition encompassing the celestial and terrestrial spheres and including a beautiful landscape background.

The iconographic theme of the Two Trinities first appeared in the Counter-Reformation literature of the late sixteenth century; it established a parallel between the Celestial Trinity (God the Father, the Holy Ghost and the Son) and the Terrestrial Trinity (the Virgin, St. Joseph and the Christ Child), Christ forming the link between Heaven and Earth. Counter-Reformation writers emphasized the humanity of Jesus and also revered both Mary and St. Joseph; his cult became increasingly popular.

Compositionally the scene adopts the iconography of the Return from Egypt, or the Return from the Temple, when the Child also appears with his parents. A precedent for this subject was the sculpture by Martínez Montañés in Seville (Hernández 1949, p. 42, pl. 18). Murillo created a strictly symmetrical composition, almost Renaissance in character. Strong light accentuates the monumentality of the figures, echoing Zurbarán's style. The landscape background, with a very low horizon, leaves a wide luminous space against which the figures are silhouetted in the style of Roelas. In the heavenly *gloria*, the angel on the left is a reversed copy of that in the 1612 *Adoration of the Shepherds* by Abraham Bloemart (Louvre) which was well-known through engravings and much appreciated in Seville, where it was copied in the works of other artists. Murillo painted the subject of *The Two Trinities* again towards the end of his life – a vast painting now in the National Gallery, London.

PROVENANCE
1848 Julian Williams, Seville; 1853 Standish sale, London; 1883 Martin Colnaghi, London; 1892 Weber, Hamburg; 1912 Berlin; Heinemann Gallery, Munich; 1918 Karl Bergsten Collection, Stockholm

REFERENCES
Angulo 1935–36, I, p. 61; Angulo 1981, I, p. 242; II, no. 189; III, pl. 6; Braham 1965, p. 445ff; Braham 1970, p. 61; Curtis 1883, no. 126; Gaya Nuño 1978, no. 5; Head 1848, p. 163; Kubler and Soria 1959, p. 274; MacLaren 1952, p. 35; Mâle 1932, p. 312, fig. 185; Mayer 1913, no. 5; Mayer 1923[1], pp. 3, 289; Méndez Casal 1936, p. 8; Stirling-Maxwell 1848, III, p. 1424

ADDITIONAL REFERENCES
Hernández, *Martínez Montañés*, Seville, 1949

4

San Diego Giving Food to the Poor

173 × 183 cm
Inscribed on the lower part, in verse:
Da de comer al Pobre y el provecho
Recive Diego de que el Pobre coma
El Pobre come y Diego satisfecho
El dar las Gracias por su quenta toma
Mira en el Pobre a Dios y de su pecho
Caridad todos a Dios le ofrece Aroma
I a un tiempo exercitando vida activa
El Santo Goza la Corona dichosa
c. 1646
Academia de San Fernando, Madrid
[repr. on p. 76]

This painting forms part of the series executed between 1645 and 1648 for the *claustro chico* (small cloister) of the Monastery of San Francisco in Seville; it was Murillo's first important public commission. The 11 pictures illustrate stories from the lives of the Franciscan saints, extolling the virtues of the Order: prayer and love of the poor. They remained in their original place until the Spanish War of Independence (1808–14), when they were dispersed. Some are in France: *The Angels' Kitchen* (fig. 4) and *San Junípero and the Beggar* (both in Musée du Louvre), *San Diego in Ecstasy before the Crucifix* (Augustinians' Museum, Toulouse) and *San Salvador de Horta before the Inquisition* (formerly in a private Parisian

4

collection and recently auctioned). The two pictures that are in the Academia de San Fernando are exhibited here: *San Diego Giving Food to the Poor* and *St. Francis Comforted by an Angel* (Cat. 5). *The Death of St. Clare* (fig. 3) is in Dresden and *St. Giles before Pope Gregory* IX is in Raleigh, North Carolina, while the Sterling and Francine Clark Institute, Williamstown has *Brother Julian de Alcalá and the Soul of Philip* II; *Two Franciscan Saints* is in the National Gallery, Ottawa.

The picture shows one of the charitable deeds of San Diego of Alcalá. The saint, who was born in San Nicolás de Puerta in the province of Seville, was sent to the Franciscan monastery at Arruzafa in the province of Córdoba and spent the last years of his life in Alcalá de Henares, near Madrid, where he died in 1463. He was canonized in 1589 through the influence of Philip II.

Although this is a religious work, it has the strong naturalistic accent of seventeenth-century Spanish painting. Murillo's early style shows the impact of the tenebrous, naturalistic paintings of Zurbarán, whose influence was especially strong in Seville. The figures are arranged in a variety of poses on parallel planes; the powerful individualism of the faces and the dignity the painter assigns to the beggars is especially impressive.

In portraying San Diego, who reappears in other pictures of the series, Murillo seems to have been inspired by the engraving by Pegna (or Pena) published in Rome in 1589 on the occasion of the Saint's canonization (*De vita et miraculis*, Rome, 1589, p. 160); this in turn was inspired by an elaborate portrait of San Diego of Alcalá, commissioned by Archbishop Carillo (d. 1482) and taken to Rome as a true likeness of the friar. The features are similar but, as Angulo has pointed out, the energy and personality of Murillo's portrayal is missing in the print.

The woman on the left holding a child in her arms, a model very similar to St. Anne in *The Virgin and St. Anne* (fig. 77), has sometimes been taken to be a portrait of Murillo's elder sister, Ana, who took him into her household on the death of their parents. In the foreground, a group of children join the saint in his prayers; they are precursors of the pictures of young children that Murillo painted throughout his career.

fig. 77 Murillo *The Virgin and St. Anne* (Museo del Prado, Madrid)

PROVENANCE
Convento de San Francisco, Seville; 1810 removed by the French to the Alcázar, Seville; 1811 Convento del Rosario, Madrid; Academia de San Fernando, Madrid; taken to Paris by Marshal Soult for the Musée Napoléon; 1814 returned to the Academia de San Fernando

EXHIBITIONS
Madrid 1927, no. 41; London and Paris 1976, no. 30

REFERENCES
Academia catalogue 1929, p. 37, no. 23; Academia inventory 1964, no. 658; Academia catalogue 1965, no. 658; Angulo 1961[1], p. 4; Angulo 1971, p. 344; Angulo 1981, I, pp. 248–49; II, no. 4; III, pl. 10–11; Ceán Bermúdez 1800, II, p. 59; Curtis 1883, no. 270; Gaya Nuño 1978, no. 10; Guinard and Baticle 1967, pp. 265–66; Kubler and Soria 1959, p. 275; Lafond 1907, p. 39; Lafuente 1935, p. 34; Mayer 1911, p. 172, pl. XLVI; Mayer 1913, p. 8; Mayer 1947, p. 352, fig. 264; Palomino 1947, p. 1031; Ponz 1947 ed., p. 787; Tormo 1929, p. 37

5

St. Francis Comforted by an Angel

127 × 183 cm
Inscribed on the lower part, in verse:
Martirio Dulçe, Gloria Repetida
Llagado siente el seraphin humano
En su mortal dolor halla la Vida
En su Tormento gozo soberano
Crece el amor y en una y otra herida
anima incendios de su ardor Ufano
Pide Aliento a Dios Hombre y dale Aliento
De un Angel la dulçura y instrumento
c. 1646
Academia de San Fernando, Madrid
[*repr. on p.* 77]

5

In this painting Murillo treats a theme common in European painting from the end of the sixteenth century, which had originated in the writing of St. Bonaventure. During St. Francis of Assisi's last illness he was comforted by the apparition of a musician-angel. Both Domenichino and Guercino painted the subject and in Spain there is a version (fig. 78) by the Valencian, Ribalta. In Murillo's picture the saint is stretched out on a rush mat while the angel appears on the left; the enormous scale of the angel shows that Murillo was still dependent on the work of Ribera and Zubarán. But, in *San Diego Giving Food to the Poor* (Cat. 4), Murillo's figures are generally smaller and there is a greater feeling for space, an indication of the way his art was to develop later.

The rather solid appearance of the angel recalls Zurbarán's figures, while its hair, falling in waves on the forehead and around the ears, is close to the work of contemporary Seville sculptors. It is earthbound and very different from Murillo's later celestial, airborne angels. St. Francis's expression is one of ecstatic absorption and

fig. 78 Francisco de Ribalta *St. Francis Comforted by an Angel* (Museo del Prado, Madrid)

6

gratitude for the gift of divine music. Naturalistic details are emphasized; his habit, the bullrush mat and his hands and feet are painted in masterly fashion. The chiaroscuro enveloping the scene accentuates the intimacy and mystery of the celestial vision.

PROVENANCE
Convento de San Francisco, Seville; 1810 removed by the French to the Alcázar, Seville; 1813 Academia de San Fernando

REFERENCES
Academia catalogue 1927, p. 37, no. 23; Academia inventory 1964, no. 658; Academia catalogue 1965, no. 660; Angulo 1961[1], p. 4; Angulo 1971, p. 344; Angulo 1981, I, p. 246–48; II, no. 1; III, pl. 7; Ceán Bermudéz 1800, II, p. 50; Curtis 1883, no. 287; Gaya Nuño 1978, no. 9; Guinard and Baticle 1967, pp. 265–66; Kubler and Soria 1959, p. 275; Lafond 1907, p. 39; Mayer 1913[1], no. 7; Mayer 1947, p. 352, fig. 264; Palomino 1947, p. 1031; Ponz 1947 ed., p. 787; Tormo 1929, p. 37

6

The Street Urchin

137 × 115 cm
c. 1645–50
Musée du Louvre, Paris
[*repr. on p.* 79]

Murillo was one of the first artists to use vagrant and begging children as a subject for paintings, a genre that has become one of the more admired themes of baroque painting. Although it is probable that Murillo knew paintings of such subjects by Ribera and in the Italian work of the Danish artist Eberhardt Keil, who specialized in scenes of daily life, Murillo's paintings in the genre achieved a spontaneity unprecedented in European art. In fact, Murillo may be seen as a spiritual precursor of eighteenth-century rococo art, especially with his attractive and stylish paintings of children of his mature period.

Murillo's paintings of children were much sought after, particularly by foreign consuls and merchants resident in Seville, who took his paintings back to their own countries, where they were highly valued on the art market. This picture can be considered the first known example of Murillo's work in this genre. Stylistically it can be dated around 1645 to 1650. The painting has a marked naturalistic accent; it shows a child seated in a shadowy room plagued by fleas, which he is trying to rid himself of. The strong play of light and shade broken by a ray of sunshine coming in through the window creates a gloomy atmosphere reinforced by the forlorn and poverty-stricken appearance of the boy. The pessimism of these works was later abandoned by Murillo and gave way to lively and optimistic paintings of children. Likewise, the thick, heavy brushstrokes with which this work was painted were later

7

replaced by a more fluent style with airy, transparent effects.

PROVENANCE
1776 Paris, art market; 1786 Jean Luis Gaignent; 1782 Radix de Sainte Foix, who sold it to the painter Lebrun; 1782 Louis XVI; Musée du Louvre

EXHIBITIONS
Paris 1963, no. 60

REFERENCES
Angulo 1981, I, p. 445, II, p. 303, no. 390; Baticle, Lacambre and Rissot, 1981, p. 120; Curtis 1883, no. 411; Gaya Nuño 1978, no. 8; Hautecour 1926, no. 1717; Mayer 1923[1], p. 206; Ricci 1913, no. 1717; Villot 1849, no. 1551

PROVENANCE
Sir William Chapman (d. 1748); James Mendez; Micham Sale, Feb. 1756; Samson Gideon, to his son Sir Sampson Gideon (Lord Eardley), Belvedere, Kent; 1871 Mrs. Culling Hanbury; 1938 Sir Francis Fremantle; 1945 sold at Christie's, London; bought by Maurice Harris; 1947 exported to U.S.A.; donated to the Detroit Institute of Arts by K.T.Keller, Leslie H.Green and Robert N.Green

EXHIBITIONS
British Institution, London 1822; British Institution, London 1845; Manchester 1857; British Institution, London 1862; Royal Academy, London 1902; London 1938

REFERENCES
Angulo 1981, I, p. 246; II, p. 208, no. 230; Curtis 1883, no. 107; Gaya Nuño 1978, no. 23; Richardson 1948, p. 78

ADDITIONAL REFERENCES
Exhibition of Works by the Old Masters including a Special Collection of Paintings and Drawings by Claude, Royal Academy, London, 1902, no. 93

7
The Flight into Egypt

207 × 162 mm
Signed: *B m e Murillo fc*
c. 1647–50
The Institute of Arts, Detroit, Gift of Mr. and Mrs. K.T.Keller, Mr. and Mrs. Leslie H.Green and Mr. and Mrs. Robert N.Green
[*repr. on p.* 78]

Murillo painted two versions of *The Flight into Egypt* at the start of his career. The first, now in the Palazzo Bianco, Genoa, is datable *c.* 1645; the second, in the Institute of Arts, Detroit, seems to be later in date and could have been painted between 1647 and 1650. The two are very similar; the only slight difference is in the figure of St. Joseph.

The painting shows that Murillo was aiming at a naturalistic treatment of subjects from the beginning of his career. In fact, without the biblical subject matter it could be said that Murillo was depicting a peasant family in transit from one country village to another. The characters' clothes are contemporary, except for St. Joseph's smock and cloak, which are timeless; similarly, their gestures and expressions are those of the ordinary people of the time. Murillo has achieved a convincing transposition of the spirit of the Gospel to the historical moment in which he lived. The expressions of the Virgin and St. Joseph reflect a deep concern for their son's and their own fate, although they also appear confident of divine help.

A broad landscape, closed on the left by woodland and opening on the right to a view of rolling country, serves as the background to the composition. The soft luminous tones imparted by the stormy sky augment the subtle lyrical atmosphere.

8
The Holy Family with the Little Bird

144 × 188 cm
Before 1650
Museo del Prado, Madrid
[*repr. on p.* 81]

This is one of Murillo's best and most popular paintings; it is generally dated a little before 1650, in the artist's early period. The naturalistic treatment of the subject and the use of light are reminiscent of the tenebrous paintings of the preceding generation; the picture echoes the intimacy of Zurbarán's paintings and, in its meticulous execution of inanimate objects such as the drapery and the work basket, the art of Ribera.

But at the same time it possesses a delicate charm and a sensation of familial tenderness, which, together with a masterly rendering of everyday life, were to be the characteristics of Murillo's mature work. It is these elements which are the reason for the picture's popularity. The sheer virtuosity in portraying infant charm, already apparent in the paintings for the *claustro chico* (small cloister) of San Francisco (Cat. 4–5), is here used to reflect the Christ Child's playful joy; it anticipates the scenes of childhood that were to follow some years later.

The Christ Child's gesture of holding up the little bird to attract the attention of the dog – readying itself to catch it – has been related to the *Madonna del Gatto* (fig. 79) by Federico Barocci, now in the National Gallery, London, which was much copied; an engraving of it by Cornelius Cort, dated 1577 survives. Murillo might have been influenced by the engraving, but could equally well have had access to one of the painted copies; there was an excellent copy in Ecija, in the province of Seville, which he may have

8

seen (Pérez Sánchez 1967). That Barocci and Murillo shared similar sensibilities, as has been often pointed out, is immediately obvious here, despite their differing techniques in the treatment of light and material.

Murillo illustrates the domestic religious scene with simplicity. It is an admirable example of the sensibility of his time; the Holy Family are shown in an intimate, domestic setting without a glimpse of heavenly or divine intervention. The painter appears to have introduced a slight iconographic variation; St. Joseph is presented as a principal character, in no way inferior to the Virgin, who is depicted seated in the semi-darkness of the middle ground. This perhaps reflects an especial devotion to the saint on the part of the person who commissioned the painting. Alternatively, it may reflect the esteem in which St. Joseph was held throughout the seventeenth century, a result of Counter-Reformation ideology. Murillo himself produced several paintings and drawings of St. Joseph and the Christ Child. In this depiction of paternal love, the painter appears to be following the texts of the Carmelite Graciano de la Madre de Dios, who in his book on St. Joseph (1597) wrote that the saint never left home without

fig. 79 Federico Barocci *Madonna del Gatto* (National Gallery, London)

9

returning with a present for the Child – a bird, for example, or apples. The devotional tone of the familiar intimacy is used in both narrative and painting.

The picture must have been restored; Ford claimed that the Virgin's face, which had been badly damaged, was repainted while the canvas was in France. Curtis concurs with this opinion and believes that the canvas was trimmed at the top and on each side, an observation made previously by Madrazo. The present measurements of the picture are no smaller than those given in the royal inventories of 1744 and 1746, but they are less than those shown in 1772 and 1794.

PROVENANCE

Miguel de Espinosa (cousin of the Conde Aguila), Seville; who gave it to Cardinal de Molina; 1744 bought from his heirs by Isabel Farnese; 1746 Palacio de La Granja, Segovia, inv. no. 667; 1772 Palacio Real, Madrid, inv. no. 667; 1810–17 Musée Napoléon, Paris; 1818 returned to Spain; 1819 Museo del Prado

EXHIBITIONS

Madrid 1972; London and Paris 1976, no. 31; Munich and Vienna 1982, no. 50

REFERENCES

Ainaud 1946, p. 43; Angulo 1971, p. 345, fig. 364; Angulo 1981, I, pp. 283–84; II, no. 193; III, pl. 51; Carriaso 1929, p. 182; Ceán Bermúdez 1800, II, p. 64; Curtis 1883, no. 137; Ford 1855; Gaya Nuño 1978, no. 29, pl. IX; Lozoya 1967, p. 83; Madrazo 1872, p. 67; Mayer 1913[1], p. 341; Mayer 1923, pp. 18, 289; Pérez Sánchez 1967, p. 229; Ponz 1947 ed., pp. 525–26; Prado catalogue 1819, no. 147; Prado catalogue 1854–58, no. 43; Prado catalogue 1872–1907, no. 854; Prado catalogue 1910–72, no. 960; Prado inventory 1849, no. 35

9

Virgin of the Rosary

166 × 125 cm
c. 1650
Musée Goya, Castres (on deposit from the Musée du Louvre, Paris)
[*repr. on p.* 82]

The Virgin and Child as a theme in its own right was not very common in Spanish painting, despite the country's Marian tradition. Fifteenth-century Flemish paintings of the subject were imported into Spain and the subject appeared in the Spanish Levant at the end of the sixteenth century, usually as the central panel of an altarpiece. During the Renaissance, Juan de Juanes y Morales executed many small-scale works of this subject. Of the generation of painters who immediately preceded Murillo, Zurbarán and Alonso Cano had painted Virgin and Child pictures, but less than half a dozen examples are known, whereas over twice that number painted by Murillo survive. Further, the Zurbarán and Cano Virgin and Child paintings date from the last years of their lives; the earliest by Zurbarán around 1640 to 1645 and those of Cano around 1646–50, making them contemporary with, and in some cases later than, the earliest by Murillo.

And, in fact, the young Murillo appears to owe little to the two established artists as far as interpretation of the subject is concerned. There is something medieval in spirit about Zurbarán's contemplative and silent Virgins, while Cano painted full-length Virgins contemplating the sleeping Child, almost invariably pyramidal compositions derived from Dürer's art. Murillo had a particular aptitude for interpreting the devotional image of the Virgin and Child; his representations combine deep religious feeling with a naturalism that appraises feminine beauty and infant charm. Several of his paintings of this theme can be placed stylistically in the ten year period following the series painted for the Monastery of San Francisco, Seville. Their size – little more than 1½ metres high – makes it probable that they were intended for private chapels.

There is general agreement that this *Virgin of the Rosary* dates from around 1650 or a little earlier. The composition is similar to a *Virgin and Child* in the Palazzo Pitti (Angulo 1981, no. 149), which may predate the Castres painting. Murillo depicts the Virgin sitting on a marble bench, wrapped in rich, enveloping drapery that falls around her. Her head is covered by a veil and her pensive, absent look gives her face a melancholy expression of great beauty. The Child, dressed in a smock, is holding the rosary and looks directly at the viewer with a sweet and soulful expression; a faint halo indicates his divinity. In this composition Murillo is still using strong chiaroscuro; powerfully lit figures stand out against a dark background. The traditional red and blue of the Virgin's drapery are modified by the white of the veil and the striped shawl. This perhaps is the most serene of Murillo's Virgins; it is the product of perfect stability and balance attained through a precise and thoughtful study of pictorial and compositional elements.

PROVENANCE

18th century Seville, where it was acquired by Sieur de Langlois; 1777 Randon de Boisset sale, Paris; 1784 Comte de Vaudreuil sale; Lebrun; acquired by Louis XVI; 1811 Musée Napoléon, Paris, no. 1056; Musée du Louvre; 1939 deposited in the Musée Goya, Castres

REFERENCES

Angulo 1981, I, p. 275; II, no. 166; III, pl. 34; Curtis 1883, no. 83; Gaya Nuño 1978, no. 32; Justi 1904, pp. 42, 45; Mayer 1913[1], no. 25; Mayer 1923; p. 27; Musée du Louvre catalogue 1913

ADDITIONAL REFERENCES

L. Viardot, *Les Musées de France*, p. 100; *Le Musée Goya de Castres*, catalogue 1961, no. 29

10

10

Virgin of the Rosary

164 × 110 cm
c. 1650–55
Museo del Prado, Madrid
[*repr. on p.* 84]

This painting, also known as *The Virgin of the Escorial*, is one of the best known and most accomplished of Murillo's interpretations of the Virgin and Child theme. A relatively youthful work, it is dated around 1650 when Murillo had yet to free himself from using strong chiaroscuro effects

fig. 80 Bartolomeo Cavarozzi *Virgin and Child* (St. Ignazio, Viterbo)

inherited from the tenebrists of the first half of the century. Something about the delicate blend of naturalistic elements and the aura of poetic sensibility characteristic of the artist's early work suggest the influence of Caravaggio, but a Caravaggio given a note of delicate and almost sentimental intimacy that is closer to the interpretation of this theme by Bartolomeo Cavarozzi (*c.* 1590–1625; fig. 80), the Italian painter whose work was widely known in Spain. Both he and Murillo evidently admired Raphaelesque models.

The change that Murillo's Virgin and Child paintings underwent was undoubtedly due to Raphael's influence; the earlier *Virgin of the Rosary* from Castres (Cat. 9) is a good example of this. Raphael's engravings and drawings were widely circulated and Murillo was particularly struck by the extraordinary elegance and mobility of Raphael's Madonnas. Whereas Murillo strove in his early work to create a sense of mass and monumentality, this gave way to a desire for refinement and elegance; his Virgins changed from mature women to young girls with delicate features that also showed the influence of Van Dyck, whose work was known in Seville. The plump children, placidly sitting on their mothers' laps, were now replaced by naked infants who stand and are more active, often playing with their mother. Like the well-known Mackintosh *Madonna and Child* by Raphael, there is a dynamic upward drive in the composition and greater elegance. Drapery is painted with a loose but masterly technique in this painting, which, despite its surface wear, displays extreme technical virtuosity in the transparency of the veil and in the fall of the full, illuminated folds of the drapery. Murillo delighted in the representation of the quality of material and it is evident that he was aware of the latest developments in Flemish and Genoese painting; the latter, particularly, was very much appreciated in Seville at that time.

This *Virgin of the Rosary* has always been an extraordinarily famous and popular work, and some excellent old copies are known. One, for some time believed to be an autograph Murillo, is in the Wallace Collection.

PROVENANCE
1788 acquired for Carlos IV, Casa del Príncipe, Escorial; 1814 Palacio Real, Madrid; 1819–27 Monastery, Escorial; 1827 Museo del Prado

EXHIBITIONS
Tokyo and Osaka 1980, no. 27

REFERENCES
Angulo 1971, p. 345, fig. 367; Angulo 1981, I, pp. 276–77; II, no. 159; III, pl. 36, 37; Ceán Bermúdez 1800, II, p. 64; Curtis 1883, no. 86; Gaya Nuño 1978, no. 35; Lefort 1892, no. 84; Mayer 1913[1], no. 29; Mayer 1923[1], p. 31; Ponz 1947 ed., p. 525; Prado catalogue 1843, no. 423; Prado catalogue 1920, no. 975

11

12

11

Virgin and Child

157 × 107 cm
c. 1650–55
Galleria Palatina, Palazzo Pitti, Florence
[*repr. on p.* 85]

Angulo dates the picture between 1650 and 1655, but other art historians have placed it much later, around 1670, and consider the style to be late. However, both its composition and light effects link it with the group of Madonnas painted by Murillo in the first half of the 1650s. It must be somewhat later than the Prado *Virgin of the Rosary* (Cat. 10), given the greater sensation of movement, particularly marked in the delicate, tentative figure of the Infant, whose acute and expressive gaze is turned towards the viewer. The sober, pyramidal composition of the *Virgin of the Rosary* is broken in this picture by the Child's playful attitude and the monumentality of the earlier painting here gives way to smaller figures, set in greater space. The clothing falls in gentler, luminous folds that are more decorative than naturalistic, and which anticipate Murillo's later pictorial technique.

In format this painting is similar to the *Virgin of the Rosary*; its novelty lies in its expressive force. As Angulo has observed, the 'soulful and uninhibited' expression of the Virgin, bordering on the romantic, emotional tenderness of the Rococo, is a foretaste of late eighteenth-century European style. The painter employs a range of exquisite tones – delicate reds, blues and pastel pinks – that were later the favourite colours of rococo artists. This is probably one of the most delicate and elegant of Murillo's Virgin and Child paintings.

As in the case of Cat. 10, there are several old copies of the picture, some of them, such as that in the collection of the Marquis of Lansdowne at Bowood House, formerly believed to be originals.

PROVENANCE
Sold from a convent at Ypres to the Grand Duke of Tuscany

REFERENCES
Angulo 1981, I, pp. 277–78; II, no. 150; III, pl. 38, 39; Curtis 1883, no. 89; Gaya Nuño 1978, no. 37; Mayer 1913[1], no. 32; Mayer 1923[1], p. 52, 290; Muñoz, 1942, fig. II

12

The Penitent Magdalen

152 × 104 cm
c. 1650–55
National Gallery of Ireland, Dublin
[*repr. on p.* 83]

13

This painting belongs to the artist's early period, datable between 1650 and 1655. After this period, Murillo repeatedly dealt with religious subjects, using dark colours and creating strong chiaroscuro effects. Between 1650 and 1655 he painted several versions of the Magdalen, with slight variations, showing the saint kneeling in prayer in a grotto.

The subject had previously been painted by Ribera. Murillo's interpretations were particularly grand in conception; the dignity of his early Magdalens mellowed with the passage of time and his later versions of the subject were much more lyrical and imbued with great sensuality, the result of the delicate beauty of his models.

This Magdalen ought, perhaps, to be considered an intermediate example, standing between the dignified versions from Murillo's earlier period, such as those in the Academia de San Fernando, Madrid and St. George's Church, New York, and the later painting belonging to the Wallraf-Richartz Museum, Cologne. In the Dublin Magdalen the artist emphasized the soft, delicate female form and gave her a youthful face, thus obtaining an effect of simplicity and asceticism.

PROVENANCE
Early 19th century in the possession of Canon Pereira, Seville; Ancieto Bravo; 1838 Louis Philippe of Orléans Paris; 1853 sold in London to William Wells; later on the London and Stockholm art markets; 1962 sold by Galerie Heim of Paris to the Gallery

EXHIBITIONS
Royal Academy, London 1871; Galerie Heim, Paris 1958, *Tableaux des maîtres anciens*, no. 29

REFERENCES
Angulo 1981, I, p. 287; II, no. 357; III, pl. 68; Baticle and Marinas 1981, no. 163, p. 119; Curtis 1883, no. 372; Stirling-Maxwell 1873, p. 94; Tubino 1864, p. 216

ADDITIONAL REFERENCES
National Gallery of Ireland Illustrated Summary Catalogue of Paintings, Dublin, 1982, no. 1720

13
The Immaculate Conception

436 × 292 cm
c. 1650
Museo de Bellas Artes, Seville
[*repr. on p.* 87]

This picture has always been called *La Concepción Grande* because of its enormous size, or, on account of its original location, *La Concepción de los Franciscanos*. Until the 1836 disentailment of church property, it was in the monastery church of San Francisco, Seville, placed high up on the chancel arch; Murillo painted it on such a grand scale because it was to be seen from afar. From a distance,

14

the Virgin appears brilliantly foreshortened, particularly if seen from the correct viewing-point (looking upwards obliquely), because Murillo designed the figure for that particular location. It is therefore, a work that can only be understood by taking its original setting into account; viewed from close to, it appears exaggerated.

It could be said that this *Immaculate Conception* represents one of the first attempts in Seville painting to add something new to the iconography of the subject. Murillo's composition incorporated the movement and dynamism characteristic of baroque art. His conception of this work probably owed something to an engraving by Ribera in which baroque stylistic solutions were already present.

Given its stylistic characteristics, the date of this painting must be early; very probably it was painted in 1650, the year in which the transept and chancel of the church of San Francisco were rebuilt after their collapse.

A painting repeating the head of the Virgin is in the Sterling Collection, Pollock House, England; according to Angulo it is possibly autograph.

PROVENANCE
Convento de San Francisco, Seville; 1810 removed by the French to the Alcázar, Seville, but later returned; 1836 Museo de Bellas Artes

REFERENCES
Alfonso 1883, p. 89; Angulo 1981, I, p. 312; II, p. 126, no. 118; Ceán Bermúdez 1806, II, p. 97; Curtis 1883, no. 21; Espinosa 1796, V, p. 22; Gaya Nuño 1978, no. 52; Gestoso 1912[2], no. 91; Gómez Imaz 1896, no. 110; González de León 1844, I, p. 52; Hernández Díaz 1967, no. 202; Matute 1886, III, p. 124; Mayer 1923[1], p. 73; Montoto 1923, p. 47; Muñoz 1942, pl. 44; Ortiz de Zúñiga 1677, V, p. 15; Ponz 1947 ed., p. 788; Quilliet 1816, p. 99

14
The Immaculate Conception with Friar Juan de Quirós

241 × 341 cm
c. 1652
Inscribed on the *verso*:
Autentico de Murillo. Pintado para la Hdad. de la Sta. Vera Cruz de Sevilla, según consta en su libro de cuentas, Agosto 12 de 1653 al folio 56, a quien pertenece
Archbishop's Palace, Seville
[*repr. on p.* 86]

On the left-hand side of the painting there is an almost illegible inscription identifying the monk in the picture as Friar Juan de Quirós, a Franciscan born in Osuna who wrote the *Glorias de María*. He is shown writing one of the volumes of his work, inspired by a painting of the Immaculate Conception placed in front of him. Murillo, therefore, has produced a picture within a picture,

15

achieving a pleasing theatrical effect by providing an architectural framework for the Virgin. The garlands of fruit hanging between the lateral columns which frame the composition are technically very accomplished. Two angels display the shield of the Brotherhood of the True Cross.

This is one of the first paintings by Murillo on the theme of the Immaculate Conception and it portrays the Virgin according to Beatriz de Silva's vision, with a blue robe and a white tunic. The figure of the Virgin with her windswept cloak moves through the celestial space, a motif that the artist was later to recreate in other versions of the subject.

The base of the painting is arched in shape due to the fact that it used to be situated above the grille at the entrance to the chapel of the Brotherhood of the Holy Cross.

PROVENANCE
1652 Chapel of the Brotherhood of the Holy Cross, Convento de San Francisco, Seville; 1810 removed by the French to the Alcázar, but returned to the Hermandad in 1814; 1836 Iglesia de San Alberto; mid-19th century Archbishop's Palace

REFERENCES
Angulo 1981, I, pp. 308–11; II, pp. 127–28, no. 119; Ceán Bermúdez 1800, II, p. 59; Gómez Imaz 1896, no. 56; Matute 1887, p. 386; Montoto 1923, pp. 45–46; Ortíz de Zúñiga 1796, V, p. 23; Ponz 1947 ed., p. 787; Valdivieso and Serrera 1979, pp. 63–64; Viñaza 1894, p. 123

15
San Rodrigo

205 × 123 cm
c. 1646–55
Staatliche Kunstsammlungen Gemäldegalerie, Dresden
[*repr. on p.* 91]

This work belongs to Murillo's early period and is usually dated between 1646 and 1655. San Rodrigo was a priest from the city of Córdoba, martyred in 857 during the Moslem domination of Spain; he was beheaded after refusing to abjure his Christian faith. Murillo placed the saint in an outside setting, standing before a balustrade; the mark of his martyrdom can be seen on his neck and in one hand he holds the palm of martyrdom. His attitude can be interpreted as that of a supplicant: he turns his eyes to heaven and demonstrates that he has offered his life to God in defence of his faith. He is rewarded with a crown of flowers that an angel is about to place on his head.

The simplicity of the composition allows Murillo's technical mastery to come to the fore. The concentrated spirituality of the saint's expression contrasts with the monumentality of his figure; it is possible that the face may have been a portrait. The rigour of the composition

16

is partly softened by the extravagance of the saint's embroidered chasuble, for which the artist must have used a sixteenth-century model.

A Seville precedent for this work, with which Murillo's painting bears a certain similarity in expression, is the *San Rodrigo* by Roelas of *c.* 1609, which is still in the Jesuit Church of the Marchena, Seville.

PROVENANCE
Convent of Santa Clara, Seville; beginning of the 19th century acquired by Canon Pereira; acquired from his heirs by Louis Philippe of Orléans and in 1838 listed in his collection ; 1853 sold in London; 1854 Dresden Gallery

REFERENCES
Angulo 1981, I, p. 295; II, p. 290, no. 369; Curtis 1883, no. 386; Ford 1853, V, pp. 28, 257; Gaya Nuño 1978, no. 54; González de León 1844, I, p. 254; Justi 1904, p. 33; Mayer 1923[1], p. 22

16
San Isidoro

193 × 165 cm
1655
Seville Cathedral
[*repr. on p.* 88]

According to the records of the Chapter of Seville Cathedral, this painting, along with its companion *San Leandro* (Cat. 17), was hung in the cathedral sacristy in August 1655; presumably it was painted in the preceding months. Juan Federigui, a cathedral canon and Archdeacon of Carmona, paid for the pair of pictures.

Ceán Bermúdez found a reference to this work in a manuscript by Antonia de la Cuesta entitled *Tesoro de la catedral de Sevilla*. It states that San Isidoro's face is a portrait of Francisco López Cavalán, a licenciate and ecclesiastic connected with the cathedral chapter, who died the year the painting was completed.

This work was designed to be seen high up on the sacristy wall. Viewed close to, the verve with which it was painted is surprising; it shows rich, fluid brushwork, particularly in the saint's vestments. This lively treatment contrasts with the saint's calm, concentrated pose and dignified expression; he is shown seated in an interior, closed off from the background by a spectacular purple curtain, holding his bishop's crozier in one hand and, in the other a book, an allusion to his religious writings. Two volumes bear the titles of works written by the saint. Preparatory drawings for Cat. 16 and 17 are in the British Museum.

EXHIBITIONS
Seville 1982, no. 43

17

REFERENCES
Angulo 1981, I, pp. 290–93; II, pp. 258–9; Ceán Bermúdez 1800, II, p. 117; Curtis 1883, no. 312; Gaya Nuño 1978, no. 61; Mayer 1923[1], p. 38; Montoto 1923, p. 47; Torre Farfán 1672, p. 191; Tubino 1834, p. 149; Standish 1840, p. 185; Valdivieso 1978, p. 84; Valdivieso and Serrera 1982, no. 43; Velázquez and Sánchez 1864, pp. 86, 200

17

San Leandro

193 × 165 cm
1655
Seville Cathedral
[*repr. on p.* 89]

This is a companion to the *San Isidoro* (Cat. 16). Both the paintings were paid for by the canon, Juan Federigui and, according to a tradition unearthed by Antonio de la Cuesta, Murillo used Alonso de Herrera, the prompter of the cathedral choir, as his model for the face of San Leandro.

Like San Isidoro, the saint appears seated in an interior, closed off by red curtains whose intensity is toned down by the shadowy background; his dignified figure, dressed in white, stands out clearly against this. The saint looks directly at the viewer and his expression reveals a vigorous and resolute moral attitude that contrasts with the phlegmatic character of San Isidoro and reflects the untiring war waged against the Arian heresy; this is symbolized in the painting by the parchment he is holding, inscribed: *Credite o gothi consubstantialem patri*, the phrase with which he defended Christ's divinity.

EXHIBITIONS
Seville 1982, no. 44

REFERENCES
Angulo 1981, I, pp. 290–93; II, p. 279, no. 353; Brown 1973, p. 30; Ceán Bermúdez 1800, II, p. 117; Curtis 1883, no. 364; Gaya Nuño 1978, no. 62; Mayer 1923[1], p. 37; Montoto 1923, p. 47; Standish 1840, p. 185; Torre Farfán 1672, p. 191; Trapier 1941, p. 36; Tubino 1864, p. 149; Valdivieso 1978, p. 84; Valázquez and Sánchez 1864, pp. 86, 200

18

Adoration of the Shepherds

187 × 223 cm
c. 1650–55
Museo del Prado, Madrid
[*repr. on p.* 80]

18

The dating of this work is uncertain, but the use of strong chiaroscuro and the realistic depiction of shepherds in the manner of Ribera makes it probable that it can be placed between 1650 and 1655. The technique is more elaborate than *The Holy Family with the Little Bird* (Cat. 8) so it is likely to post-date that picture, but it must come before the works of the second half of the 1650s when the artist began to brighten his palette and to paint clear, luminous backgrounds.

The scene is lit from the upper right-hand corner; in the foreground a shepherd kneels, the soles of his feet wrinkled and dusty in the manner of Caravaggio. The shepherd recalls one of the beggars in *San Diego Giving Food to the Poor* (Cat. 4), which helps to establish a dating close to the paintings executed for the Convento de San Francisco. Despite the scene's strong naturalistic accent (the two chickens and the lamb show his keen observation of nature), Murillo demonstrates his innate sense of elegance in figures such as the Virgin and the young shepherd standing on the right. The predominating ochre, brown and reddish colours make the figure of the Child, wrapped in a white cloth, stand out with even greater luminosity. But Murillo uses light realistically and does not make the Child the composition's luminous focal point in the Venetian manner, as he did in an earlier painting of the same theme that is now in the Hermitage.

Given the measurements in the 1772 inventory of the Palacio Real, Madrid, it would appear that this painting has been enlarged by some 8 cm.

PROVENANCE
1764 acquired from the English painter Kelly by Charles III; 1772 Palacio Real, Madrid, inv. no. 34; 1813 Musée Napoléon, Paris; 1819 Museo del Prado

EXHIBITIONS
Madrid 1972

REFERENCES
Angulo 1971, p. 351; Angulo 1981, I, p. 285; II, no. 222; III, pl. 78–79; Beroqui 1933, pp. 88, 155; Braham 1965, p. 446; Ceán Bermúdez 1800, II, p. 64; Curtis 1883, p. 165; Gaya Nuño 1978, no. 29; Justi 1904, p. 19; Madrazo 1884, p. 296; Mayer 1913[1], no. 22; Mayer 1923[1], pp. 24, 290; Ponz 1947 ed., p. 574 (letter of Mengs); Prado catalogue 1819, Room I, no. 154; Prado catalogue 1872, no. 859; Trapier 1964, p. 269

19

The Vision of St. Bernard

311 × 249 cm
c. 1650–55
Museo del Prado, Madrid
[*repr. on p.* 93]

This painting and its companion, *St. Ildefonso Receiving the Chasuble from the Virgin* (Cat. 20), of identical dimensions and depicting a similar theme, are first mentioned in 1746 when they are listed in the palace inventory at La Granja among the works belonging to

19

Isabel Farnese. This suggests that they, together with paintings by other artists, were acquired by Queen Isabel during her years in Seville.

Their large scale suggests that they were intended to be altarpieces, but there is no information about their original location. Angulo is inclined to think that they came from a Cistercian foundation since both St. Bernard and San Ildefonso belonged to that order, and this – and their royal provenance – suggests that they came from twin chapels in the Convent of San Clemente in Seville, rather than from separate altars in the churches of St. Bernard and St. Ildefonso.

The dating is controversial: Mayer places them between 1665 and 1670, Gaya Nuño dates them around 1660 and Justi believes them to be before 1655, a date accepted by Angulo, who emphasizes the naturalistic elements and contrasted lighting in these pictures that appear also in other works of the period.

fig. 81 Juan de Roelas *The Vision of St. Bernard* (Hospital de San Bernardo, Seville)

The theme of Marian exaltation is frequent in the iconography of St. Bernard: in one of his visions he was rewarded with a jet of milk from the Virgin's breast for the writings and eulogies he had dedicated to her.

St. Bernard kneels on the left, wrapped in the ample white Cistercian habit – fuller and more ornamental than the vestments of Zurbarán's monks – and this makes him stand out in the half-light of the room, in which one can discern a table covered with books and a vase of white lilies. The Virgin appears on the right holding the Child and accompanied by numerous angels who swirl about her, creating the most spectacular *gloria* painted by Murillo up to this date; they anticipate those in his Immaculate Conceptions. Against the bright orange-coloured background, the Virgin's blue cloak swirls up as in the large *Immaculate Conception* (Cat. 13); it is reminiscent of the swirling draperies in the painting by Ribera in the Convento de las Agustinas Descalzas, Salamanca.

Perhaps Murillo took as an example the picture of the same subject painted by Roelas in 1611 for the Hospital of San Bernardo, Seville (fig. 81). The coincidence of the table placed behind the saint's back, with books, inkwell and a small vase of white lilies arranged in almost the same manner is curious, but Murillo's work is endowed with a positively baroque grandeur compared to the restrained austerity of Roelas's painting. Alonso Cano's painting of the same subject of around 1658–60 in the Prado is almost contemporary, but cannot have been known by Murillo; it is a sweeter and more gentle vision of the subject.

There is a small sketch for the Virgin and the Child, known only through a photograph, which Angulo accepts as a possible original by Murillo; its present whereabouts is unknown. It was reproduced by Sentenach (1911) who claimed it was in the Museo del Prado, Madrid although Angulo was unable to trace it.

PROVENANCE

1746 Palacio de la Granja, Segovia, inv. no. 646; 1794 Palacio Real, Madrid, inv. no. 646; 1810 Council Room, Palacio Real, Madrid; 1819 Museo del Prado

REFERENCES

Angulo 1961, p. 19; Angulo 1981, I, pp. 289–90; II, no. 287; III, pl. 83–86, 88; Beroqui 1932, p. 94; Prado catalogue 1910–72, no. 978; Curtis 1883, no. 262; Gaya Nuño 1978, no. 75; Justi 1904, p. 15; Lafond 1922, p. 68; Mayer 1913[1], no. 59; Ponz 1947 ed., p. 894; Prado catalogue 1819; Prado catalogue 1854–58, no. 315; Prado catalogue 1872–1907, no. 868; Saltillo 1933, p. 80; Sentenach 1911, p. 193

20

20

St. Ildefonso Receiving the Chasuble from the Virgin

309 × 261 cm
c. 1650–55
Museo del Prado, Madrid
[*repr. on p.* 92]

The dimensions of this picture and the theme of the Virgin appearing to a saint suggest that it is a pair with *The Vision of Saint Bernard* (Cat. 19). Both are first mentioned among Isabel Farnese's pictures in the palace at La Granja, but some writers have considered that *St. Ildefonso* should be regarded as an independent work and have dated it later in Murillo's *oeuvre* because of its elaborate composition and spatial effects. Curtis, Justi and Mayer believe that it dates from the last years of the artist's life, between 1675 and 1680. However, Angulo thinks it is contemporary with *The Vision of St. Bernard*, made for a twin chapel, and suggests that it might come from the Cistercian convent of San Clemente in Seville. Devotion to St. Ildefonso was less fervent in Seville than in Toledo (of which he is patron saint), but he was brought up in Seville and was a follower of San Isidoro. There are paintings of this subject in Seville, the most famous by Velázquez, dated 1623, now in Seville Museum.

The painting illustrates the miracle associated with the saint, which was described by Cyxila, Archbishop of Toledo and successor to St. Ildefonso (774–783):

'Prostrating himself before the altar of the Most Holy Virgin, Ildefonso found the self-same Lady seated in the cathedral where the bishop was wont to sit and to greet the people . . . and lifting up his eyes he looked about him and saw all the arches of the church full of troops of Virgins who were singing the psalms of David, with a very sweet and soft harmony. Then, the Virgin looking at him, did speak to him in this manner: Approach thou me, most upright servant of God, and take from my hand this gift that I have brought thee from the treasuries of my Son; blessing it, thou hast to use it on my feastdays.'
(Flórez, *Espãna Sagrada*, V, p. 482)

Murillo follows Cyxila's account, but introduces a new element from popular legend that gives his painting a strong naturalistic accent: the old woman, kneeling and holding a candle. She is a character from José de Valdivieso's *Auto*, or religious play, about St. Ildefonso, written in 1616, and also features in one of Lope de Vega's plays: instead of returning the candle to the angels who gave it to her, she kept it for the hour of her death. Murillo focuses attention on the divine gift, which gives him an excuse to unfold the rich embroidered cloth in the centre and accentuates the composition's diagonal movement. The facial types are close to others of those years: the old woman is similar to her counterpart in the *Adoration of the Shepherds* (Cat. 18), and the angel recalls the Virgin in that painting and in *The Holy Family with the Little Bird* (Cat. 8).

PROVENANCE
1746 Palacio de la Granja, Segovia, inv. no. 647; 1794 Palacio Real, Madrid, inv. no. 647; 1810 Council Room, Palacio Real, Madrid; 1819 Museo del Prado

REFERENCES
Angulo 1961, p. 18; Angulo 1981, I, pp. 287–88; II, no. 316; III, pl. 87, 89–91; Ceán Bermúdez 1800, II, p. 64; Curtis 1883, no. 311; Gaya Nuño 1978, no. 76; Justi 1904, p. 47; Mayer 1913[1], no. 194; Ponz 1947 ed., p. 894; Prado catalogue 1819, Room II, no. 129; Prado catalogue 1854–58, no. 326; Sánchez Cantón 1942, no. 979

21

21

The Resurrection of Christ

243 × 164 cm
c. 1650–60
Academia de San Fernando, Madrid
[*repr. on p.* 90]

The painting came from the Capilla de la Expiración in the convent-church of the Merced Calzada in Seville. Angulo dates it before the *St. Antony of Padua* of 1656 in Seville Cathedral since the chiaroscuro is still very marked, although Murillo has lessened the extremely strong contrasts of his earlier compositions.

Iconographically, the painter complied with the dictates of the Church as summarized by Pacheco in his *Arte de la Pintura* (II, p. 295); the sepulchre is closed and the soldiers asleep. This gives the scene a sober, solemn character, differing from the interpretation of some artists who show the soldiers confronted by the risen Christ, astonished and gesticulating. The only elements of baroque theatricality are the red banner and Christ's shroud, which has been unfurled by the impetus of his ascent.

Murillo's exquisite draughtsmanship is apparent in his painting of the naked body of Christ; it is probably one of the best figures he painted. In the lower part of the painting, the sleeping soldiers serve as a silent counterpoint to the spectacular Resurrection. The one sitting with his head on his knees is copied from the engravings of Schöngauer and Dürer, obviously known by Murillo. There are reminiscences of Caravaggio in the dusty, wrinkled bare feet of the soldier in the right foreground; Murillo had already used this motif in his *Adoration of the Shepherds* (Cat. 18) and it was frequently used in

22

seventeenth-century painting, deriving ultimately from Caravaggio's *Virgin of the Pilgrims* of 1603 (St. Agostino, Rome). Here Murillo skilfully combined vivid realism in the sleeping soldiers with the profound spirituality expressed in the face of Christ.

PROVENANCE
Capilla de la Expiración, Convento de la Merced Calzada, Seville; 1810 removed by the French to the Alcázar, Seville, inv. no. 291; 1811 taken to Paris by Marshal Soult; 1813 or 1814 returned to the Academia de San Fernando

REFERENCES
Academia catalogue 1929; Academia catalogue 1865, no. 641; Academia inventory 1964; Angulo 1981, I, pp. 285–86; II, no. 271; III, pl. 72; Beroqui 1932, p. 96; Ceán Bermúdez 1800, II, p. 59; Ceán Bermúdez 1806, p. 98; Curtis 1882, no. 228; Gaya Nuño 1978, no. 69; Gómez Imaz 1916 ed., no. 291, p. 78; Mayer 1913[1], no. 41; Ortiz de Zúñiga and Espinosa 1796, V, p. 25; Pacheco 1866, II, p. 295; Ponz 1947 ed., p. 790; Saltillo 1933, p. 27; Vignau 1903

22

St. John the Baptist Pointing to Christ

269 × 183 cm
c. 1655
The Art Institute of Chicago, Louise B. and Frank H. Woods Purchase Fund
[*repr. on p.* 95]

This painting belongs to the cycle of four scenes of the life of St. John the Baptist painted for the refectory of the Convent of San Leandro, Seville around 1655.

The composition is simple; the artist has placed the two protagonists facing the viewer and at the same height. Only St. John, pointing towards Jesus to indicate that he is the Messiah, breaks the static solemnity of the picture, enhanced by the extensive landscape with the River Jordan flowing down the centre.

The symbols of the evangelists, the eagle (St. John) and the bull (St. Luke), appear in the upper part of the painting; above them are inscriptions: OMNES CREDERENT PER ILLUM, from *John*, I, 7 and HIC ERIT MAGNUS CORAM DOMINO, from *Luke*, I, 15.

PROVENANCE
Refectory, San Leandro, Seville; 1812 bought by Antonio Bravo; 1837 his brother, Ancieto Bravo, sold it to Dauzat for the collection of Louis Philippe of Orléans and in 1838 listed in his collection; 1853 bought in London by Thomas Townsend; 1883 in the Château Randon owned by the Duke of Montpensier; 1954 on the London art market; 1958 bought by Agnew's; 1960 entered the Chicago Art Institute

REFERENCES
Alfonso 1883, p. 152; Angulo 1981, II, p. 21, no. 14; Curtis 1883, no. 177; Gaya Nuño 1978, no. 411

23

23

The Baptism of Christ

233 × 160 cm
Signed: *Murillo*
c. 1655
Staatliche Museen Preussischer Kulturbesitz, Gemäldegalerie, Berlin
[*repr. on p.* 96]

This painting is one of a group of four of the life of St. John the Baptist, painted by Murillo for the refectory of the Convent of San Leandro, Seville. Murillo gave the work a profoundly spiritual feeling revealed through the attitudes of the two characters; St. John's expression has an intense emotional quality, while that of Jesus shows a modest humility. The two figures are harmoniously related to each other, the composition based on a diagonal.

Later, Murillo painted the same subject for the altarpiece in the Chapel of St. Antony, Seville Cathedral. Murillo's technical advances by the time of the later painting, especially in his drawing and in his handling of paint, must have been due, in part at least, to his stay in Madrid, where he studied the royal collection and was influenced by sixteenth-century Venetian painting and by Flemish artists.

PROVENANCE
1812 sold by the Convent of San Leandro to Nathan Wetherell; 1897 his son, John, sold it in London to Mr Bevington; passed to the collection of W.M. Burdon; 1848 listed by Burdon in Hartford House, Durham; 1963 sold by his heirs and acquired by the Museum

EXHIBITIONS
Manchester 1857, *Art Treasures of the United Kingdom*, no. 653; Berlin Gemäldegalerie 1971, no. 4

REFERENCES
Angulo 1981, II, no. 15; Calvert 1907, p. 164; Curtis 1883, no. 176; Gaya Nuño 1978, no. 39; Kubler and Soria 1959, p. 387; Mayer 1913[1], p. 286; Oertel 1968, pp. 215–17; Soria 1960, pp. 12–14; Standish 1840, pp. 283–84; Stirling-Maxwell 1848, p. 1429

ADDITIONAL REFERENCES
Schleier, *Kat. der ausgestellten Werke des 13–18 Jahrhunderts*, Berlin, 1975, pp. 290–91

24

St. John the Baptist and the Pharisees

261 × 179 cm
c. 1655
Fitzwilliam Museum, Cambridge
[*repr. on p.* 94]

Like *The Baptism of Christ* (Cat. 23), this painting was one of a series of four illustrating the life of St. John the

24

Baptist painted for the Convento de San Leandro, Seville around 1655. The text is taken from *John*, I, 19–27, in which the priests of Jerusalem sent Scribes and Pharisees to ask the Baptist if he was the Messiah. He replied that he was 'the voice of one crying in the wilderness, Make straight the way of the Lord.' In the sky on the left is St. Matthew's symbol of an angel together with a text from *Matthew*, XI, 11, which reads 'INTER NATOS MULLIERUM NON SURREXIT MAIOR', while on the right, above the lion of St. Mark, is the inscription 'VOX CLAMANTIS IN DESERTO PARATE VIAM DOMINO' (*Mark*, I, 3).

The figures are shown full-length, arranged in a semicircle; the commanding presence of the foremost Pharisee who questions the Baptist is especially effective, being set against the light. The river in the background is obviously the Jordan where St. John baptized his converts. The gentleness of the setting contrasts with the psychological tension created between the main characters.

A precedent for Murillo's picture is the painting of the same subject by Francisco de Herrera the Elder now at Rouen (fig. 82).

PROVENANCE
1812 acquired from the Convento de San Leandro, Seville by Mr. Nathan Wetherell, who sold it at Christie's, London in 1827; 1849 sold at Christie's by Thomas Purvis to John Anderson; on the London art market until 1868, when it was acquired by the Museum

REFERENCES
Angulo 1981, II, p. 23, no. 16; Carriazo 1929, p. 180; Curtis 1883, no. 334; Gaya Nuño 1978, no. 38; Mayer 1925, p. 220; Soria 1960, p. 14; Townsend 1972, II, p. 335

ADDITIONAL REFERENCES
J.W. Goodison and D. Sutton in Fitzwilliam Museum *Catalogue of Paintings*, I, Cambridge, 1960, no. 334, pl. 110

fig. 82 Francisco de Herrera the Elder *St. John the Baptist and the Pharisees* (Musée des Beaux-Arts, Rouen)

25

Virgin and Child

188 × 137 cm
c. 1655–60
Rijksmuseum, Amsterdam (on deposit from the Mauritshuis, The Hague)
[*repr. on p.* 97]

This beautiful painting belongs to the series of pictures of the Virgin and Child dating from 1650–60; Angulo places it towards the end of the decade, around 1658. As in the *Virgin of the Rosary* (Cat. 10) and the *Virgin and Child* (Cat. 11), the Child is standing up on the Virgin's lap; perhaps Gabriel, one of the painter's sons, born in 1657, served as a model.

The fundamental difference between this interpretation of the Virgin and Child theme and Murillo's earlier ones is the placing of the Virgin on a throne of clouds against a background of bright orange-coloured scudding clouds. The colour scheme of this painting thus links it to *The Vision of St. Bernard* (Cat. 19) and both pictures break with the deep chiaroscuro of Murillo's earlier painting.

The composition is of impressive simplicity; there are no small angels to distract the viewer. The arrangement of the figures, full face and motionless, enhances the fundamental simplicity. Not that Murillo has produced a monotonous painting; there is variety in the attitude and expression of both Virgin and Child, in the arrangement of the clothing and in the changing cloud formations, which gradually grow lighter towards the top of the canvas. Everything in the scene is conceived to create a feeling of serenity. The Virgin's face, with its fine and delicate characteristics, has similar features to those of the earlier

25

Virgin (Cat. 11), but here it is imbued with a gentle spiritual calm, to which is added the Child's serenity as he gives a blessing; it is with this mood of peace and timelessness that Murillo expresses the religious ideal of divine contemplation, in a similar manner to that achieved by Zurbarán in his *Virgin and Child* in the Seville Museum (fig. 83).

PROVENANCE
Jan Adrien Snyders; 1818 bought by King William I at the sale of the Snyders collection, when it was said to have come from a convent at Ypres; the Mauritshuis, The Hague; 1948 passed to the Rijksmuseum

REFERENCES
Angulo 1981, I, p. 280; II, no. 143; III, fig. 101; Curtis 1883, no. 82; Gaya Nuño 1978, no. 66; Mayer 1913, no. 34

ADDITIONAL REFERENCES
Cátalogue de la peinture moderne, Musées Royaux de Belgique, 1927; Descamps, *Voyage pittoresque de la Flandre et du Brabant*, Paris, 1792, p. 238; Vliet in *Bull. Rijksmuseum*, 1966, pp. 132, 160

fig. 83 Zurbarán *Virgin and Child* (Museo de Bellas Artes, Seville)

26

26

Virgin and Child with Angels

137 × 112 cm
c. 1660
Collection of Margot and Albert Ernst, Saarbrücken
[*repr. on p.* 99]

This is one of Murillo's most popular paintings on the theme of the Virgin and Child and was frequently copied. It is also known as *The Virgin of the Sash*. Stylistically it seems to date from around 1660, when the painter was at the height of his powers.

In the conception of this work, Murillo was inspired by daily life; the Virgin is tenderly wrapping the Child in swaddling clothes before binding around him the sash, which is seen on the left-hand side of the painting. A sad, preoccupied expression clouds Mary's face as she looks at the Child, as if she were foreseeing his future Passion. These presentiments are allayed by the musician angels while cherubs look down on the scene from above.

The composition is based on a play of diagonal lines, which partly frames the figures. A delicate colour scheme, bathed in warm tones, with harmonizing ochres, pinks and yellows adds to the intimate and poetic sensation of the scene. There is an echo of Van Dyck's influence in this painting.

PROVENANCE
Early 19th century Conde de Aguila, Seville; 1837 Baron Isidore de Taylor; 1838 Louis Philippe of Orléans, Paris; 1866 Duke of Montpensier, Palacio de San Telmo, Seville; 1883 Palacio de Sanlúcar de Barrameda; inherited by Antonio de Orléans; 1908 mentioned in the Palacio de Sanlúcar de Barrameda; later on the Paris and German art markets

EXHIBITIONS
Boston 1875

REFERENCES
Angulo 1981, I, p. 429; II, p. 161, no. 167; Calvert 1907, p. 136; Curtis 1883, no. 101; Davies 1819, p. 76; Gaya Nuño 1978, no. 183; González de León 1884, I, p. 131; Mayer 1923[1], p. 66; Standish 1840, p. 315

27

The Good Shepherd

123 × 101 cm
c. 1660–65
Museo del Prado, Madrid
[*repr. on p.* 100]

Of Murillo's religious subjects the most popular were scenes of the infancy of the Christ Child and of St. John the Baptist. The subject of the present picture is taken from *John*, X, 11–14, in which Christ is compared to the

27

Good Shepherd who gives his life for his sheep. Madrozo suggested that the sheep with the Christ Child is the one that had gone astray, as recounted in *Matthew*, XVIII, 12: 'How think ye? If a man have an hundred sheep, and one of them be gone astray, doth he not leave the ninety and nine, and goeth into the mountains, and seeketh that which is gone astray?'. *The Good Shepherd* is still valued today as a devotional image; it is a brilliant example of Murillo's interpretation of religious themes; he can explain religious mysteries in a manner that is popular and accessible, yet subtle artistically. The Infant Christ is endowed with that mysterious, intimate charm faintly tinged with melancholy that is characteristic of his most beautiful religious paintings.

The picture seems to belong to a relatively late period in Murillo's *oeuvre*, close to the paintings of 1665 for Santa María la Blanca, Seville (Cat. 36–39). This work has previously been identified as one of the paintings which, together with *The Infant St. John* (Cat. 35) and an *Immaculate Conception*, decorated one of the altars erected for the procession in honour of the church's consecration (Torre Farfán, 1666). Angulo, however, has convincingly shown that this painting presents sufficient differences from the chronicler's description to force us to reject this identification – although its date may be close to the group in question – and he places it between 1655 and 1660 because of some coldness in the colouring and a certain technical stiffness usually found in his work of that period.

Ceán Bermúdez was the first to point out the similarity between the Christ Child and the *Cupid* engraved by Stefano della Bella to illustrate an edition of Ovid's *Metamorphoses* (fig. 84); in effect, it is only a superficial similarity in the pose, and the deep spiritual content of Murillo's painting inevitably alters the subject.

Angulo has identified two drawings similar in composition to this painting (1961, fig. 34; 1974, fig. 74; Cat. fig. 63). There are both similarities and differences between these drawings and this painting. This suggests to Angulo that they may be studies for a later composition, now lost – a theory that Brown supports (Brown 1976, nos. 90 and 91) – rather than preparatory studies for the Prado painting. It might have been this work that Torre Farfán mentioned in connection with the festivities at Santa María la Blanca.

The painting was originally smaller (107 × 85 cm), but it was enlarged sometime before 1744, probably to pair it with *The Infant St. John* in the Prado (fig. 24).

PROVENANCE
1744 Palacio de la Granja, Segovia, bought by Isabel Farnese from the heirs of Cardinal de Molina; listed in Inventory of La Granja 1746, no. 831; 1794 Palace at Aranjuez (as *St. John*), Inv. no. 831; Ceán Bermúdez claimed to have seen it before 1770 in Seville and in 1792 in Cádiz, where it was bought by Charles IV, but this may be due to a confusion since an identical composition is described in the inventory of Palacio de La Granja in 1746 (no. 831)

EXHIBITIONS
London and Paris 1976, no. 32; Tokyo and Osaka 1980, no. 28; Munich and Vienna 1982, no. 52

REFERENCES
Angulo 1961[1], pp. 15–16; Angulo 1974[1], p. 106; Angulo 1981, I, pp. 437–38; II, no. 202; III, pl. 141–42; Ceán Bermúdez 1800,II, p. 65; Ceán Bermúdez 1826, I, fig. XXXII; Curtis 1883, no. 962; Ewald-Schubeck 1965, p. 56; Gaya Nuño 1978, no. 108; Lafond 1922, pp. 49, 52; Madrazo in Prado catalogue 1872–1907, no. 864; Madrazo 1878, p. 571; Mayer 1913[1], no. 86; Mayer 1923[1], pp. 90, 291; Mayer 1926[1], p. 251; Prado catalogue 1819, Room I, no. 14; Prado catalogue 1854–58, no. 46

fig. 84 Stefano della Bella *Cupid*; illustration to Ovid's *Metamorphoses*

28

Adoration of the Kings

190 × 146 cm
c. 1660–65
The Toledo Museum of Art, Toledo, Ohio, Gift of Edward Drummond Libbey
[*repr. on p.* 98]

This work shows Murillo's assimilation of the spirit of seventeenth-century Flemish art; it is clearly inspired by Rubens, more specifically by his *Adoration of the Kings* (Brussels Museum), which Murillo would have known from the 1620 engraving by Lucas Vosterman.

In his version, Murillo has modified the robust nature of Rubens's picture, discarding the lavish dress of the king's retinue and endowing the scene with a simplicity and humility closer to the spirit of the Gospel. The two small pages in the king's retinue are a delightful addition;

28

fig. 85 Murillo *The Adoration of the Kings* (private collection, Paris)

Murillo might well have used two of his sons as models.

Stylistically this painting can be dated between 1660 and 1665. A preparatory drawing for the composition is preserved in a private collection (fig. 85).

PROVENANCE
Bought by Mr. Stanhope in Spain; 1729 at Belvoir Castle; by descent to the Dukes of Rutland; acquired for Contini Bonacossi Coll., Florence; 1972 Christie's, London; Wildenstein, New York; bought by Edward Drummond Libbey, who donated it to the Museum

EXHIBITIONS
Rome 1930, no. 49; Princeton 1982, no. 26

REFERENCES
Angulo 1981, II, p. 206, no. 227; Brown 1976, p. 68; Gaya Nuño 1978, no. 49; Mayer and Longhi 1930, p. 207; Suida 1930, p. 144; Sullivan and Mallory 1982, no. 26

29

30

29

Santa Justa

93 × 64 cm
c. 1660
Meadows Museum, Southern Methodist University, Dallas
[*repr. on p.* 102]

Santa Justa and Santa Rufina were frequently represented in seventeenth-century Seville, but Murillo only painted them twice; together for the altarpiece of the Seville Capuchin Church around 1665 (Cat. 41), and in this painting of *Santa Justa* and its companion, *Santa Rufina* (Cat. 30), which are generally considered to have been painted around 1660. Because of the small scale of this picture and its companion piece, it can be assumed that they were meant for private devotion; this allowed the artist to secularize the figures in such a way that they are closer to lay portraits than sacred images.

These tendencies were already hinted at in the painting of 1555 by Hernando del Sturmio for the altarpiece of the Chapel of the Evangelists in Seville Cathedral (fig. 86). Given that it was painted a hundred years earlier, its composition and expressive quality are close enough to Murillo's paintings to make it likely that he knew del Sturmio's work.

PROVENANCE
In the collection of the Marqués de Villamanrique, Seville (probably with its companion piece, *Santa Rufina* [Cat. 30]); Conde de Altamira; 1827 Marquis of Stafford, London; 1858 Duke of Sutherland; 1913 Christie's, London; sold to the Boehler Gallery when the pair was split up; 1967 the pair appeared together on the Paris art market; 1972 Schickman Gallery, New York; sold to the Museum

EXHIBITIONS
British Institution, London 1828; Royal Academy 1870; Princeton, 1982 no. 27

REFERENCES
Angulo 1981, II, no. 346–47, p. 276; Curtis 1883, no. 359; Gaya Nuño 1978, no. 278–79; Haraszti-Takacs 1978, no. 28; Justi 1904, p. 23; Jordan 1974, p. 47; Sullivan and Mallory 1982, nos. 27, 28

fig. 86 Hernando del Sturmio *SS Justa and Rufina* (Seville Cathedral)

31

30

Santa Rufina

93 × 64 cm
c. 1660
Meadows Museum, Southern Methodist University, Dallas
[*repr. on p.* 103]

This is a companion piece to the *Santa Justa* (Cat. 29).

PROVENANCE
In the collection of the Marqués de Villamanrique, Seville (probably with its companion piece, *Santa Justa* [Cat. 29]); Conde de Altamira; 1827 Marquis of Stafford, London; 1858 Duke of Sutherland; 1913 Christie's London; sold to the Boehler Gallery when the pair was split up; 1917 *Santa Rufina* in the collection of Bernax Back of Szeged, Hungary; 1929 sold to Boehler; 1967 the pair reappeared together on the Paris art market; 1972 Schickman Gallery, New York; sold to the Meadows Museum

EXHIBITIONS AND REFERENCES
See Cat. 29

31

Immaculate Conception of the Escorial

206 × 144 cm
c. 1660–65
Museo del Prado, Madrid
[*repr. on p.* 104]

With the exception of the famous *Immaculate Conception of los Venerables* (Cat. 75) that belonged to Marshal Soult, this is the most popular and best known of the many Immaculate Conceptions Murillo produced throughout his career; it is one of four in the Prado. Until 1945, it was wrongly catalogued as the *Immaculate Conception of La Granja* (or of St. Ildefonso) because it was believed to have come from the Palacio Real de La Granja. Today, it is generally known as the *Immaculate Conception of the Escorial* after the palace where it hung during the eighteenth century. Mayer dated it around 1665–70, but Angulo considers this much too late, arguing that stylistically it cannot be later than the painting for Santa María la Blanca (Cat. 38) of 1665; he dates it around 1660.

It is one of Murillo's most seductive works, perhaps on account of the youth and beauty of the model and the refined colouring. Light tones predominate and the Virgin's silhouette stands out against a yellowish, luminous background. The composition's upward drive is emphasized by the diagonal movement of her hands.

For the Virgin's face, Murillo used a model who appeared in his work from the beginning of the 1650s; she is more youthful than the Virgin in the two earlier Immaculate Conceptions and many of the ones that were to follow. He was hereby obeying the iconographic instructions laid down by Pacheco in his *Arte de la Pintura*. In the silhouette of the figure and the luminous background, Murillo kept to the oval format recommended by the Seville artist and theoretician, whose influence can also be seen in the blue and white colouring of Mary's clothing, which accords with Beatriz de Silva's vision of the Virgin.

The Escorial *Immaculate Conception* echoes the diagonal movement of the Loja version, now in the Meadows Museum, Dallas, but here Murillo presented the beautiful, serene features of the Virgin in full face. One novelty is the disposition of the angels in the lower part of the painting; instead of forming a closed group they carry Marian symbols and play among the clouds. This open, dynamic grouping, used here for the first time, was a compositional device Murillo continued to improve on in later versions of the subject. He used thick brush strokes to convey the broken surface brilliance of the dress and deep tones in the shadows of the shawl. Although the painting of the upper part of the canvas has been somewhat erased, the way the cherubim's heads dissolve into the clouds is very beautiful.

Several preparatory drawings for this painting are known, each of them containing elements utilized in the final picture. Curtis has already pointed out the relationship between this *Immaculate Conception* and a drawing in the Hispanic Society of New York. Two other drawings connected with this painting are in New York, one in the Schaab collection and the other in the Pierpont Morgan Library; some critics consider them to be autograph, other believe them to be copies. Only the group of angels on the right in both drawings has some slight correlation with the Prado *Immaculate Conception* (see Angulo 1962, pl. I, fig. 3; 1974, p. 98, no. 3; Brown 1976, nos. 38 and 54).

The provenance of this painting is unknown. It is perhaps the one mentioned by Ceán Bermúdez, bought by Charles III in Seville at the same time as a *St. Jerome* – perhaps the Prado picture (no. 987).

PROVENANCE
1788 Royal Collections, Casa del Príncipe, Escorial; 1809 Palacio de Aranjuez; 1819 Museo del Prado

EXHIBITIONS
London and Paris 1976, no. 33

REFERENCES
Angulo 1962, p. 232; Angulo 1981, I, pp. 315–16; II, no. 112; III, pl. 172, 173; Ceán Bermúdez 1800, II, p. 64; Curtis 1883, no. 26; Elizalde 1955 p. 113; Gaya Nuño 1978, no. 70; Guinard and Baticle 1950, p. 131, fig. 132; Lefort 1892, no. 27; Mayer 1913[1], no. 74; Mayer 1923[1], p. 113; Mayer 1947, p. 363; Prado catalogue 1819, Room II, no. 21; Prado catalogue 1854–58, no. 229; Prado catalogue 1872–1907, no. 878; Prado catalogue 1910–72, no. 972; Saltillo 1933, pp. 59, 71

32

32

Jacob Setting the Peeled Rods before the Flocks of Laban

221 × 361 cm
c. 1660
Meadows Museum, Southern Methodist University, Dallas, Texas
[*repr. on pp.* 106–07]

This painting belongs to a series illustrating scenes from the life of Jacob. In the eighteenth century they were mentioned in the collection of the Marqués de Santiago in Madrid, but they had already been dispersed by the beginning of the nineteenth century. Several have been located: *Jacob Blessed by Isaac* and *Jacob's Ladder* are in the Hermitage, Leningrad, *Laban Searching for his Stolen Household Gods in Rachel's Tent* (Cat. 33) is in The Cleveland Museum of Art and Angulo has noticed a reference to a *Meeting of Jacob and Rachel*, mentioned in the 1817 London sale of Alexis Delahaute's collection as coming from the Marqués de Santiago; given its similar measurements and the subject matter, it might well be a companion piece.

The series is first mentioned by Palomino who extols Murillo's landscape backgrounds:

Not to be omitted is the remarkable facility our Murillo had for landscapes, such as we are offered in his stories. And thus it happened that the Marqués of Villamanrique decided to make a game with the stories from the Life of David by Murillo, saying that the landscapes were to be done by Ignacio Iriarte. Murillo said that Iriarte should do the landscapes, and he would fit in the figures afterwards. Iriarte said that Murillo should do the figures and he would then fit in the landscapes. Murillo, angered, said to him that if he thought he needed him for landscapes, he was deceiving himself; and so he alone did these paintings with stories and landscapes, a thing as marvellous as his; and the said Marquis brought them to Madrid.

Palomino is wrong about 'stories from the Life of David', but even in the seventeenth century Torre Farfán mentions in his description of the façade of the Marqués de Villanmanrique's house – on the occasion of the festivities for the consecration of Santa María la Blanca in 1655 – the presence of paintings of Abraham and Jacob, some by Murillo and some by another hand, among which were those that have come down to us. This reference allows Angulo to date the Jacob series certainly before 1665, and stylistically he thinks they were painted slightly before 1660; other critics, including Mayer, Soria, Jordan, Stechow and Gaya Nuño, date them after 1665.

fig. 87 Joos de Momper *Landscape* (private collection, Munich)

Cumberland saw this series at the Marqués de Santiago's house in Madrid in 1787. He wrote of five pictures depicting tales from Jacob and considered them the best that Murillo had painted: 'Miraculous – I preferred them to all those I had seen, only excepting Titian's *Venus*. In fact, the serene beauty of the landscape, shady, with blurred mountainous outlines dissolved in the clear brightness of the background, and the perfect fusion of the figures within it, make this work one of the artist's most beautiful and interesting compositions.'

Murillo illustrates the episode in *Genesis*, XXX, 37–40 when Jacob discovers Laban's deceit: the latter had promised him, as payment for long years of tending his flocks, all the spotted and speckled sheep in the herd, but then he had given them to his sons to hide.

And Jacob took him rods of green poplar, and of the hazel and chestnut tree; and pilled white strakes in them, and made the white appear which was in the rods.

And he set the rods which he had pilled before the flocks in the gutters in the watering troughs when the flocks came to drink, that they should conceive when they came to drink.

And the flocks conceived before the rods, and brought forth cattle, ringstraked, speckled and spotted.

And Jacob did separate the lambs, and set the faces of the flocks toward the ringstraked, and all the brown in the flock of Laban; and he put his own flocks by themselves, and put them not unto Laban's cattle.

The painter reproduces the biblical description with great exactitude, even including the pairing of the sheep. Murillo introduced elements of Flemish landscape painting into his background, the central rocky crag covered with trees and undergrowth, for example, and the theatrical chiaroscuro effects, derived from Momper (fig. 87). Angulo also sees in this work the influence of landscapes by Rubens and his school, as well as the contemporary Italian landscapes of Gaspar Dughet.

PROVENANCE
1724 Marqués de Villamanrique, Madrid; 1775–76 Marqués de Santiago, Madrid; 1859 the Earl of Northwick, Cheltenham; 1883 Sir John Hardy, Bart., Dunstall Hall, Staffordshire; 1951 Sidney Sabin, London; 1959 David M. Koester Gallery, Zurich; 1968 Wildenstein, New York; acquired by the Meadows Museum

EXHIBITIONS
Frank T. Sabin, London 1951, no. 29

REFERENCES
Angulo 1981, I, pp. 472–74; II, no. 31; III, pl. 121–23; Calvert 1907, pp. 155–56; Cumberland 1787, II, pp. 101–02, 123–25; Curtis 1883, pp. 119–20, no. 9; Gaya Nuño 1978, no. 207; Head 1848, pp. 176, 186; Jordan 1968[1], pp. 288–96; Jordan 1968[2], pp. 30–31; Justi 1904, p. 14; Kubler and Soria 1959, p. 277; Lefort 1892, p. 70; Mayer 1913[1], p. 19; Mayer 1929, p. 79; Palomino 1947 ed., p. 1036; Stechow 1966, p. 367–77; Stirling-Maxwell 1891, III, p. 204; Waagen 1854, II, p. 204

33

33
Laban Searching for his Stolen Household Gods in Rachel's Tent

242 × 375 cm
c. 1660
The Cleveland Museum of Art, Cleveland, Gift of the John Huntington Art and Polytechnic Trust
[*repr. on pp.* 108–09]

This is from the same series of scenes from the Life of Jacob as Cat. 32: both were originally in the collection of the Marqués de Villamanrique in Seville. It depicts another episode from the Life of Jacob, a theme which was interpreted as a prefiguration of the tribulations of Christ's disciples. It appears to have been a favourite Old Testament subject in Seville.

The story of Laban's searching for the stolen images was first painted at this date: this is one of its finest interpretations. Murillo depicted the meeting between Jacob and Laban on Mount Galad; Jacob fled from his father-in-law's house, and the latter pursued him, accusing him of stealing the family idols (*Genesis*, XXXI, 20–25). Jacob, innocent of this and not knowing that his wife Rachel has taken them, encourages Laban to search:

'With whomsoever thou findest the gods, let him not live: before our brethren discern thou what is thine with me, and take it to thee. For Jacob knew not that Rachel had stolen them. And Laban went into Jacob's tent, and into Leah's tent, and into the two maidservants' tents; but he found them not. Then went he out of Leah's tent, and entered into Rachel's tent. Now Rachel had taken the images, and put them into the camel's furniture, and sat upon them. And Laban searched all the tent, but found them not. And she said to her father, Let it not displease my lord that I cannot rise up before thee; for the custom of women is upon me. And he searched , but found not the images.'
(*Genesis*, XXXI, 32–35)

Jacob and Laban are disputing in the centre of the picture. On the left are Laban's daughters: Leah, standing surrounded by children, and Rachel, sitting at the entrance of the tent; on the right are Laban's followers and shepherds guarding the flocks. The extensive, luminous landscape shows the influence of Flemish painting. One testimony to the painting's beauty is the fact that the Duke of Westminster, who purchased the painting at the beginning of the nineteenth century, exchanged for it two landscapes by Claude Lorrain, a painting by Poussin and £1,200 into the bargain.

34

PROVENANCE
1665 Marqués de Villamanrique, Seville (?); 1724 Marqués de Villamanrique, Madrid; 1775–76 Marqués de Santiago, Madrid; 1809 Duke of Westminster, Grosvenor House, London; 1924 Christie's, London, sale of Westminster Collection bought by Hibbard; 1926 Jacques Canson, Paris; 1931 Carlos Guinle, Rio de Janeiro; 1965 donated to The Cleveland Museum by the John Huntington Art and Polytechnic Trust

REFERENCES
Angulo 1981, I, pp. 473–74; II, no. 32; III, fig. 124–27; Cumberland 1787, II, pp. 101–02, 123–25; Curtis 1883, no. 10; Gaya Nuño 1978, no. 206; Head 1848, p. 176; Justi 1904, p. 14; Kubler and Soria 1959, p. 277; Mayer 1913[1], no 107; Mayer 1926[2], p. 173; Mayer 1929, p. 79; Palomino 1947 ed., p. 1036; Stechow 1966, p. 367

ADDITIONAL REFERENCES
The Cleveland Museum of Art Catalogue of Paintings, III, *European Paintings of the 16th, 17th and 18th Centuries*, Cleveland, 1982, no. 220

34
The Hunter: Portrait of Don Antonio Hurtado de Salcedo

238 × 135 cm
c. 1664
Private collection, Spain
[*repr. on p.* 105]

This portrait of Antonio Hurtado de Salcedo is an exceptional work, both in the context of Murillo's *oeuvre* and of seventeenth-century painting in general. The representation of a character in a hunting dress was rare; we have, of course, to except the magnificent portraits by Velázquez of Philip IV, the Cardinal Infante and Prince Baltasar Carlos, all dressed as hunters, for the Torre de la Parada hunting lodge, painted around 1635. It was, perhaps, these which prompted Antonio Hurtado – Philip IV's Secretary of State – to commission such a portrait.

The painting has been dated between 1647, the year Hurtado was created a Knight of the Order of Santiago (his cross is displayed on his chest), and 1664, when he received the title of Marqués de Legarda, since there is no marquis's coronet on the coat-of-arms lying on the ground behind him. Critics date the portrait around 1655–58, before the painter visited Court. But if the Marqués de Legarda's date of birth – 1625 – is taken into account, this would seem to be too early in relation both to the apparent age of the knight and the style of his apparel. Angulo has suggested that this work was painted a little before 1664, perhaps in Seville, where the Marquis had a house close to Murillo's. In October 1665, the Marquis was received as a Brother of the Hospital de la Caridad, as Murillo had been in June of the same year. It seems logical to suppose that the Marquis would have known the painter and would have wanted to be portrayed by him since he was already considered Seville's most famous artist.

Technically the picture is quite close to the painter's work of the mid-1660s and there are similarities between the treatment of the landscape background here and in the two large pictures painted between 1662 and 1664 for Santa María la Blanca (Cat. 36 and 37).

The portrait does not appear to owe its inspiration to the portraits by Velázquez, which Murillo might not have even seen during his stay in Madrid. There is a slight resemblance to Velázquez's hunting portraits in the pose of the figure standing with his legs slightly apart and holding the gun with its butt resting on the ground. However, the Knight faces forward and is closer to portraits of the following generation, such as those by Carreño, painted at about the same date. Murillo accentuates the scene's hunting theme, emphasizing the figure of the young man in charge of the three magnificent hunting dogs and the pile of game. The grouping of the dogs, something absolutely new in Murillo's art, is one of the most successful naturalistic touches in his *oeuvre*.

The picture's large scale (this is the biggest portrait Murillo painted) indicates that it was executed for a grand setting such as the main salon in the Marquis's house. The noble, commanding attitude of the Marquis, standing in a fine landscape – with a possible reference to the Salcedo tower in the distance – makes this portrait one of the most outstanding in Spanish painting.

EXHIBITIONS
IV *Congreso de Estudios Vascos* 1926; Barcelona 1929, no. 453, p. 491; Madrid 1951

REFERENCES
Angulo 1981, I, pp. 462–63; II, no. 410; III, pl. 461; Gaya Nuño 1978, no. 60; Montesa 1951, p. 158 ff; Young 1980, no. 60

ADDITIONAL REFERENCES
La Caza en el arte, exhibition catalogue, Madrid, 1951

35
The Infant St. John the Baptist and the Lamb

164 × 106 cm
c. 1660–65
The Trustees of the National Gallery, London
[*repr. on p.* 101]

This painting is a companion to *The Good Shepherd* in the Lane Collection (fig. 88). It probably also belonged to Justino de Neve and may have been one of the paintings which decorated the altar erected in the Plaza de Santa María la Blanca in 1665 during the festivities for the church's inauguration; it can be dated between 1660 and 1665.

The young St. John embraces the lamb and looks straight at the viewer as in other versions of the theme,

35

such as that in Vienna and the one that formerly hung in the Hospital de la Caridad. Everything about St. John, from his seductive smile to his finger pointing towards heaven, engages the viewer's attention. His relaxed pose is a delicate and charming anticipation of eighteenth-century sensibility, as is *The Good Shepherd*, the painting's companion piece. Murillo employs a greyish-brown colouring and lights the figure from behind. As with the Lane Collection *Good Shepherd* this work was extensively copied, a confirmation of a successful iconographic innovation. One copy, a drawing now in the Chrysler Museum, Norfolk (USA), was once considered a preparatory sketch for this painting.

PROVENANCE
c. 1665 in Seville (Justino de Neve?); 1750 Comte de Lassay; Comte de la Guiche; 1771 sold in Paris to Donjeux; 1792 de Presle sale, Paris; 1801 Robit sale, Paris; bought by Paillet for Bryan; 1802 sold to Sir Simon Clarke; 1840 sale of Clarke Collection, London; bought by Lord Ashburton, who donated it to the Gallery

fig. 88 Murillo *The Good Shepherd* (Lane Collection, London)

36

EXHIBITIONS
Manchester 1857; Royal Academy, London 1870

REFERENCES
Angulo 1981, I, pp. 437–38; II, no. 335; III, p. 185–86; Brown 1976, see no. 25; Buchanan 1824, II, p. 35; Curtis 1883, no. 322; Gaya Nuño 1978, no. 181; MacLaren and Braham 1970, p. 65, no. 176; Mayer 1913[1], no. 85; Mayer 1923[1], pp. 86, 291

36
The Dream of the Patrician

232 × 522 cm
c. 1662–65
Museo del Prado, Madrid
[*repr. on pp.* 114–15]

Between 1662 and 1665 Murillo undertook one of the most important commissions of his career: a series of four large pictures to decorate the interior of Santa María la Blanca in Seville. The papal brief, promulgated by Pope Alexander VII in 1661 in favour of the Immaculate Conception of Mary, extolled Seville's devotion to this Marian mystery. It was around this time that Santa María la Blanca, formerly a medieval synagogue, was converted into one of the city's most spectacular baroque churches. The driving forces behind this work were the parish priest, Domingo Velázquez Soriano, portrayed by Murillo in one of the pictures (Cat. 38), and Justino de Neve, a canon of the Cathedral and a figure of great social standing in Seville at the time. Neve, although wishing to remain anonymous, must have paid for some of the work, and he may also have chosen the themes of Murillo's pictures. The church was completed in 1665 and its inauguration was one of the great religious and artistic events of the time, with celebrations that were minutely described by Torre Farfán in the same year.

Murillo must have been commissioned to paint the four large pictures around 1662 when the work on the church began; and they were in place for the re-opening of the church in 1665. The large lunettes (Cat. 36, 37) decorated the central nave and were lit from above by the skylights in the cupola (fig. 33). They represent the foundation of the Roman basilica, Santa Maria Maggiore, the mother church of Santa María la Blanca. The smaller lunettes, which occupied the walls of the side aisles, were dedicated to the Immaculate Conception (on the Gospel side) and to the Eucharist (on the Epistle side). The pictures remained in the locations for which they were painted until the Spanish War of Independence (1808–14), when they were taken as war booty by Marshal Soult. Two of them were subsequently returned to Spain.

The Dream of the Patrician, which occupied the left

hand side of the nave according to Torre Farfán, illustrates the legend of the foundation of Santa Maria della Neve, in which the Virgin appeared to a Roman patrician and his wife while they were asleep. Because of their devotion to the Virgin, they had nominated her as heir to all their wordly goods; in return for their prayers she appeared to them while they slept and told them that it was her wish that they should build a church in her honour on the Esquiline Hill and that its plan should follow the outline traced on the ground by a miraculous fall of snow in summer.

Murillo set the scene in an interior of a house in surroundings that, as Angulo points out, recall some of Zurbarán's paintings of everyday domestic life – the young Virgin sleeping, for example, in the Jerez Colegiata, or the Infant Jesus making the crown of thorns. There is also an echo of Murillo's own composition, *The Holy Family with the Little Bird* (Cat. 8), although here the painter has abandoned the tenebrism of his early pictures. The chiaroscuro is blended here with light that gives a sensation of depth, highlighting details in the room.

The dream theme, a tradition in Bolognese painting, is extended to all the participants in the scene: the little dog lies curled up at the wife's feet; the wife herself has abandoned her work and is sleeping; the exhausted patrician reclines against a table. On the left the Virgin and Child appear, the former pointing towards the Esquiline Hill and its miraculous snowfall. Murillo diverged from the prototype of the mosaic in Santa Maria Maggiore, Rome: instead of depicting the married couple asleep in a bed he shows them slumbering in their living quarters, an ingenious solution. Indeed this is one of the highest achievements of Spanish painting. The fluid and assured technique, the outlines no longer sharply defined but merging into the background, heralds Murillo's later style.

The drawing in the Kunstalle, Hamburg (Cat. D20), showing a woman – possibly the Magdalen – asleep, has been suggested as a preparatory study for this composition by Angulo; there are similarities in the handling of the drapery and in the pose of the Patrician's wife.

PROVENANCE
1665 Santa María la Blanca, Seville; 1813 Musée Napoléon, Paris; 1816 Academia de San Fernando, Madrid; 1901 Museo del Prado, Madrid

EXHIBITIONS
Geneva 1939, no. 68

REFERENCES
Inventario manuscripto de la Academia, 1824; Angulo 1969, pp. 13, 55; Angulo 1974, p. 102; Angulo 1981, I, pp. 327–29; II, no. 39; III, pl. 198–200; Beroqui 1932, p. 97; Beroqui 1933, p. 88; Curtis 1883, no. 229; Gaya Nuño 1978, no. 103; Mayer 1913[1], no. 77; Madrazo 1884, p. 300; Passavant 1877, p. 287; Ponz 1947 ed., p. 194; Sánchez Cantón in Prado catalogue 1942, no. 994; Torre Farfán 1666, fol. 4

37

37
The Patrician John and his Wife before Pope Liberius

232 × 522 cm
c. 1662–65
Museo del Prado, Madrid
[*repr. on pp.* 116–117]

This lunette is a companion piece to *The Dream of the Patrician* (Cat. 36). The patrician John and his wife present themselves to Pope Liberius and tell him of their vision and of the Virgin's command. The Pope, who had the same dream during the night, wished to verify the miracle and called together the clergy and the faithful, exhorting them to gather at the Esquiline Hill, where, despite the heat of August, they find an area covered with snow in the shape of a church's ground plan. The composition of both lunettes is based on a receding diagonal that would have been especially effective when the paintings hung in their original locations on either side of the nave of Santa María la Blanca, leading up to the high altar where the venerable image of the *Virgen de Santa Maria* was placed.

This is the more complex of the two compositions, but Murillo successfully integrated two scenes in the one lunette. The group on the left are shown against a grandiose architectural setting decorated with swags of rich drapery reminiscent of Venetian painting, particularly Tintoretto and Veronese. Monumental architecture is rare in Murillo's work; he only used it once again in the later paintings for the Hospital de la Caridad. Light falls from the left, silhouetting the Pope and the great velvet curtain. Angulo has suggested that the Pope's features are based on those of Pope Alexander VII (during whose pontificate the church of Santa María la Blanca was renovated), the author of the papal brief on the Immaculate Conception.

In the distance the procession to the Esquiline Hill is glimpsed; the Pope walks under a canopy surrounded by an excited group of bystanders. Murillo used light and shade effectively to animate the scene.

The two paintings' handsome neo-classical frames were designed by the architect Percier while the pictures were in France; their spandrels are decorated with symbols of the papacy and ground plans and elevations of Santa Maria Maggiore in Rome.

PROVENANCE
1655 Santa María la Blanca, Seville; 1813 Musée Napoléon, Paris; 1816 Academia de San Fernando, Madrid; 1901 Museo del Prado

EXHIBITIONS
Geneva 1939, no. 69

38

REFERENCES
Angulo 1969, p. 13; Angulo 1981, I, pp. 329–32; II, no. 40; III, pl. 201–04; Beroqui 1932, p. 97; Beroqui 1933, pp. 88, 155; Ceán Bermúdez 1800, II, p. 52; Ceán Bermúdez 1806, p. 62; Curtis 1883, no. 230; Gaya Nuño 1978, no. 104; González de León 1844, I, p. 102; Madrazo 1884, p. 300; Mayer 1913[1], no. 78; Ortiz de Zúñiga 1667, fol. 817; Ponz 1947 ed., p. 794; Sánchez Cantón in Prado catalogue 1942, no. 995; Stirling-Maxwell 1848, p. 206; Torre Farfán 1666, fol. 4

38
The Immaculate Conception

172 × 285 cm
Inscribed: IN PRINCIPIO DILEXIT EAM
c. 1662–65
Musée du Louvre, Paris
[*repr. on p.* 113]

This picture is a companion to *The Triumph of the Eucharist* (Cat. 39) in the series painted by Murillo to decorate Santa María la Blanca; it hung on the Gospel side of the aisle. The two works were originally full lunettes and have been unevenly trimmed on either side; perhaps also in height. Originally, they must have measured 194 × 320 cm, with the Virgin's hands at the centre of the painting.

The pair are linked both in compositional terms and thematically, for the association between the Virgin and the Eucharist originated in the Middle Ages, and the Virgin Mary, who bore the Son of God, came to represent the first tabernacle. It may have been either Justino de Neve or Velázquez Soriano, the church's parish priest whom Torre Farfán described as a theological scholar, who suggested to Murillo the subject matter for the paintings. And, in fact, during the festivities to mark the re-opening of Santa María la Blanca in 1665 the two mysteries – the Immaculate Conception and the Triumph of the Eucharist – were both lauded, and they were always related to each other in the praises that prefaced every sermon.

Using a very loose technique, Murillo portrayed the Virgin alone against a background of orange-coloured scudding clouds, with swirling cherubim and putti. The painting differs from his other Immaculate Conceptions in the introduction of the group of half-length figures adoring the Virgin, a motif often used by El Greco, Pacheco, and Zurbarán in his *Immaculate Conception* (Edinburgh). But by the time of Murillo this was already a somewhat archaic device, although it seems to have come back into fashion about this time and had been used a few years earlier by Alonso Cano in his 1658 *Presentation of the Virgin* in Granada Cathedral, and again in Cano's *Virgin*

39

of the Rosary of 1665–66 in Málaga Cathedral.

According to Torre Farfán the group contains several portraits, but he mentions only Domingo Velázquez Soriano, the parish priest, identified as the man with his hands crossed on his chest. Angulo has suggested that the figure behind him might be Salvador Rodríguez, who was Soriano's parochial assistant and later succeeded him as parish priest. The man seen from behind could possibly be the Marqués de Villamanrique who, as both parishioner and member of the church's fraternity, no doubt contributed to its redecoration; the child accompanying him could be his son, Melchor, who was 13 years old at the time.

A drawing of the Immaculate Conception in Copenhagen (Brown 1976, no. 24) is of doubtful authenticity: the drawing is too close to the painting, while the Virgin is clumsily drawn.

PROVENANCE
1665 Santa María la Blanca, Seville; 1817 M. Lom, who bought it from Marshal Soult; sold to Louis XVIII; Musée du Louvre

REFERENCES
Angulo 1969, p. 13; Angulo 1981, I, pp. 335–37; II, no. 41; III, pl. 205; Ceán Bermúdez 1800, II, p. 52; Ceán Bermúdez 1806, p. 62; Curtis 1883, no. 30; Gaya Nuño 1978, no. 105; González de León 1844, I, p. 102; Hautecoeur 1926, p. 1708; Louvre catalogue 1848, no. 546; Louvre catalogue 1981, II, p. 102; Madrazo 1884, p. 300; Mayer 1913, no. 76; Ortiz de Zúñiga 1677, fol. 817; Ponz 1947 ed., p. 794; Stirling-Maxwell 1848, p. 206; Torre Farfán 1666, fol. 4

39
The Triumph of the Eucharist

196 × 250 cm
Inscribed: IN FINEM DILEXIT EOS, *Joanis Cap.*[e] XIII
c. 1662–65
Collection of the Faringdon Trust, Buscot Park, Faringdon
[*repr. on p.* 112]

A companion piece to *The Immaculate Conception* (Cat. 38), this picture was situated above the altar rail on the Epistle side of the church of Santa María la Blanca.

In his description of the painting, Torre Farfán described it as *Faith*, although neither the scriptures nor the keys are attributes of that particular virtue; they are more consistent with an allegorical representation of the Church. The Sacrament of the Eucharist is given great prominence; the dove, symbolizing the Holy Ghost, hovers over the Sacrament, and the personification of the Church is represented administering the Eucharist. On the right of the painting a group of figures adore the Sacrament; through them, Murillo seeks to portray the faith and fervour of the common people.

40

PROVENANCE
Santa María la Blanca, Seville; during the Spanish War of Independence (1808–14) stolen from Spain by either Marshal Soult or Marshal Faviers; 1865 Pourtalès sale, Paris; 1895 Lyne Stevens sale, London; 1908 Sir Alexander Henderson; 1934 Lord Faringdon

EXHIBITIONS
Burlington Fine Arts Club, London 1908, no. 16; Grafton Galleries 1913–14, no. 79; London 1920–21, no. 85; London 1981, no. 50

REFERENCES
Angulo 1969, p. 13ff.; Angulo 1981, I, pp. 337–39; II, no. 42; III, pl. 206; Braham 1981, no. 50; Ceán Bermúdez, 1800, II, p. 59; Ceán Bermúdez 1806, p. 62; Gaya Nuño 1978, no. 106; Justi 1904, p. 28; Ortiz de Zúñiga 1677, fol. 817; Ponz 1947 ed., p. 794; Torre Farfán 1666, fol. 5

40
San Leandro and San Buenaventura

200 × 176 cm
c. 1665–1666
Museo de Bellas Artes, Seville
[*repr. on p.* 111]

This painting was part of the high altarpiece of the Capuchin Church in Seville. It formed the right wing, the left being the *Santa Justa and Santa Rufina* (Cat. 41).

San Buenaventura is one of the principal Franciscan saints and San Leandro, according to tradition, founded the church erected on the site where SS Justa and Rufina were martyred and where the Capuchins later built their monastery. The picture is an allegorical representation of the donation of the old church to San Buenaventura by the saintly bishop of Seville, symbolized by the model of the church in San Buenaventura's hands; however, its gothic architecture bears no relation to the Capuchin church and can probably be explained by Murillo having worked from an engraving.

The composition is impressive and solemn, although Murillo has enlivened it by means of the gestures of the saints who seem to be holding a conversation. San Leandro's figure has precedents in Murillo's earlier work; his features are similar to those in the San Leandro of 1656 (Cat. 17), and to the tondo of San Leandro of 1668 in the chapter house of Seville cathedral. In both paintings he holds a bishop's crozier in one hand and, in the other, a piece of paper with the inscription CREDITE O GOTHI CONSUBSTANTIALEM PATRI, an allusion to his fight against the Arian heresy. A child angel supports his bishop's mitre.

This is the only time that Murillo portrayed San Buenaventura; the saint's face is charged with emotion, he is bearded and tonsured in the manner of Capuchin monks and his expression conveys the spiritual transcendence that Murillo often confers on his saints.

The two characters are in harmony in both the spiritual sense and in terms of colour; whites, ochres and browns are perfectly balanced, but this austere range of colours is brightened by the purplish red of San Buenaventura's cloak.

PROVENANCE
Capuchin Church, Seville; 1810 temporarily transferred to Gibraltar; 1814 returned to the Capuchin Church, Seville; 1836 transferred to the Museo de Bellas Artes on the disentailment of church property

REFERENCES
Angulo 1981, I, p. 66; II, no. 65 pl. 239–41; Ceán Bermúdez 1800, II, p. 61; Curtis 1883, no. 336; Gaya Nuño 1978, no. 116; Gestoso 1912[2], no. 83; Hernández Díaz 1967, no. 206; Mayer 1923[1], p. 137; Ponz 1947 ed., p. 799

41
Santa Justa and Santa Rufina

200 × 176 cm
c. 1665–66
Museo de Bellas Artes, Seville
[*repr. on p.* 110]

This is one of Murillo's most famous paintings and forms part of the high altarpiece of the Capuchin Church in Seville, which was built over the site of the saints' martyrdom.

The saints appear with their attributes, ceramic pots; these allude to their occupation as potters and to the reason for their martyrdom, which occurred during the Roman domination of Spain. Tradition has it that the clay vessels produced by the saints were exceptionally beautifully made and were therefore solicited by the Roman priests who wanted them as cult objects for their idol, Salambo. The saints, being Christian, opposed the idea of their vessels being used to honour a pagan god, and for this they were martyred.

The other symbol usually associated with SS Justa and Rufina is the Giralda, the tower of Seville Cathedral. According to another legend, it was saved from destruction during the earthquake of 1504, which devastated the city of Seville and endangered the tower, by the descent from heaven of the two saints, who clasped the Giralda in their arms to prevent its collapse.

The earliest surviving painting of the two saints is by Hernando de Esturmio (1555) in the altarpiece of the Chapel of the Evangelist in Seville Cathedral. In 1558, Luis de Vargaso frescoed the saints on one of the walls of the Giralda, but this has almost completely disappeared. Another example is the painting signed by Miguel de Esquivel, datable around 1615–20, which is kept in the Seville Cathedral Archive (fig. 89). The Cathedral also has a painting of SS Justa and Rufina, attributed to Ignacio de Ries and datable around 1655.

41

In his version of the subject, Murillo portrayed the two saints as young girls with delicate and beautiful features; they hold a miniature Giralda in their hands; they are dressed in robes of a harmonious blend of greens, ochres and reds. The painted sketch for this work is in the Tokyo museum, and there is a preparatory drawing in the Musée Bonnat, Bayonne (fig. 48).

PROVENANCE
Capuchin Church, Seville; 1810 temporarily transferred to Gibraltar; 1814 returned to the Capuchin Church, Seville; 1836 transferred to the Museo de Bellas Artes on the disentailment of church property

REFERENCES
Angulo 1981, I, p. 360; II, p. 65, no. 64; Ceán Bermúdez 1800, p. 61; Curtis 1883, no. 125; Gaya Nũno 1978, no. 114; Gestoso 1912[2], no. 81; González de León 1884, II, p. 261; Hernándes Díaz 1967, no. 197; Lafond 1946, p. 85; Latour 1855, II, p. 182; Mayer 1923[1], pl. 138; Montoto 1923, p. 79; Ortíz de Zúñiga 1667, p. 773; Ponz 1947 ed., p. 799; Sánchez Cantón 1930, V, pl. 420; Valencina 1908[1], IV, pp. 119, 124; Velázquez and Sánchez 1864, p. 178

fig. 89 Miguel de Esquivel *SS Justa and Rufina* (Seville Cathedral)

42

42
St. Thomas of Villanueva

283 × 188 cm
c. 1668
Museo de Bellas Artes, Seville
[*rep. on p.* 121]

Both technically and in terms of composition this is one of Murillo's greatest works and, in fact, Palomino tells us that the artist considered it to be one of his best paintings.

It comes from the church of the Capuchin friars in Seville where it was in the first chapel on the right. St. Thomas of Villanueva was not a Franciscan but an Augustinian; however, he was a saint devoted to charity, and charitable deeds were one of the principal missions of the Franciscans. Angulo has observed that the choice of this subject is due to the fact that several friars in Seville's Capuchin community were of Valencian origin. Since St. Thomas of Villanueva was Valencian and since his cult was widespread in the second half of the seventeenth century, it is natural that he should be honoured in a Seville monastery. He had preached before the Emperor Charles V and was elected Archbishop of Valencia in 1544; in 1658 he was canonized. He was famous for his charity, which also explains why he was chosen as a subject for a Franciscan church, although not of that order himself.

The scene is set in a church interior, the spatial depth of which is created through a succession of alternating planes of light and shade. The composition is dominated by the figure of the saint, who has abandoned his study of theological texts to give alms to some beggars. Kneeling at his feet is a cripple. To the right are several beggars, each strongly characterized: the expectant expression of the poor child waiting to be helped, the satisfaction of the old man who is looking greedily at the money he holds in the palm of his hand and the anxiety of the old woman in the background, who fears there will be nothing left for her because she is the last to arrive. This group is contrasted with the equilibrium of the mother and son on the lower left, whose serenity, after receiving alms from the saint, is one of the most beautiful glimpses of popular life ever caught by the artist.

PROVENANCE
Capuchin Church, Seville; 1810 temporarily transferred to Gibraltar with the church's other paintings by Murillo to evade Marshall Soult's rapacity; 1836 transferred to the Museo de Bellas Artes on the disentailment of church property

REFERENCES
Angulo 1981, I, p. 369; II, no. 76; Céan Bermúdez 1800, II, p. 62; Curtis 1883, no. 395; Gaya Nuño 1978, no. 141; Gestosoy Perez 1912, no. 90; Hernández Díaz 1967, no. 201; León 1805, fol. 19; Mayer 1923[1], p. 144; Montoto 1923, p. 85; Palomino 1947 ed., p. 1033; Ponz 1947 ed., p. 799

43

44

45

43
St. Francis Embracing the Crucified Christ

282 × 188 cm
c. 1668
Museo de Bellas Artes, Seville
[*repr. on p.* 122]

This painting is one of the extensive series that Murillo painted for the Capuchin Church in Seville. It was situated in the first chapel on the left of the nave.

The subject extols the deep devotion to the crucified Christ of the Franciscans and alludes to St. Francis's youthful decision to renounce all worldly goods and to dedicate himself to preaching the Christian message: to love God and thy neighbour. Two angels hold a book inscribed QUI NON RENUNTIAT OMNIBUS QUI POSSIDET NON POTEST MEUS ESSE DISCIPULUS LVC XIIII ('whosoever he be of you that forsaketh not all that he hath, he cannot be my disciple'; *Luke*, XIV, 33). The globe symbolizes St. Francis's rejection of worldly goods.

The mystical subject of the crucified Christ embracing St. Francis had previously been represented in Spanish painting, most notably in Francisco Ribalta's *St. Francis Embracing the Crucified Christ*, painted for the Capuchin monastery in Valencia (fig. 13).

The great popularity of this painting is due to the intense spiritual intimacy between St. Francis and Christ, which breaks away from the hieratic treatment of such religious themes in Seville during the first half of the seventeenth century; thus, the viewer feels himself involved in the mystical event. The delicate chromatic harmony between Saint Francis's habit, the flesh-coloured hues of Christ's body and the greenish background, adds to the intensity of the deeply intimate emotion.

Cat. D6 is a study for this composition.

PROVENANCE
Capuchin Church, Seville; 1810 temporarily transferred to Gibraltar; 1835 transferred to the Museo de Bellas Artes, Seville on the disentailment of church property

REFERENCES
Angulo 1981, I, p. 367; II, p. 71, no. 72; Ceán Bermúdez 1800, II, p. 61; Curtis 1883, no. 228; Gaya Nuño 1978, no. 187; Gestoso y Perez 1912, no. 93; Hernández Díaz 1967, no. 203; Mayer 1923; Montoto 1923[1], p. 84; Ponz 1947 ed., p. 799; Valencina 1908[1], IV, p. 119

44
Adoration of the Shepherds

282 × 188 cm
c. 1668
Museo de Bellas Artes, Seville
[*repr. on p.* 120]

This is one in the extensive series of paintings made by Murillo for the Capuchin Church in Seville, and was placed in the third side chapel on the right of the nave. It is a work of exceptional quality with a masterful composition; the figures of the shepherds and the Holy Family are set within a framework of interweaving diagonal lines and a harmonious effect of contrasted lighting is realized by balancing the bright diagonal shaft of light coming from the left with the soft half-light of the stable interior.

There is a sense of the elation of ordinary people in this work. Murillo introduces four shepherds who, together, represent the cycle of life from infancy to old age: a child who offers a hen, a pretty young peasant girl who carries a basket of eggs, a shepherd of mature years who kneels and offers a lamb and, finally, an old man who, lost in thought with his hands clasped to his breast, contemplates the Christ Child.

The Holy Family is portrayed with sweetness and simplicity. Joseph leans on his crook and gazes at the Child with a benevolent expression, while the Virgin gently lifts the swaddling clothes which cover the newly-born child so that the shepherds may see him better. The pose of the Virgin is one of the most beautiful effects achieved by Murillo; he endowed the Virgin with a modest and simple beauty.

There is a sketch for this work in the Courtauld Institute on the *verso* of a preparatory drawing for *St. Francis Embracing the Crucified Christ* (Cat. D6).

PROVENANCE
Capuchin Church, Seville; 1810 temporarily transferred to Gibraltar; 1835 transferred to the Museo de Bellas Artes, Seville on the disentailment of church property

REFERENCES
Angulo 1981, I, p. 372; II, p. 72, no. 73; Ceán Bermúdez 1800, II, p. 61; Curtis 1883, no. 118; Gestoso 1912, no. 92; Hernández Díaz 1967, no. 200; Mayer 1923[1], p. 147; Montoto 1923, p. 90; Ponz 1947 ed., p. 799; Valencina 1908[1], IV, p. 119.

45
The Healing of the Paralytic at the Pool of Bethesda

237 × 261 cm
1668
The Trustees of the National Gallery, London
[*repr. on p.* 118]

This painting is one of the series of the Acts of Mercy painted by Murillo for the Hospital de la Caridad in Seville, commissioned by Miguel de Mañara. It was painted in 1668 and was placed in the church the same year.

46

The subject is taken from *John*, V, 2: Jesus cures a paralytic by immersing him in the Pool of Bethesda at Jerusalem. It illustrates one of the Acts of Mercy, attending the sick, and is identified as such in the Caridad's inventory of 1674.

Murillo created an admirable architectonic perspective in this painting, the most daring in his *oeuvre*. The Gospel text says that the pool had 'five porches', two of which are shown by Murillo; to accentuate the sense of depth he used alternating planes of light and shade.

The figures are concentrated in the left-hand side of the composition, where Jesus, with St. Peter, St. John and another apostle, are grouped around the paralytic who lies on the ground, his body strongly foreshortened.

Numerous copies of this painting were made, the most important being those by the Seville painter, Joaquin Cortés, who also copied the other Acts of Mercy paintings by Murillo in the Hospital de la Caridad. These copies, now at the Palacio de Aranjuez near Madrid, were exhibited in the Hospital's church on the third centenary of the painter's death; they were hung in the places occupied by the originals before they were stolen by Marshal Soult.

PROVENANCE
1810 Church of the Hermandad de la Caridad, Seville; removed by Marshal Soult to the Alcázar, Seville; 1812 Soult Collection, Paris; 1847 George Tomline, Orwell Park; inherited by G. Pretyman; 1933 sold to Owen Hugh Smith; 1949 Agnew's, London; sold to the executors of W. Graham Robertson; 1950 donated to the Gallery

EXHIBITIONS
Royal Academy, London 1910, no. 46; London 1981, no. 51

REFERENCES
Angulo 1981, I, p. 391; II, p. 85, no. 82; Braham 1981, no. 51, fig. 103; Brown 1970, pp. 265–77; Curtis 1883, no. 182; Gaya Nuño 1978, no. 252; MacLaren and Braham 1970, pp. 67–70; Mayer 1923, p. 131; Valdivieso and Serrera 1980, p. 71; Young 1980, no. 148; Waagen 1854, 3, p. 439

ADDITIONAL REFERENCES
Works by Old Masters and the Deceased Masters of the British School, Royal Academy, London, 1910, no. 46

46
The Return of the Prodigal Son

236 × 262 cm
1668
National Gallery of Art, Washington, Gift of the Avalon Foundation
[*repr. on p.* 119]

This painting belongs to the group of pictures painted for the Hospital de la Caridad in Seville to illustrate the Acts of Mercy. The *Catechism of Christian Doctrine* lists seven Corporal Works of Mercy, based on *Matthew*, XXV, 35–36. In the institution's 1674 inventory, the picture was connected with the act of 'clothing the naked'. The picture was hung in the church in 1668 and it is very probable that it was painted that year.

Luke, XV, 22 recounts the parable of the return of the Prodigal Son: after having squandered his fortune he returns, repentant, to his father's house. The father, seeing his ragged, battered son, embraces him and orders his servants to dress him in rich clothing, to shoe his bare feet, and to put a ring on his finger; at the same time he orders a calf to be sacrificed and arranges a banquet to celebrate the return of the son he had given up for lost. Murillo has faithfully included all the details of the gospel text. The composition is centred around the embrace of father and son; on the right are the servants who have carried out the old man's instructions, and whose faces are jubilant. To the left is another servant and a smiling child who lead in the sacrificial calf.

Murillo had already painted this subject in a series recounting the story of the Prodigal Son that is now in the Beit Collection (Cat. 52). However, the earlier version lacks the intensity of psychological reaction expressed by the characters in the present painting; the earlier version is also of very inferior quality technically.

PROVENANCE
1810 Church of the Hermandad de la Caridad, Seville; 1812 removed to the Alcázar, Seville; 1812 Soult Collection, Paris; 1835 Duke of Sutherland; 1952 sold to Agnew's, London; sold to the Avalon Foundation, who donated it to the Gallery in 1948

EXHIBITIONS
British Institution, London 1836; Grafton Galleries, London 1913, no. 83; London 1938, no. 217

REFERENCES
Angulo 1971, p. 352; Angulo 1981, I, p. 396; II, p. 86, no. 83; Brown 1970, p. 265; Carnaid 1952, p. 84; Ceán Bermúdez 1806, p. 19; Curtis 1883, no. 193; Gaya Nuño 1978, no. 253; Gómez Imaz 1896, no. 5; Mayer 1923[1], p. 126; Montoto 1923, p. 97; Ponz 1947 ed., p. 802; Valdivieso and Serrera 1982, p. 71

47
The Prodigal Son Receiving his Portion

104 × 145 cm
c. 1660–70
Sir Alfred Beit Collection, Russborough, County Wicklow
[*repr. on* p. 124]

Murillo painted a series of six scenes illustrating the parable of the Prodigal Son (Cat. 47–52), which, according to Dorival, were based on engravings by Callot of the same subject. Their dating is problematical; Curtis, Mayer, Stechow and Jordan, among others, place the

47

48

49

series late in the artist's career, but Angulo thinks that they are stylistically close to Murillo's work of around 1660, even if the use of back lighting suggests a later date. It is not known who commissioned these pictures: in 1670 the artist agreed to paint a series of six paintings for de la Puente and the licenciate Duarte; there is no mention of the subject but it might have been the Prodigal Son series, despite the late date.

Here Murillo shows the Prodigal Son collecting his patrimony: the gospel narrative (*Luke*, XV, II) is very brief, and Murillo had no literary text to which he was obliged to conform. This gave him the opportunity of elaborating a theme which could be adapted to a scene of contemporary life. There are no biblical references in either the surroundings or in the characters' costume: Murillo has dressed them in contemporary fashion. The room is lit though the open door on the left and there is a suggestion perhaps of contemporary Dutch painting – we can imagine the Dutch treating the scene in a similar manner; simply and intimately, as in the small Prado oil sketch (Cat. 53). Murillo suggests the feelings of the characters confronted with the son's departure – the dignity of the father and the quiet regret of the older brother and sister – with the same psychological understanding that he shows throughout the series.

PROVENANCE
Mid 19th Century, Marqués de Narros, Zarauz; José de Madrazo, Madrid; 1850 Marqués de Salamanca, Madrid; 1867 sold in Paris; bought by Earl of Dudley; 1896 bought by Sir Alfred Beit

EXHIBITIONS
Leeds 1868, nos. 2917–21; Royal Academy, London 1871, no. 411; New Gallery, London 1895–96, p. 30; Arts Council, London 1947, nos. 17–22

REFERENCES
Angulo 1981, I, pp. 304–05; II, nos. 18–23; III, pl. 154–60; Beruete 1901, p. 258; *Chronique des Arts* 1867, i, VI, p. 1; Curtis 1883, p. 193, nos. 183–91; Dorival 1951, p. 94; Gaya Nuño 1978, nos. 260, 262, 264, 266–67, 269, MacLaren 1947, p. 13; Mayer 1913[1], nos. 109–15; Mayer 1923[1], p. 115; Stechow 1966, p. 367; Velázquez and Sanchez 1864, p. 176; Young 1980, nos. 247, 249, 251, 252, 254, 255

ADDITIONAL REFERENCES
W. Bode, *The Art Collection of Mr. Alfred Beit*, 1904

48
The Prodigal Son Leaving his Father's House

105 × 135 cm
c. 1660–70
Sir Alfred Beit Collection, Russborough, County Wicklow
[*repr. on p.* 125]

In the second scene from the parable, the Prodigal Son bids farewell to his father, brother and sister. As in the other paintings of the series, the painter takes evident pleasure in capturing everyday details and faithfully recording contemporary dress. Murillo places the action in the foreground, where the figures stand out against the luminous background.

The work is very close to the small Prado sketch (Cat. 54).

PROVENANCE; EXHIBITIONS AND REFERENCES
See Cat. 47

49
The Prodigal Son Feasting

105 × 136 cm
c. 1660–70
Sir Alfred Beit Collection, Russborough, County Wicklow
[*repr. on p.* 126]

In terms of composition, this is perhaps the most beautiful of the Prodigal Son series. Again echoing Callot's engraving, Murillo shows the young man squandering his inheritance on banquets, finery and harlots. But, as in the other pictures, the painter departed quite considerably from the engraving; the numerous small figures and sense of space are reduced to a clearer and more sober composition, the figures are framed in a portico and the emotional content of the work springs from Murillo's imagination, and owes nothing to Callot.

The setting and costumes place the scene firmly in the seventeenth century and make no concession to historical accuracy, playing down the moral significance of the subject. Two servants wait at the table, which is abundantly laden with extravagant dishes and a young man plays a lute and looks towards the main group, which consists of the Prodigal Son and two beautiful women who are, like him, dressed in rich costumes. Murillo adds a charming anecdotal element to the picture, reminiscent of the Venetians – the little dog eating under the table. And he bathes the whole composition in a careful play of light which stresses the warm tonal values: reds, whites, and browns tinged with gold. The technique, using rich, succulent brushstrokes, adds to the feeling of movement and atmosphere.

There are slight variations between this painting and the Prado oil sketch (Cat. 55).

PROVENANCE, EXHIBITIONS and REFERENCES
See Cat. 47; London 1981, no. 48

50

51

52

50
The Prodigal Son Driven Out

105 × 135 cm
c. 1660–70
Sir Alfred Beit Collection, Russborough, County Wicklow
[*repr. on p.* 127]

This composition is not included in the series of small Prado sketches; it is the most closely dependent on the Callot engraving, in both the architectural setting and – especially – the women's poses. As in the other scenes, the painter places the figures in the foreground, but in contrast to the preceding painting, here the young man is dressed in rags. A man silhouetted against an illuminated doorway and an old bawd complete the group.

PROVENANCE, EXHIBITIONS AND REFERENCES
See Cat. 47

51
The Prodigal Son Feeding the Swine

105 × 135 cm
c. 1660–70
Sir Alfred Beit Collection, Russborough, County Wicklow
[*repr. on* p. 128]

Whereas Callot's series of engravings devoted to the story of the Prodigal Son numbered ten, Murillo reduced his scenes to six. This may have been in accordance with his client's wishes, or it may have been because the painter wanted to concentrate on the most dramatic and expressive scenes, such as this one, which shows the Prodigal Son wretched and poverty-stricken, praying amid a herd of swine. Murillo emphasized the theme of repentance by showing the half-naked young man on his knees in a bleak and desolate landscape instead of in Callot's luxuriant setting.

There is a small preparatory oil sketch for this work in the Prado (Cat. 56).

PROVENANCE, EXHIBITIONS AND REFERENCES
See Cat. 47

52
The Return of the Prodigal Son

105 × 135 cm
c. 1660–70
Sir Alfred Beit Collection, Russborough, County Wicklow
[*repr. on p.* 129]

The last scene in the series of the parable of the Prodigal Son is similar in composition to the large painting in the series for the Hospital de la Caridad (Cat. 46), a much more elaborate and grandiose presentation than this modest and intimate work. Angulo observed that in this scene Murillo departed from the Callot engraving; it is much closer in spirit to another engraving on the same theme by the Italian Pietro Testa (Bellini, 1976, no. 24), particularly in the poses of the father and son.

PROVENANCE
Mid-19th century Marqués de Narros, Zaranz, José de Madrazo; 1850 acquired by Queen Isabel who gave it to Pope Pius IX; 1868 the Vatican exchanged it with the Earl of Dudley in return for a Fra Angelico and a Bronzino

EXHIBITIONS AND REFERENCES
See Cat. 47

ADDITIONAL REFERENCES
P. Bellini, *L'opera incisa di Pietro Testa*, Milan, 1976, no. 24

53
The Prodigal Son Receiving his Portion

27 × 34 cm
c. 1660–70
Museo del Prado, Madrid
[*repr. on* p. 123]

The Prado owns four small oil sketches on the theme of the Prodigal Son. They repeat the compositions of the Beit Collection scenes (Cat. 47–52), although with slight variations; two scenes, *The Prodigal Son Driven Out* and *The Return of the Prodigal Son*, are missing.

Although in the past some critics considered they were no more than copies of the larger series, their high quality suggests they are autograph Murillos, possibly preparatory sketches for the other series. The unfinished aspect of the work, with small brushstrokes suggesting form and leaving details incomplete, accords with the artist's method in other oil sketches for paintings, and it is this rapid technique that makes these four small Prado pictures genuine masterpieces – intimate scenes of everyday reality caught instantaneously. In this picture, with its back lighting and its figures dissolving into the room's shadows, Murillo is almost the equal of Rembrandt.

PROVENANCE
1814 Palacio Real, Madrid; 1819 Museo del Prado

REFERENCES
Inventario del Palacio 1814, no. 312; Angulo 1981, II, nos. 24–27; III, pl. 162–65; Curtis 1883, nos. 184, 186, 191; Gaya Nuño 1978, nos. 261, 263, 265, 268; Lefort 1875, pp. 3, 5; Mayer 1911, p. 174; Mayer 1922, p. 342; Mayer 1928, p. 324; Prado catalogue 1819, Room II; Prado catalogue 1928, nos. 161–65; Sánchez Cantón in *Catalogue del Prado* 1963–72, nos. 997–98

53

54

55

56

54

The Prodigal Son Leaving his Father's House

27 × 34 cm
c. 1660–70
Museo del Prado, Madrid
[*repr. on p.* 123]

Like the previous picture, this is probably a preparatory sketch for the painting on the same subject in the Beit Collection (Cat. 48). It has slight variations in relation to the painting, mainly in the figures' dress. The picture must have been trimmed on the left-hand side and added to at the top, as the present measurements do not agree with those given in the inventory of the Palacio Real in Madrid (21 × 42 cm).

PROVENANCE, EXHIBITIONS AND REFERENCES
See Cat. 53

55

The Prodigal Son Feasting

27 × 34 cm
c. 1660–70
Museo del Prado, Madrid
[*repr. on p.* 123]

Of the four Prado sketches, this is the one that diverges most from its counterpart in the Beit Collection (Cat. 49). This is not only apparent in the figures' poses and in the objects on the table, but also in the spatial arrangement, which is reduced in the upper part and extends further in the lower part and in the foreground. The beauty of the colouring makes the picture one of the most attractive of the series. In spite of its sketchy nature, Murillo has included the little dog retrieving bones under the table.

PROVENANCE, EXHIBITIONS AND REFERENCES
See Cat. 53

56

The Prodigal Son Feeding Swine

27 × 34 cm
c. 1660–70
Museo del Prado, Madrid
[*repr. on p.* 123]

This is perhaps the most finished of the four Prodigal Son oil sketches and, like the others, it shows some variations from the painting in the Beit Collection (Cat. 51); the architecture on the left is different and the landscape background is even more bleak. The scene's lighting effects, as in the other three sketches, have been exquisitely conceived.

PROVENANCE, EXHIBITIONS AND REFERENCES
See Cat. 53

57

The Marriage of Cana

179 × 235 cm
c. 1670–75
The Barber Institute of Fine Arts, the University of Birmingham
[*repr. on pp.* 130–31]

The Marriage of Cana gave Murillo scope to create a composition with a large cast of characters in a spacious architectural setting. It is stylistically very close to the large paintings for the Hospital de la Caridad of 1671–73 in its interpretation of space and human types; Angulo dates the picture between 1665 and 1675 because the setting and the use of light are still similar to that in *The Patrician John and his Wife Before Pope Liberius* (Cat. 37) of a little before 1665.

More than 20 figures are gathered round the table of the bridal pair, which is placed in the centre of the composition and accentuated by a ray of lateral light that illuminates the bride and bridegroom and the dishes laid out on the table. With little attention to historical accuracy, Murillo supplied oriental clothing for some of the characters while others are dressed in tunics and cloaks or wear fantastic turban-like head-dresses. The spacious setting, with some beautiful classicizing architecture in the background, together with the large number of guests and the group of servants including a black boy, inevitably recalls Veronese's paintings of banquets, one of which is in the Prado. Of course young black servants had already appeared in Murillo's secular pictures (Cat. 68) and they would not have been unusual in seventeenth-century Seville.

Murillo emphasized the miracle of the changing of water into wine; he painted an assortment of ceramic jars – examples of Seville craftsmanship – in the foreground, one of which serves as the centre and axis of the composition. On the left there is a still-life of a splendid enamelled vase – a fine example of those still found in Seville churches – on top of a table draped with cloths. The tablecloth which appears under the lace edged white cloth is embroidered with Chinese pheasants and is a reminder of the presence of oriental goods in Seville.

57

Angulo argues that this gives an idea of Murillo's taste; his inclusion of oriental objects in his painting anticipated the success they were to have in European courts a century later.

PROVENANCE
1737 Jean Julienne, Paris; 1767 Julienne sale; 1769 Abbé Guillaume sale; 1777 de Conti sale; 1796 Mr. Askew, Carhan Hall; 1797 Presle sale; 1801 Robit sale, bought by George Hibbert, acquired for Lord Aylesbury; 1883 M. de A. Curtis, Wiltshire; 1915 Christie's, London sale; 1947 bought for the Barber Institute by H.B. Binney

EXHIBITIONS
British Institution, London 1816; British Institution, London 1831; Royal Academy, London 1881

REFERENCES
Angulo 1981, I, pp. 423–24; II, no. 237, pl. 296; Curtis 1883, no. 179; Gaya Nuño 1978, no. 31; Kubler and Soria 1959, p. 276

58
The Holy Family

74 × 71 cm
c. 1670–75
The Trustees of the Chatsworth Settlement, Chatsworth, Derbyshire
[*repr. on p.* 134]

fig. 90 After Ribera *The Holy Family* (Museo de Santa Cruz, Toledo)

58

Murillo produced numerous paintings of *The Holy Family*; this is one of the most pleasing. Stylistically it can be dated between 1670 and 1675 when the artist was at the height of his powers. Murillo unfolds an intimate, domestic scene, placing the figures in the humble workshop at Nazareth. Mary briefly interrupts her sewing to look at the sleeping child, lifting up one of the sheets that cover him, while Joseph pauses in his carpentry and turns to gaze at the Infant. The tenderness of the intimate family group is enhanced by a group of four angels who appear in the upper part of the painting, sharing the feeling of domestic tranquillity.

The composition is based on a diagonal, which includes the figures of the Virgin and St. Joseph; this is balanced by an opposing diagonal created by the cot where the Child is sleeping. The composition's atmospheric intimacy is reinforced by the use of softly contrasted lighting; the main protagonists stand out from the heavy shadow of the room. The lighting effects are reminiscent of Ribera, as is the figure of St. Joseph, who is holding a piece of wood in one hand and an adze in the other, similar to copies (Santa Cruz Museum, Toledo [fig. 90]; Monastery of the Escorial) of a lost Ribera original.

PROVENANCE
First half of the 18th century acquired by the 2nd or 4th Duke of Devonshire

EXHIBITIONS
Derby 1948, no. 9; Sheffield 1948–49, no. 9; Leeds City Art Gallery 1954–55, no. 20; Graves Art Gallery; Sheffield 1955, no. 20; Arts Council 1955–56, no. 19; London 1980–81, no. 36; London, 1981, no. 53, fig. 105

REFERENCES
Angulo 1981, I, p. 420; II, p. 171, no. 187; III, pl. 309; Braham 1981, no. 53; Curtis 1883, no. 143; Gaya Nuño 1978, no. 174; Mayer 1923[1], pl. 58; Waagen 1854, 3, p. 351; Young 1980, no. 192

ADDITIONAL REFERENCES
Treasures from Chatsworth, Royal Academy, London, 1980–81, no. 36

59
The Infant St. John

142 × 107 cm
c. 1670
Collection of the Duke of Buccleuch and Queensberry, K. T., Boughton House, Kettering
[*repr. on p.* 133]

The theme of the infant St. John the Baptist in the desert, known in Spanish as 'San Juanito', is frequent in Murillo's work and similar to the Infant Christ portrayed as the Good Shepherd, with which it is sometimes paired. Both are a product of seventeenth-century religious sensibility, which favoured gentle subjects with a sentimental streak, as also

59

in popular devotional images.

The subject comes from *Luke*, I, 80, which is devoted to the infancy of St. John: 'And the child grew, and waxed strong in spirit, and was in the deserts till the day of his shewing unto Israel.' This enables Murillo to set the figure in a landscape; to emphasize the child's helplessness, Murillo portrayed him half-wrapped in a leather tunic with all the frailty of infancy expressed in his delicate features.

The composition is similar to the Prado *Good Shepherd* (Cat. 27), but reversed. St. John sits holding the cross in his left hand while resting his right hand on the lamb's back; Murillo stresses the child's contemplative life. The sombre nature of the landscape, the penumbra which envelops the figure and the peace and calm pervading the composition, emphasize the child's expression of controlled ecstasy, his gaze raised towards the divine light; in the upper part of the picture two putti watch over the saint. This is probably the most sober of all the versions of this theme. In the National Gallery picture (Cat. 35), Murillo emphasized the playful aspect of the child hugging a lamb; in the Prado version the painter extols infant ecstasy; here it is the solitary child's innocence and delicacy that moves the viewer. Together with the Good Shepherd, the Infant St. John is the religious parallel to Murillo's secular scenes of childhood.

This was not, as Gaya Nuño erroneously stated, the *St. John* which, along with a *Good Shepherd*, decorated the open-air altar for the 1655 Santa María la Blanca festivities (see Cat. 35); stylistically it is closest to Murillo's work of around 1670.

There are several drawings of the Infant St. John (see Brown 1976), although none is a preparatory sketch for this version.

PROVENANCE
1757 Bagnal sale, London, bought by Lady Cardigan; *c.* 1770 Duke of Montagu, by descent to the Duke of Buccleuch

EXHIBITIONS
British Institution, London 1870, no. 24; Edinburgh 1951, no. 50

REFERENCES
Angulo 1981, I, pp. 438–39; II, no. 334; III, pl. 351; Curtis 1883, no. 336e; Gaya Nuño 1978, no. 107; Young 1980, no. 111

ADDITIONAL REFERENCES
Catalogue of the Pictures in Montague, 1898, no. 25

60

The Christ Child Asleep on the Cross

141 × 108 cm
c. 1670–80
City Art Galleries, Sheffield
[*repr. on p.* 132]

60

The iconographic theme of the sleeping Christ Child was introduced into Spain in the mid-seventeenth century. One of the earliest known versions was probably that by Alonso Cano (Gudiol Coll., Barcelona, see H. Wethey 1955), dated around 1650, which makes it earlier than any Murillo of the subject.

Giacomo Francia's engraving showing the child asleep on the Cross – a premonition of his death – of 1557 was made in Bologna. Many versions of the subject, including paintings by Guido Reni and Albani, were produced in Bologna during the seventeenth century. These painters helped to disseminate the theme in other countries through their engravings. The foretelling of the Passion and the triumph of Jesus over death – symbolized by the Child's hand resting on a skull – were linked together from an early date.

Such a complex religious theme, with great potential for the expression of tenderness and drama, must have appealed to Murillo, whose sensibility was always aroused by the opportunity of painting children, as is apparent from the numerous variations on the theme of the sleeping Christ Child, both autograph and workshop, which exist.

The most simple composition, with the Child resting on a board perhaps symbolizing the sepulchre, is in the Wernher collection at Luton Hoo (Angulo 1981, pl. 323). Another type of composition – to which this present picture belongs – portrays the Child asleep on the Cross with his hand on a skull; this is to be seen in its simplest form in the Prado version (Angulo 1981, pl. 103), where the Child appears alone. The Sheffield version is more complex: the artist has enlarged the composition and placed the sleeping infant against a landscape background with two putti swirling above him. The interpretation of this theme reaches its culmination in another work (Angulo 1981, pl. 140; present whereabouts unknown) in which the putti draw back a large awning, while another angel bids them to be silent. This painting, perhaps the most beautiful and technically the finest of the known interpretations of the subject by Murillo, can be dated at the beginning of the 1670s; the technique and the treatment of the children both correspond to other works of that period. The Louvre has a preparatory drawing for the canvas (Cat. D16) of the same date.

There are several copies of the painting, possibly studio versions, some of high quality, which demonstrate the composition's success. At the end of the eighteenth century Manuel Salvador Carmona, a Spanish engraver, reproduced the work in an engraving dedicated to the king, for which a Maella drawing exists in the Prado. However, some slight variations in relation to the Sheffield original might indicate that it was, perhaps, inspired by another version of the subject.

61

PROVENANCE
1766 Charles Jennings, London; inherited by Earl Howe through his father, a cousin of Charles Jennings; 1933 Howe sale; Christie's, London, bought by Graves

EXHIBITIONS
British Institution, London 1824 no. 14; British Institution, London 1858, no. 1; Barnard Castle 1967, no. 71

REFERENCES
Angulo 1981, I, p. 422; II, no. 215; III, pl. 321; Curtis 1883, no. 157; Stirling-Maxwell 1873, p. 80

ADDITIONAL REFERENCES
Festival of Britain, Graves Art Gallery, Sheffield 1952, no. 49; *Primitives to Picasso*, Royal Academy, London 1962, no. 108; *The English Conoisseur* 1766, I, pp. 36, 81; *The Illustrated London News* Nov. 1933, p. 777; *The Studio* Jan. 1952, p. 20; H. Wethey, *Alonso Cano, Painter, Sculptor and Architect*, Princeton University, 1955, figs. 159, 161

61

Self Portrait

122 × 107 cm
Inscribed: *Bart.^{us} Murillo seipsum depin/gens pro filiorum votis acpreci/bus explendis*
c. 1670
The Trustees of the National Gallery, London
[*repr. on p.* 148]

Only two of the Murillo self portraits that have come down to us can be considered autograph. The first is in an American private collection (Angulo 1981, no. 413), in which the painter's portrait is placed in a fictive marble frame. In that portrait, Murillo appears to be aged about 30, which would date it around 1650 and make it an example of his early portrait style. The second self portrait, exhibited here, is the better known of the two and has been the accepted likeness of Murillo since the seventeenth century. Commissioned by his children, as indicated by the Latin inscription, its dating has been much debated, but it is now placed around 1670: the artist, born in 1617, appears to be about 50 years old.

The *Self Portrait* was engraved in Antwerp in 1682 at the request of Nicolás de Omazur, a Flemish merchant established in Seville and a friend of Murillo (Cat. 63). If we except the self portrait of Velázquez in *Las Meninas*, in which the painter wears the Cross of a Knight of Santiago and is seen in the company of the royal family, this is one of the most significant self portraits of its time, emphasizing the rank and social status attained by Spanish artists in the seventeenth century. The painter used a device characteristic of Flemish and Dutch portraits of the late sixteenth century: the artist appears in an oval frame in front of which a tablet is inscribed with the sitter's identity, and on either side are arranged a palette and brushes, a drawing, red chalk, a compass and ruler.

62

Murillo depicts himself with a dignified, untroubled gaze, and a very slight expression of melancholy. His absolute mastery of portraiture is apparent in the psychological understanding of this self portrait. The ambiguity of the pictorial space is accentuated by his hand resting on the gilt frame which apparently contains his portrait.

PROVENANCE
1682 taken to Antwerp to be engraved; 1709 perhaps one of the two self portraits by Murillo listed in the inventory of Murillo's son, Canon Bartolomé Esteban Murillo, Seville; acquired by Sir Daniel Arthur in Spain; 1729 collection of Mr. Bagnall who married Sir Daniel Arthur's widow, London; 1740 collection of Frederick, Prince of Wales; 1751 sold to Sir Lawrence Dundas; 1794 sold to Lord Ashburnham; 1850 collection of Earl Spencer, from whose heirs the Gallery acquired it in 1953

EXHIBITIONS
British Institution, London 1855, no. 53; Manchester 1857, no. 640; Leeds 1868, no. 342; South Kensington Museum, London 1876, no. 77; The New Gallery, London 1895–96, no. 103; Grafton Galleries, London 1913–14, no. 99; Birmingham 1934, no. 7; Agnew's, London 1947, no. 22; Edinburgh 1951, no. 28; London 1981, no. 43

REFERENCES
Angulo 1981, I, p. 462; II, p. 322; Braham 1970, p. 71; Braham 1981, no. 43; Ceán Bermúdez 1800, II, p. 55; Curtis 1883, no. 462; Gaya Nuño 1978, no. 281; Harris 1951, p. 314; Kubler and Soria 1959, p. 277; Maclaren and Braham 1970, p. 71, no. 6153; Mayer 1923[1], p. 7; Palomino 1947 ed., p. 1034; Viñaza 1889, III, p. 139; Waterhouse 1951, p. 23

62

Portrait of Josua van Belle

125 × 102 cm
1670
Inscribed on the *verso*: *Josua van Belle Bartome. Murillo en Sevilla an° 1670*
National Gallery of Ireland, Dublin
[*repr. on p.* 151]

Josua van Belle, of Dutch nationality, was probably born in Rotterdam. From 1663 he worked in Seville as a shipping merchant, like so many of his compatriots resident in the city. He died in Rotterdam in 1710.

Murillo probably had seen Dutch portraits in the collections of the Dutch consuls and merchants who lived in Seville. This portrait of Van Belle bears the essential characteristics of Dutch portraiture: it describes the sitter's dress accurately, displays him elegantly and pays attention to the delineation of his character. The picture is particularly reminiscent of the work of Bartolomeus van der Helst (fig. 91). Van Belle is shown standing with a dignified expression; his sober yet elegant dress is typically Dutch, as is his fair complexion. A red curtain frames the composition on the left, while an extensive landscape is indicated to the right.

63

The inscription on the *verso* is probably a transcription of one on the original canvas before it was relined, so the date of 1670 can be taken to be accurate.

PROVENANCE
Josua van Belle's collection, Rotterdam; 1730 sold by his heirs; 1886 National Gallery of Ireland

REFERENCES
Angulo 1981, I, p. 465; II, p. 314, no. 46; Minor 1882, p. 73

ADDITIONAL REFERENCES
National Gallery of Ireland, Illustrated Summary Catalogue of Paintings, Dublin, 1982, no. 30

fig. 91 Bartolomeus van der Helst *Portrait of a Lawyer* (Thyssen Collection, Lugano)

63
Portrait of Nicolás de Omazur

83 × 73 cm
1672
Museo del Prado, Madrid
[*repr. on p.* 149]

This is a portrait of the Flemish poet and merchant Nicolás de Omazur who was a friend of Murillo. Born in Antwerp either in 1603 or in 1609, he worked in the silk trade in Seville. When still very young, he married Susana Belens in his home town; in 1665 he married again, this time Isabel Malcampo in Sicily. It was probably a little after his second marriage that he returned to Seville, where he lived until he died – he was still there in 1691. His friendship with Murillo led him to commission an engraving of the *Self Portrait* (Cat. 61 and p. 152) on the artist's death in 1682. As a sign of his affection and regard, he inscribed the engraving with a Latin text.

The portrait has been trimmed on all sides; Ceán Bermúdez saw a copy of it in Seville in which the oval frame was decorated and which bore a Latin inscription alluding to the skull held by De Ozamur in the lower part. Ceán Bermúdez added that the portrait was signed and dated 1672. It originally formed a pair with a portrait of his wife, Isabel Malcampo, known today by way of a copy in the Stirling-Maxwell collection, Glasgow, in which she is holding a rose. The date of 1672 is problematical, for if De Ozamur's date of birth is correct, he would then have been some 70 years old,which is not reflected by the portrait. Possibly the earlier date of birth is wrong, or perhaps his portrait was painted earlier and De Ozamur commissioned Murillo to paint his wife to form a companion piece much later.

The portraits of both De Ozamur and Isabel Malcampo fall more within the Flemish and Dutch tradition than the Spanish. The use of decorative oval frames, a northern convention probably known to Murillo through engravings, is evidence of this, as is the moralizing severity of the images: the sitters hold a skull and a rose, symbols of death and of the vanity of possessions and beauty. Angulo cites precedents for these allegories in portraits by Cornelius de Vos, while the connection between the skull and the rose as a symbol of *Vanitas* appeared in the work of H. Andrienssen, A. van Nieulandt and Nicholas van Verendael. Perhaps De Ozamur remembered this traditional type of portrait in his native country when he was painted by Murillo, but it must not be forgotten that the same austere, moralizing climate existed in religious circles in Seville too. Miguel de Mañara, a friend of Murillo and an influential citizen of his time who was the driving force behind the foundation of the Hospital de la Caridad, made a special point of discussing death and the skull in his *Discurso de la Verdad*. The skull's religious connotation is evident in Murillo's portrait.

The portrait of De Ozamur also shows Murillo to be one of the great portrait painters of his time; the character's psychological make-up is captured in a masterly way by his close friend. The elegance of the pose and the sober colouring – reduced to black and white – recall the most harmonious portraits of Van Dyck's English period.

64

PROVENANCE
1806 Bernardo Iriarte, Madrid; 1842 sold by his heirs in Paris, bought by Dubois; 1883 R.S. Holford, London; 1928 Sir George Lindsay Holford, Dorchester House; De Boer, Adler; 1964 bought from Mme Adler by the Museo del Prado

EXHIBITIONS
New Art Gallery, London 1895, no. 67

REFERENCES
Angulo 1964[2], p. 269; Angulo 1981, I, pp. 468–70; II, no. 416; III, p. 464; Ceán Bermúdez 1806, p. 105; Curtis 1883, no. 471; Gaya Nuño 1978, no. 243, fig. L; Mayer 1923[1], p. 232; Sánchez Cantón 1972, no. 3060

ADDITIONAL REFERENCES
The Holford Collection, Dorchester House, 1928, fig. 117

64

St. Thomas of Villanueva as a Child Dividing his Clothes amongst Beggar Boys

219 × 148 cm
c. 1670
Cincinnati Art Museum, Donation of Mary M. Emery
[*repr. on p.*135]

This painting formed part of an altarpiece dedicated to St. Thomas of Villanueva, formerly in the Cavaleri chapel of the church of the Convent of San Agustín, Seville. St. Thomas of Villanueva (1488–1555) was an Augustinian who preached to Charles V. He was appointed Archbishop of Valencia in 1544, and was canonized in 1658 for having dedicated his life to acts of charity and for having attended the sick and needy.

This painting emphasizes St. Thomas's charitable vocation even in childhood; a group of young beggars dress themselves in clothes that the child saint is discarding. Murillo has captured an intense quality of suppressed emotion in the young beggars' faces, demonstrating his understanding of child psychology, a natural attribute given that he was born into a large family and was himself the father of nine children. The view of the street has been given more prominence than usual, perhaps to emphasize the small scale of the juvenile characters.

PROVENANCE
Convent of San Agustín, Seville; before 1806 sold by the convent, passing into the possession of Godoy who gave it to the French General Sebastiani; 1814 Buchanan Collection, London; sold to Mr. Baring; passed to Lord Ashburton and sold at an unknown date; 1912 bought by Mrs Thomas Emery of Cincinnati; 1927 bequeathed to the Cincinnati Museum

EXHIBITIONS
Royal Academy, London 1871; Metropolitan Museum, New York 1928; Toledo Museum, 1941; Carnegie Institute, Pittsburgh 1954

65

66

REFERENCES
Angulo 1973[1], p. 71; Angulo 1981, II, pp. 54–55, no. 55; Ceán Bermúdez 1800, II, p. 60; Ceán Bermúdez 1806, p. 95; Gaya Nuño 1978, no. 131; González de León 1844, II, p. 177; Mayer 1923[1], p. 166; Montoto 1923, p. 70; Ponz 1947 ed., p. 789

65

Two Boys Eating a Pie

123 × 102 cm
c. 1665–75
Bayerische Staatsgemäldesammlungen, Munich
[*repr. on p.* 136]

The pessimism and introspection apparent in Murillo's earlier scenes of the everyday life of peasant children had disappeared in his paintings of similar themes dating from 1665–75. Here the artist set the scene out-of doors, bathed in warm light, and although the children are just as ragged as their predecessors, their expressions are happy and carefree. Murillo emphasizes their childish delight and greed in their feast; they have plenty of bread and fruit and a dog as a companion.

PROVENANCE
1756 Palace Mannheim; 1802 Hofgartengalerie, Munich; 1836 Alte Pinakothek, Munich

EXHIBITIONS
Brussels, Paris and Amsterdam 1848; London 1949; Cologne and Oslo 1955; Stockholm 1959–60, no. 77

REFERENCES
Angulo 1981, I, p. 448; II, p. 302, no. 388; Curtis 1883, no. 436; Fischer 1953, p. 81; Justi 1904, p. 18; Mayer 1923[1], p. 218; Soehner 1963, p. 122

ADDITIONAL REFERENCES
Treasures from Munich, Masterpieces from the Alte Pinakothek, National Gallery, London, 1949; *Store Spanska Mästare*, Stockholm, 1959–60

66

Children Playing Dice

140 × 108 cm
c. 1665–75
Bayerische Staatsgemäldesammlungen, Munich
[*repr. on p.* 137]

Together with *Two Boys Eating a Pie* (Cat. 65), with which it has close stylistic ties, this painting can be dated between 1665 and 1675.

The composition is simple; a diagonal is formed by the children's heads. The focus of attention is the dice, around which the boys form a circle. A warm light is diffused over the scene; a ruined building draped with ivy is indicated on the right of the picture.

67

The children are carefree and vivacious, removed from the problems of their daily existence; their natural quick wittedness can procure them enough food to survive, leaving them free to idle their time away at games.

PROVENANCE
1698 attributed to Murillo in an inventory in Antwerp; early 18th century Gisbert van Ceulen, Munich (acquired for Manuel of Bavaria); 1748 the Residenz; 1781 Hofgestengalerie; 1836 Alte Pinakothek, Munich

EXHIBITIONS
Madrid 1981, no. 29; Munich and Vienna 1982, no. 55

REFERENCES
Angulo 1981, I, p. 449; II, p. 303, no. 389; Curtis 1883, no. 435; Fischer 1950, p. 81; Gaya Nuño 1978, no. 238; Justi 1904, p. 18; Mayer 1923[1], p. 217; Soehner 1963, p. 117; Sonnenburg 1980, p. 57

67

Invitation to the Game of Pelota

165 × 110.5 cm
c. 1670
The Governors of Dulwich Picture Gallery, London
[*repr. on p.* 138]

This is a companion piece to the *Three Boys* (Cat. 68) and can be dated around 1670 on stylistic grounds. Angulo has interpreted the subject convincingly: the standing boy is a serious and obedient child who is running an errand for his parents while the other is a mischievous street urchin who is trying to entice him to play a game of *pelota* (a Basque game like rackets) – the bats and balls lie on the ground beside him. So the scene presents a kind of moral argument: the serious child, faced by a tempting offer to delay his errand and to play with the urchin, is being put to the test. The tempted child's uncertain expression does not, however, indicate what his decision will be.

The setting is typical of Murillo's treatment of this genre in his late period. The figures are in the open air, on the right is a ruined building, a diffuse sky is broken by clouds. As in similar paintings, the two figures form a diagonal line across the painting; at the same time, Murillo emphasized the opposing psychological expressions on the face of each boy.

PROVENANCE
1786 Noel Desenfans sale, Christie's, London; 1804 listed at Dulwich Picture Gallery

EXHIBITIONS
British Institution, London 1828, no. 66; London 1981, no. 46

REFERENCES
Angulo 1981, I, p. 450; II, no. 382; III, pl. 444; Braham 1981, no. 46; Cook and Hall 1926, no. 224; Curtis 1883, no. 435; Fischer 1953, p. 80; Gaya Nuño 1978, no. 167; Justi 1904, p. 16; Mayer 1913[1], no. 208; Mayer 1923[1], p. 212; Muñoz 1942, pl. 21; Murray 1980, no. 224; Young 1980, no. 185

68

69

68

Three Boys

168 × 110 cm
c. 1670
The Governors of Dulwich Picture Gallery, London
[*repr. on p.* 139]

In this painting, which has also been called *The Poor Black Boy*, the artist shows two children about to begin a picnic; a third boy with a pitcher on his shoulder approaches and asks for a piece of the pie they are about to eat.

Psychological reactions are well contrasted: while one of the boys turns his head towards the viewer with a smile, the other hastens to protect the pie with his hand, at the same time showing an expression of mistrust. Meanwhile, the young black boy – most probably a slave whose owner has sent him to fetch water – has a friendly appearance and expresses the wish to be invited to take part in the feast.

We know that Murillo had a black slave called Juan, born in 1657, who could well have been the model for this painting; stylistically the work can be dated around 1670, when Juan would have been 12 or 13 years old.

The composition of this painting is triangular, the apex being formed by the black boy's head and the sides by the other two boys.

PROVENANCE
1786 Noel Desenfans sale, Christie's, London; 1804 listed at Dulwich Picture Gallery

EXHIBITIONS
British Institution, London 1828, no. 69; London 1981, no. 45

REFERENCES
Angulo 1981, I, p. 449; II, no. 383; III, pl. 445; Braham 1981, no. 45; Cook and Hall 1926, no. 222; Curtis 1883, no. 452; Gaya Nuño 1978, no. 168; Justi 1904, p. 6; Mayer 1913[1], no. 209; Mayer 1923[1], p. 213; Murray 1980, no. 222; Young 1980, no. 186.

69

The Flower Girl

121 × 99 cm
c. 1670
The Governors of Dulwich Picture Gallery, London
[*repr. on p.* 141]

Although rarer than his paintings of boys and young children, Murillo also produced genre paintings of young girls. Good examples of these are the *Fruit Vendor* (Pushkin Museum, Moscow), the *Young Girl Taking off her Bonnet* (English private coll.; Angulo 1981, nos. 394, 396) and this *Flower Girl*, one of the painter's most

70

beautiful late works, which can be dated around 1670.

As Angulo has pointed out, the girl is not merely a flower-seller, like the village girl in the Moscow painting, but an allegory of the fleeting passage of beauty and youth; their transience is mirrored in the full-blown and faded roses that are lying on the girl's fine shawl. Villegas, a Seville poet and a contemporary of Murillo, had linked the happiness of youth and the transience of beauty in his poem to the Rose. The theme of *Vanitas*, so frequent in baroque art and in seventeenth-century Seville, is echoed in this painting. Because the picture is contemporary with the *Gypsy Virgin* in the Corsini Gallery it has been suggested that the model was either a gypsy or a young Moorish girl, but there is no foundation for this romantic hypothesis.

As in the *Gypsy Virgin*, the setting suggests the outskirts of a city, with a landscape background and a dry-stone wall on the right. The warm tones of the painting are enhanced by the strong light which illuminates the figure, leaving the surrounds in partial shade. The girl's happy smile and her charming turban decorated with a flower in Andalusian fashion, mask the melancholy of the *Vanitas* theme – if, indeed, such a meaning is intended.

The appeal of the painting is testified by the numerous copies that exist in various European collections.

PROVENANCE
1775 Countess de Verrue; sale of Count de Lassay; 1776 sale of Blondel de Gagny, Paris; Collection de Bassan, Randon de Boisset; 1795 C.A. Calonne sale, London; 1804 Desenfans Collection; passed to Sir Francis Bourgeois, who donated it to the Picture Gallery

REFERENCES
Angulo 1981, I, p. 452; II, no. 395; III, pl. 448; Cook and Hall 1926, p. 118; Curtis 1883, no. 426; Fischer 1950, p. 81; Gaya Nuño 1978, no. 169; Kubler and Soria 1959, p. 276; Mayer 1913[1], no. 212; Mayer 1923[1], p. 216; Murray 1980, no. 199

ADDITIONAL REFERENCES
Museo Pintoresco, 1852, p. 41

70

Santa Rosa of Lima

145 × 95 cm
Inscribed: *Bart^{meus} Murillo f.*, possibly not autograph; appearing from the Child's mouth:
ROSA CORDIS MEI TV MIHI SPONSA ESTO
c. 1670
Museo Lázaro Galdiano, Madrid
[*repr. on p.* 143]

In this composition Murillo depicted Santa Rosa of Lima (1586–1618), who was canonized on the 15 April 1668. As she was the first saint of American origin this event had a tremendous effect in the Catholic world and particularly in Seville, since it was closely connected with the Peruvian religious community through the Dominicans. It must have been a gratifying subject for Murillo to paint: his only daughter, Francisca María, took vows in 1671 in the Dominican Convent, Madre de Dios, and assumed the name of Sister Francisca María de Santa Rosa. Murillo's canvas may be dated around that time, about 1670, and Angulo has suggested that it had some connection with his daughter's vows, a theory borne out by the fact that there are two copies of the work in the Seville convent.

The painter portrayed an incident from the life of Santa Rosa; she was praying in the convent garden and sewing to make money for her parents when the Child Jesus appeared to her, seated on her work-basket. The series of paintings decorating the Vatican in commemoration of the saint's canonization were commissioned from the Roman painter, Lazzaro Baldi, in 1668 (Pampalone 1979, p. 24). The celebrations were described in detail by Francisco de Córdova y Castro. Although Murillo does not appear to have been influenced by any of these pictures in his choice of subject, there is an echo of the scene engraved by Thiboust (Pampalone 1979, fig. 16) from a Baldi drawing, in which the saint holds the Child in her arms while he embraces her. The features of the idealized and very beautiful face of Murillo's Santa Rosa recall the engraving and other representations of her, such as Baldi's painting of the saint worshipped by Indians in Santa Maria Sopra Minerva, Rome. So it seems likely that engravings of her true likeness had been circulated and were used by both artists as a model.

In this composition Murillo emphasized the contemplative aspect of the Saint's life; this is one of his most poetic visions of prayer and contemplation of the divine.

There is another version of this subject known through two versions, which probably are not autograph Murillos but of his school (Angulo 1981, no. 371); one is in the Lázaro Galdiano Museum, Madrid, the other is in an English private collection; this is different in composition, showing the saint half-length, with a branch of roses in her right hand and the child Jesus seated amongst the roses. The Ciro Ferri print mentioned by Mayer should probably be attributed to Lazzaro Baldi.

PROVENANCE
1872 Isaac Pereire sale, Paris, as coming from the Standish and Urzaiz collections; 1929 Christie's, London, when it was said to have been bought in Cádiz in 1821 and to have come from the Brackenbury Collection; 1931 Tomás Harris, London; sold to the Museum

EXHIBITIONS
British Institution, London 1832; British Institution, London 1862; London, 1931, p. 3

REFERENCES
Angulo 1981, I, pp. 434–35; II, nos. 370, 371; III, pl. 412; Curtis 1883, no. 391c; Gaya Nuño 1978, no. 309; Young 1980, no. 301

71

ADDITIONAL REFERENCES
Camón Aznar, *Guía del Museo Lázaro Galdiano*, 1962, p. 124; A. Pampalone, *Disegni di Lazzaro Baldi*, Rome, 1979; Francisco de Córdova y Castro, *Festivos cultos, célebres aclamaciones que la siempre triunfante Rome dio a la bienaventurada Rosa de S. María en su solemne beatificación*, Rome, 1668

71

Laughing Boy

52 × 38 cm
c. 1675
The Trustees of the National Gallery, London
[*repr. on p.* 140]

In the last years of his life Murillo intensified the sensation of optimism and happiness in his genre scenes. This painting can be dated to that period, and demonstrates how the smile became the real subject of his late pictures of children. A boy is leaning out of a window looking towards someone who is making a funny gesture or saying something that makes him smile. The frankness of his expression is emphasized with particular sharpness by the bright light that illuminates his figure and makes it stand out against the shadowy, neutral background.

The picture is painted in Murillo's late technique: loose, lively brush-strokes give the figure something of the aspect of a sketch, although the painting is completely finished.

It has sometimes been suggested that this is a companion to *A Laughing Boy Crowned with Ivy* (J.C. Carras, Collection, London): although both works are of similar scale and subject matter it is possible that the latter picture was cut down in the eighteenth century so that the works would form a pair.

PROVENANCE
1737 Paris, Comtesse de Verrue (as companion piece to *A Laughing Boy Crowned with Ivy*); 1777 Randon de Boisset sale; 1806 Marquis of Lansdowne sale, London; 1921 M. Zachary; 1929 donated to the Gallery

EXHIBITIONS
British Institution, London 1821; London 1947, no. 23, pl. 20

REFERENCES
Angulo 1981, I, p. 451; II, p. 297, no. 380; Curtis 1883, no. 412; Gaya Nuño 1978, no. 299; Maclaren and Braham 1970, p. 64, no. 74; Mayer 1923[1], p. 209; Muñoz 1942, p. 18; Soria 1948, p. 22

72

72

The Virgin and the Child with Santa Rosalia

190 × 147 cm
c. 1670
Baron Thyssen-Bornemisza Collection, Lugano
[*repr. on p.* 142]

Angulo has correctly identified the subject as the Virgin and Child with Santa Rosalia of Palermo, a young Sicilian whose cult was popularized during the Counter-Reformation. Previously it was believed to represent Santa Rosa of Viterbo, a Franciscan nun of the late thirteenth century, owing to the roses, an attribute common to both saints. Angulo has dated the work around 1670 or a little later. The loose, sketchy technique used by Murillo for the group of Saints and the *gloria* of putti accords with his work of this date.

The saint is depicted offering the child some roses; the Virgin and Child seated on a cushion of clouds are accompanied by several virgin martyrs. Their grouping recalls the large painting of *St. Clare* (Dresden), painted for the small cloister of the Convento de San Francisco, but the poses of the present picture are more varied.

The theme of the Virgin and Child appearing to saints was common in seventeenth-century altarpieces and Murillo did not depart from the traditional schema; the principal group are placed in the foreground, within a triangular, almost Renaissance format. The colouring progresses from dark, warm tones in the foreground to light, delicate shades in the background.

There is a painting with a similar composition in the Wallace Collection; Angulo believes this to be a copy of a lost autograph Murillo, which is known through a rather poor quality drawing, now in the National Library, Turin. It is slightly different from the painting exhibited here (see Angulo 1974, p. 108, fig. 21).

PROVENANCE
1729 Mr Stanhope, Lord Harrington, formerly British Ambassador in Madrid; 1883 Duke of Rutland, Belvoir Castle; 1926 Christie's sale of property of the Duke of Rutland; 1930 Contini Bonacossi Collection, Florence; 1968 Baron Thyssen-Bornemisza Collection, Castagnola, Switzerland

EXHIBITIONS
Rome 1930, no. 51, fig. XLIV

REFERENCES
Angulo 1961[1], pp. 1–24; Angulo 1974[1], p. 108; Angulo 1981, II, no. 373, III, pl. 355, 617, 619; Calvert 1907, p. 159, Curtis 1883, no. 114; Davies 1819, p. 91; Gaya Nuño 1978, no. 73; Longhi and Mayer 1930, no. 51; Waagen 1854, p. 398

ADDITIONAL REFERENCES
The Thyssen-Bornemisza Collection, 1969, no. 228, fig. 292

73

74

73

The Martyrdom of St. Andrew

123 × 162 cm
c. 1675–1682
Museo del Prado, Madrid
[*repr. on p.* 144]

It is generally accepted that this is one of Murillo's late works; it is exceptional in that it is one of the few occasions on which the artist dealt with a dramatic subject. It is an example of his soft style, obviously influenced by Rubens; although there is no element in the painting taken directly from a known Rubens composition, some of the figures – for instance, the executioner lit from behind and framed by the wooden props of the cross, the soldier isolated on the extreme right of the painting and the general disposition of the horsemen – exemplify Murillo's familiarity with the engravings of the Antwerp master. As Angulo has pointed out, the general arrangement of the scene is also partly inspired by Rubens's picture of the same subject, painted for the Hospital de San Andrés de los Flamencos in Madrid (now in the Museo del Prado), of which there were many engravings in circulation at that time.

The delicate range of golden tones is emphasized by the darkness enveloping the group of female figures in the left foreground, placed there to accentuate the luminosity at the centre. This was a standard device of seventeenth-century Seville painters and of them all Murillo knew best how to utilize it with astonishing ease and realism. The light technique, with loose, spongy brushstrokes, gives the painting a soft quality; and there are certain details of marvellous realism, like the soldier's dog on the right, the woman with the child, and the girl weeping at the death of the saint.

The painting is almost identical in size to the *Conversion of St. Paul* (Museo del Prado, no. 981 [fig. 92]; 125 × 169 cm) and has been considered its companion piece since the eighteenth century, when they were listed together in the inventory of the Aranjuez Palace. A studio (or school) copy has been in the Detroit Museum since 1889.

PROVENANCE
Acquired by Carlos IV; listed in 1814 Palacio de Aranjuez, inv. no. 419; 1819 Museo del Prado

EXHIBITIONS
London and Paris 1976, no. 35; Munich and Vienna 1982, no. 57

REFERENCES
Angulo 1981, I, p. 435; II, no. 277; III, pl. 340; Calvert 1907, p. 120; Curtis 1883, no. 237; Gaya Nuño 1978, no. 283; Guinard and Baticle 1950, p. 131; Kubler and Soria 1959, p. 278, fig. 150; Lafond 1922, p. 59; Lefort 1982, no. 235; Mayer 1913[1], no. 192; Mayer 1923[1], pp. 196, 293; Mayer 1947, p. 359; Prado catalogue 1819, Room II; Prado inventory 1849, no. 182; Prado catalogue 1854–58, no. 182; Prado catalogue 1872–1907, no. 881; Prado catalogue 1910–72, no. 982

fig. 92 Murillo *The Conversion of St. Paul* (Museo del Prado, Madrid)

74

Cherubs Scattering Flowers

191 × 246 cm
c. 1675
The Marquess of Tavistock and the Trustees of the Bedford Estate, Woburn Abbey
[*repr. on p.* 146]

This is a good example of Murillo's compositional facility. The cherubim and child angels who usually people his religious canvases, Immaculate Conceptions in particular, are here represented on their own.

Palomino, who saw the work in Madrid when it belonged to Francisco Artier in 1724, said of it: 'a *gloria* of child angels in different poses, boisterous and playing with flowers, it is truly a glory to see'. Several critics have thought it a preparatory study for the *gloria* of angels in *The Vision of St. Francis at the Portiuncula* painted in 1668 for the Capuchin Monastery in Seville and now in the Wallraf-Richartz Museum (fig. 9), or a copy after it. But in fact the paintings have little in common. There is a copy of this painting in Cádiz Cathedral, and Angulo has suggested that the original was painted for that location; he also discerned the hand of the same assistant who had helped Murillo with another late work, the *Immaculate Conception* in San Felipe, Cádiz.

75

This painting of putti could well have been an independent work, but the symmetrical grouping of the figures, leaving a central space, and the fact that several of the putti are directing their gaze towards heaven suggest that this may have been painted as a background for an altar on which there was a sculpted image. This could have been an Immaculate Conception, a subject for which Murillo habitually supplied his *glorias*, which became even more densely peopled in the last phase of his life. The charm of the different groups of putti and the pearly colouring of their flesh show Murillo evolving towards the rococo style; it is likely that this painting would have been highly thought of in the eighteenth century. If it had been the background for a sculpture, the upper portion may have been cut, leaving only the more animated lower section.

PROVENANCE
1724 D. Francisco Artier, Seville, who was identified by Waterhouse as the son [?] or close relative of the Irish merchant Sir Daniel Arthur, who died in Spain; mid-eighteenth century Mr. Bagnol, who married the widow of Sir Daniel Arthur; sold to the Duke of Bedford

EXHIBITIONS
British Institution 1821, 1851; Royal Academy, London 1851; London 1950, no. 68; Portland Art Museum 1961, no. 15

REFERENCES
Angulo 1981, II, no. 102; III, pl. 376; Curtis 1883, no. 234; Gaya Nuño 1978, no. 218; Justi 1904; Mayer 1913[1], no. 68; Mayer 1923[1], p. 291; Montoto 1923, p. 107; Palomino 1947 ed., p. 1033; Stirling-Maxwell 1848, III, p. 416; Waagen 1854, III, p. 465; Waterhouse 1947, p. 78; Young 1980, no. 111

ADDITIONAL REFERENCES
Klesse, *Wallraf-Richartz Museum*, Cologne, 1973, p. 85; *Lord Oxford's Works*, 1798, II, p. 251

75
Immaculate Conception of Los Venerables

274 × 190 cm
c. 1678
Museo del Prado, Madrid
[*repr. on p.* 147]

This is probably one of Murillo's most popular Immaculate Conceptions. Known as the *Immaculate Conception of los Venerables* after the Hospital de los Venerables, Seville, from which it comes, it is sometimes called the Soult *Immaculate Conception* since it later belonged to the French marshal.

The picture is painted in Murillo's most mature style. The figure of the Virgin is smaller than usual, which creates a space that is thronged with some of the most delightful putti the artist created; diminutive and charming, they are intertwined in spiralling curves that surround the Virgin, and anticipate the delicacy and mobility of rococo art. The group in the upper right-hand corner is an almost literal repetition of the Capuchin *Immaculate Conception* (Seville Museum), and the angel flying with arms extended is a direct quotation in reverse of one of the putti in Titian's *Rape of Europa* (Isabella Stewart Gardner Museum, Boston), a painting that was in the Spanish Royal Collection during the seventeenth century. Murillo might well have seen the painting during his visit to Court in 1658.

Ceán Bermúdez said that the painting was commissioned by Justino de Neve in 1678 for one of the altars in the Hospital de los Venerables, together with two other pictures, *St. Peter*, now in the Townsend Collection, Newick, and the *Virgin and Child Distributing Bread to a Priest* in the Budapest Museum, which is documented in 1679 (Angulo, no. 145). The *Immaculate Conception* is mentioned as one of two altars in the Seville hospital in a document of 1701, but, apart from Ceán's testimony, there is no record of when it was commissioned. Justino de Neve owned an *Immaculate Conception* of similar dimensions, listed in his 1685 inventory; it had the Virgin's attributes carved on its frame, and he may well have sent it to the Hospital instead of commissioning another; the frame is still preserved in the Iglesia de los Venerables. Angulo believes that this *Immaculate Conception* could have been the one lent by an anonymous donor, mentioned in connection with the altar raised for the consecration of Santa María in Blanca in 1665; this also had a frame carved with Marian symbols. However, such an identification runs counter to the traditional dating of this picture to *c.* 1678.

The fame of this *Immaculate Conception* was sparked off by Ceán Bermúdez, who wrote that it was '. . . superior to all the ones by him [Murillo] in Seville, as much for the beauty of the colouring as for the good effect and contrast of the chiaroscuro'. The bottom right corner is in deep shadow, a standard device used to enhance the luminous glow of the vision. In 1813 Marshal Soult took the *Immaculate Conception of los Venerables* from Spain. In the nineteenth century the work was considered one of the most beautiful pieces in the history of painting by the Parisians; Balzac referred to it in *Peau de Chagrin* (1831). At a public sale in 1852, it was acquired by the Musée du Louvre for 615,300 gold francs, the highest figure ever paid for a single painting at that time. In 1941, at a time when aesthetic criteria were less favourable to Murillo, it was swapped for the magnificent portrait of *Marianne of Austria* by Velázquez, during an exchange of works of art between the Spanish and French governments.

76

PROVENANCE
1685 Justino de Neve, Seville; 1701 Hospital de los Venerables, Seville; 1810 removed by the French to the Alcázar, Seville, but returned to the hospital soon afterwards; 1813 stolen by Marshal Soult; 1852 Soult sale, no. 57, acquired by the Musée du Louvre; 1941 returned to Spain, passed to the museum.

REFERENCES
Angulo 1976, p. 43; Angulo 1981, I, p. 414; II, no. 110; III, pl. 371–72; Ceán Bermúdez 1800, II, p. 60; Ceán Bermúdez 1806, p. 93; Curtis 1883, no. 29, p. 130; Gaya Nuño 1978, no. 311; Mayer 1913[1], no. 166; Mayer 1923[1], p. 293; Palomino 1947 ed., p. 1033; Ponz 1947 ed., p. 794

76

The Presentation of the Virgin in the Temple

155 × 208 cm
c. 1680
Private collection, Switzerland
[*repr. on p.* 145]

This is both an exceptional composition and an extremely rare subject in Murillo's *oeuvre*. It is known that he painted a series of scenes from the life of the Virgin and it is possible that this painting belonged to it. Angulo suggests that it may be identified with the painting in the Convento de la Vírgenes, Seville, which was sold to an English peer sometime before 1737.

The work can be placed in the last decade of Murillo's life; Mayer dated it as late as around 1680. Some very thick, rapid brushstrokes, with little attention to detail, help to create the masses and shapes. Murillo manipulated this technique to produce a sparkling luminosity which, in some figures – such as the young Virgin and the priests in the background – bears a certain affinity to works by Rembrandt. Reducing the size of figures in relation to space is also characteristic of Murillo's late style. Here the space is very extensive, with the same atmospheric quality created by Velázquez; Murillo had already begun to use this technique in his 1656 *Vision of St. Antony* for Seville Cathedral (fig. 5).

As in all his paintings from the Santa María la Blanca masterpieces (Cat. 36, 37), Murillo lit the scene with exquisite refinement and variety. A shaft of light, coming from a hidden source, falls upon the beggar lying in the foreground; the Virgin and her companions are illuminated by light entering from a side doorway and the effect of light on the background is even more pronounced: the figures of the priests stand out boldly against an illuminated arch. The Virgin is the focal point of the scene; this diminutive *Inmaculada*, gracious and determined, ascends the temple steps before the solicitous, understanding gaze of her parents.

77

PROVENANCE
A painting of this subject was in the Convento de la Vírgenes, Seville; 1840 Archbishop of Sorrento, Capri; Vermeer Gallery, London; 1926 Reinhardt Galleries sale, New York; 1936 Julius Böhler, Munich; sold to Fischer Gallery, Lucerne; 1964 private coll., Switzerland

EXHIBITIONS
New York 1927

REFERENCES
Angulo 1981, II, no. 131, 867; III, pl. 384; Mayer 1926, p. 251

ADDITIONAL REFERENCES
Sevilla Mariana, II, 1882, no. 214

77

Portrait of Don Juan Antonio de Miranda y Ramírez de Vergara

197 × 108 cm
1680
Inscribed: *Aetatis suae vigessimo quinto anno 1680*
Collection of the Duke of Alba, Madrid
[*repr. on p.* 150]

Juan Antonio de Miranda was born in 1658 and died in 1709. He followed an ecclesiastical career and, after discharging the duties of prebendary – a post he obtained with the help of his uncle, Canon Fernando de Miranda – he was himself appointed a canon of Seville Cathedral in 1679.

The portrait is dated the year after his appointment as canon and it was probably painted to record the event. The identification of the sitter was made by the Marqués de Saltillo who identified the coat of arms on the base of the column. It had been thought previously that the sitter was Gaspar Murillo, the painter's son, who was also a canon of Seville Cathedral.

Technically the painting is remarkable: the loose, fluid brushwork contrasts with the sitter's sober demeanour. The canon's solemnity is a little surprising, for, according to the inscription, he was only 25 years old. The muted colour scheme with whites and blacks predominating was dictated by the vestments of the canon.

PROVENANCE
Entered the Alba collection at an unknown date; inherited by the Duke of Berwick; 1877 put up for sale by him in Paris, but not sold and later returned to the House of Alba

EXHIBITIONS
Seville 1982, no. 50

REFERENCES
Angulo 1981, II, p. 319, no. 412; Barcia 1911, pp. 89, 255; Gaya Nuño 1978, no. 315; Montoto 1923, p. 118; Saltillo 1947, p. 78; Sánchez Cantón 1937, p. 74; Serrera and Valdivieso 1982, no. 50

Catalogue of the Drawings

D1

D1

A Scene from the Life of St. Francis Solano

222 × 335 mm
Pen and sepia wash over black chalk on yellowish paper
Signed in lower right corner: *bartolome murillo f.*
Verso in black chalk
Museum of Fine Arts, Boston, Frances Draper Colburn Fund (no. 20811)

Published simultaneously by Angulo and Brown, this drawing is a preparatory sketch for a painting which Angulo discovered in the Alcázar, Seville.

It represents an episode from the life of St. Francis Solano, recounted by his seventeenth-century biographer, Diego de Córdoba: the saint and his companions were attacked by a bull, but the saint pacified it. The Franciscan theme, the format and the early style, led Angulo to suggest that this was a preparatory drawing for the series of paintings in the *claustro chico* (small cloister) of the Convento de San Francisco (Cat. 4, 5). The vigour of Murillo's pen stroke and the virtuoso use of wash, which produces strong contrasts of light and shade, are already noticeable.

The *verso*, lightly drawn in black chalk, has another study for the figure of St. Francis Solano and, barely legible, a sketch for the figure of San Salvador from another painting for the *claustro chico* (small cloister) of *San Salvador of Horta and the Inquisitor of Aragon*, now in a private collection.

PROVENANCE
Cathedral Library, Seville; A. Fitzherbert, Baron St. Helens (1753–1839); 1840 acquired by W. Buchanan at Baron St. Helen's sale, London; C. Morse; 1873 sold to Gaskell; H. Adams; Mrs H.D. Quincy; 1920 bought for the Museum.

EXHIBITIONS
Princeton 1976–77, no. 2

REFERENCES
Angulo 1973[4], pp. 435–36, fig. 1; Angulo 1974[1], p. 97; Angulo 1981, II, see n. 315; Brown 1973, p. 30; Brown 1976, no. 2; McKim Smith 1974, p. 49

ADDITIONAL REFERENCES
Diego de Córdoba, *Vida, virtudes y milagros del nuero apóstol del Perú, el Venerable P.F.Francisco Solano*, Lima, 1630, p. 195

D1 (*verso*)

D2

D2

A Miracle of St. Antony of Padua

346 × 265 mm
Pen and bistre wash on yellowish paper
Inscribed: *S*^{n} *Antonio* and *de Cano*
The Trustees of the British Museum, London (1920–11–16–20)

The drawing was correctly identified as the work of Murillo by Brown; he rejected the former attribution to Cano whose name appears at the foot of the drawing.

Its relationship to other drawings of the artist's early period places it around the mid-1640s, and Brown thinks it may have been a preparatory study for the series of works for the *claustro chico* (small cloister) in the Convento de San Francisco in Seville. These depict incidents or miracles from the lives of the Franciscan saints, and, although this miracle of St. Antony of Padua does not appear in the series, it could well have been a preliminary idea.

Some characteristics typical of Murillo's drawing style – above all the masterly use of wash, which produces the same chiaroscuro effects the painter was using in his paintings at that time – can already be seen here. The very fine strokes, the feeling of movement suggested by the figures and the clear spatial disposition remained constant throughout his career.

PROVENANCE
J. Rushout, 2nd Earl of Northwick; 1920 E. G. Spencer-Churchill sale; donated to the British Museum

EXHIBITIONS
Princeton 1976–77, no. 5

REFERENCES
Brown 1973, p. 30, fig. 4; Brown 1976, no. 5

ADDITIONAL REFERENCES
H. Wethey, 'Alonso Cano's Drawings', *Art Bulletin*, XXXIV, 1952, pp. 217–34

D3

D3
San Isidoro

238 × 167 mm
Pen and sepia wash on yellowish paper
Inscribed in ink in lower right corner: *Morillo*
(The sheet is made up at the top by some 4 cm)
Cabinet des Dessins, Musée du Louvre, Paris (no. 18445)

The drawing is close to the painting of *San Isidoro* (Cat. 16), which Juan de Federigui, Archdeacon of Carmona, donated with *San Leandro* in 1655 to decorate the sacristy of Seville Cathedral.

It can therefore be dated around that time and is an example of Murillo's earliest drawing style while he was still very influenced by the drawings of Herrera the Elder, the great master of the previous generation. From him derive the incisive and forceful pen strokes and the ordered manner of shading, both in the cross-hatching to create shadows, as in etching, and in the looser sweep with parallel or zigzag lines, which clarify the depth of shadow and creates tension and movement within the composition.

Angulo has stressed the differences between this drawing and the finished painting; these are not just small variations in the figure's pose but a total conceptual change. In the painting Murillo emphasized the saint's studious nature – he is engrossed in reading a book – but in the preparatory sketch San Isidoro's commanding posture, his left hand clasping the closed book, the crozier held in a firm grasp and the saint's gaze directed at the viewer sharpen the sense of San Isodoro's energy and strength. There is also a change in the figure's surroundings; Murillo allowed a spacious setting in the drawing, while on the canvas the setting is more constricted.

Angulo has also suggested that Murillo might have made this sketch for a second version of the subject; a meeting of the Cathedral Chapter on 4 December 1656 proposed dedicating a chapel and an altarpiece to San Isidoro because he was the city's patron saint. But there is no subsequent information to suggest that this project was realized.

D4

It seems unlikely that a second drawing of San Isodoro – closer to the painting (British Museum; Brown 1976, no. 12) – is by Murillo, and it should perhaps be considered a copy of a lost work by the artist.

PROVENANCE
P. Crozat

EXHIBITIONS
Princeton 1976–77, no. 8

REFERENCES
Angulo 1974[1], p. 101, fig. 5; Baticle and others 1961, p. 82, ill. p. 50; Brown 1976, no. 8

D4

The Archangel Michael

267 × 189 mm
Pen over faint black chalk marks on yellowish paper
Inscribed at the bottom: *Bartolome Murillo fa*[t]
The Trustees of the British Museum, London (1873–6–14–216)

This is one of Murillo's most attractive drawings and is typical of his use of the pen; he modelled the figure and created the chiaroscuro and a sense of movement through a variety of pen strokes. The pen's vigour and sureness, with parallel and zigzag strokes, place it in the same period as the preparatory sketch (Cat. D3) for the *San Isidoro* painting in Seville Cathedral, *c.* 1655.

Brown points out that Murillo only painted the Archangel Michael once: for the altarpiece of the Capuchin Church in Seville which was lost during the French invasion. Dated around 1665 to 1666, stylistically it would have been rather late to be connected with this drawing.

PROVENANCE
1873 J. H. Anderdon, London, who donated it to the British Museum

EXHIBITIONS
Princeton 1976–77, no. 10

REFERENCES
Angulo 1974[1], p. 102, fig. 7; Brown 1976, no. 10

D5

D5

Studies of Angels and the Head of the Virgin

284 × 198 mm
Pen with brown ink (angels)
Black and red chalk (Virgin's head)
Yellowish-white paper
Signed in black chalk at the bottom: *Murillo f*
and in ink in the centre: *M° fe* and *15*
The Trustees of the British Museum, London (1873-6-14-213)

This group of child angels, a preparatory study for the Loja *Immaculate Conception*, is an example of Murillo's more forceful and vibrant style and shows the way he worked up a composition. It seems evident that he resolved the group of child angels supporting the Virgin before he started to paint, and, despite some slight variations in the poses, the lighting of these figures is identical in both drawing and painting. Murillo created a shadow across the heads of the cherubim with a few parallel and cross hatched lines and highlighted the angel flying in the foreground.

The lower part of the sheet is a detailed study of a female head in black and red chalk, which, because of the Virgin's tearful aspect, can be related to the theme of the *Mater dolorosa*. Angulo thinks it might be related to the Prado painting of that subject or to the *Dolorosa* in the Seville Museum. The sketch has a naturalistic intent in the use of red chalk for the skin and black chalk for the drapery, frequent in the work of other seventeenth-century artists.

The drawing, given its relation to the Loja *Immaculate Conception*, can be dated around 1655 or 1660. The inscriptions on the drawing are considered to be Murillo autographs.

PROVENANCE
J.H. Anderdon, London, who donated it to the British Museum

EXHIBITION
Princeton 1976–77, no. 15

REFERENCES
Angulo 1974[1], pp. 103–4, fig. 6; Angulo 1981, II, no. 104; Brown 1976, no. 15

D6

D6

St Francis Embracing the Crucified Christ

339 × 226 mm
Black chalk on yellowish white paper
Signed in ink at the bottom: *Murillo fc*
Verso in black chalk
Courtauld Institute Galleries, London (no. 4650)

This is a preparatory study for the picture of the same subject painted between 1668 and 1669 for the altarpiece of the Capuchin Church in Seville (Cat. 43); there are, however, slight differences, the most notable being the variation in the position of the globe at the saint's feet. The drawing may be an example of a rapidly sketched study to determine the details of the composition, to be gone over later in pen. The unfinished appearance is, however, the most attractive aspect of the sketch; in addition to the atmospheric sensation created by the scribbled lines, we are able to follow the painter's creative process as he modified the image to obtain its utmost expressive force.

There is a faint sketch on the *verso* in black chalk, scarcely visible on the paper, a preparatory study for another of the Capuchin paintings, the *Adoration of the Shepherds*, now in the Museum, Seville (Cat. 44).

PROVENANCE
J. Rushout, 2nd Earl of Northwick; Lady E. A. Rushout; 1920 E. G. Spencer-Churchill sale; 1956 acquired by the Courtauld Institute.

EXHIBITIONS
Courtauld Institute Galleries, London 1965–66, no. 48; Princeton 1976–77, no. 27; London 1978, no. 32; Nottingham 1980, no. 55

REFERENCES
Angulo 1981, II, nos. 72 & 73; Brown 1976, no. 27

ADDITIONAL REFERENCES
Newly Acquired Drawings for the Witt Collection, exhibition catalogue by P. Murray, Courtauld Institute Galleries, 1965–66

D7

D7
Assumption of the Virgin

215 × 197 mm
Pen and light brown wash over black chalk on yellowish paper
Inscribed: *Bartolome Murillo fact*
Kunsthalle Kupferstichkabinett, Hamburg (no. 38570)

The *Assumption of the Virgin* is one of the most beautiful, and most typical, of Murillo's drawings. Brown dates it around 1665 or 1666 in the artist's middle period, because of its similarity to the preparatory study in the Bonnat Museum, Bayonne, for the *SS Justa and Rufina* (fig. 48). However, given the broken strokes of the rippling and undulating outline, and the dynamic composition, it is possible that it may be somewhat later; in fact, it could date from the following decade.

It has long been thought that the drawing was a preliminary sketch for the Hermitage *Assumption*, with which it has some points in common, such as the figure's upward impetus and the pose of the arms. Pérez Sánchez believes that it may have been for an alternative version of that painting or an abandoned project, since Murillo usually used more tranquil designs for Marian subjects. Both Angulo and Brown reject the suggestion that it is related to the Hermitage painting.

PROVENANCE
Possibly from the library of Seville Cathedral; 1840 acquired by W. Buchanan at Baron St. Helens sale London; 1881 C.S. Bale sale, sold to J.A. Echevarría; 1891 B. Quaritch, who sold it to the Museum

EXHIBITIONS
Hamburg 1966, no. 164; Princeton 1976–77, no. 34; Madrid 1980, no. 178

REFERENCES
Angulo 1962, pp. 234–236; Brown 1976, no. 34; Gradmann 1939, no. 15; Gómez Sicre 1949, pl. 62; Mayer 1934, p. 16; Pérez Sánchez 1970, pl. XXVIII; Pérez Sánchez 1980, no. 178; Richards 1968, p. 238, fig. 4

D8

D8

The Agony in the Garden

254 × 175 mm
Pen and sepia wash over black chalk on yellowish-white paper, lightly squared in black chalk
Verso in black chalk
Biblioteca Nacional, Madrid (B. 348)

Few of Murillo's drawings can be accurately dated, but Brown places this one in the 1660s given its stylistic closeness to others of that decade. The attempt to render atmospheric effects was characteristic of Murillo's work in that period; the artist obtained these in his drawings by means of a transparent wash, which subtly suggested light and shade and tonal gradations. The mastery of this drawing makes both Brown and Pérez Sánchez believe it is an autograph Murillo, even if the poor quality sketch of a kneeling female saint on the *verso* is by another hand; however this attribution has not been unanimously accepted. A small oil painting on black marble (Musée du Louvre, no. 931), which has been considered to be either by Murillo or an artist from his close circle, has a similar composition, although in reverse, to the Madrid drawing, and they may both be connected with a lost painting. The careful framing of the drawing with a semi-circular top indicates that it was conceived as a preparatory study for an altarpiece.

PROVENANCE
Carderera Collection

EXHIBITIONS
Hamburg 1966, no. 169; Princeton 1976, no. 35; Madrid 1980, no. 177

REFERENCES
Barcia 1906, no. 348; Brown 1976, no. 35; Lafuente Ferrari 1937, p. 55, fig. 12; Pérez Sánchez 1980, no. 177

D9

D9

St. Joseph and the Christ Child

250 × 192 mm
Pen and sepia wash on yellowish paper
Yvette Baer Collection

The theme of St. Joseph with the Christ Child appears frequently in Murillo's paintings and also occurs in several drawings. However, on no other occasion did the artist present Joseph sitting and playing with the Child in such a relaxed manner; it is closer to the many versions of the Virgin and Child. There is no painting for which this drawing could be a preparatory sketch.

Brown has dated it towards the end of the 1660s, but the modelling of St. Joseph, the rendering of his loose and enveloping robe and the marked contrast of light and shade might place it earlier, perhaps in the decade beginning 1650; it has obvious points of comparison with the figure of St. Joseph in *The Holy Family with the Little Bird* (Cat. 8).

PROVENANCE
Possibly C. Morse (Sotheby's sale, London, 4 July 1873, lot 153).

EXHIBITIONS
Cambridge (Mass.) 1958, no. 12, pl. 12; Princeton 1976–77, no. 36

REFERENCES
Brown 1973, p. 33, no. 4; Brown 1976, no. 36

ADDITIONAL REFERENCES
Drawings from the Collection of Curtis O. Baer, Fogg Art Museum, Harvard University, Cambridge (Mass.), 1958

D10

D10

Angel with a Lantern and Sword

216 × 142 mm
Pen sepia wash over black chalk on yellowish white paper
Inscribed in ink in lower right corner: *B. Morillo f.*
Cabinet des Dessins, Musée du Louvre, Paris (no. 18435)

This drawing, together with Cat. D11 and D12, belongs to a series depicting angels with the symbols of Christ's Passion; several are in the Musée du Louvre and one, the *Angel with the Veil of St. Veronica*, is in the Bonnat Museum, Bayonne (Brown 1976, no. 43), although the latter has slightly different proportions.

All the drawings in the series are in the same technique, pen and wash over red and black chalk, and the signatures are autograph. The strong definition of the figures and the fact that the drawings are enclosed by borders in ink or red chalk led Brown to believe that perhaps they were conceived not as preparatory sketches for paintings, but as an independent series. Another possibility is that they were preparatory sketches for engravings, although no such prints survive.

Because the strong modelling and the chiaroscuro recall the paintings in the small cloister of the Convento de San Francisco, Seville, Angulo has dated the series in Murillo's early period; there is a certain similarity between these angels and those in *The Angels' Kitchen* (fig. 4). But Brown believes they are also stylistically related to drawings dated in the early 1660s in which there is a similar use of wash and wavy, rippling outlines.

The Angel is carrying a lantern and a sword to which a

DII

severed ear is attached; this alludes to St. Peter cutting off the ear of the centurion, Malchus, in the Garden of Olives.

The iconography of the series is discussed by Weil. There are copies of five of the angel drawings, all by the same hand.

PROVENANCE
J.I. de Espinosa y Tello de Guzmán, 3rd Conde de Aguila; J. Williams; F.H. Standish; Louis Philippe of Orléans

EXHIBITIONS
Princeton 1976–77, no. 45

REFERENCES
Angulo 1974, pp. 98–99; Brown 1976, nos. 40–49; Standish 1842, no. 441; Stirling-Maxwell 1848, III, p. 1447

ADDITIONAL REFERENCES
M. Weil, *The History of the Decoration of the Ponte S. Angelo*, 1974

DII

Angel with a Banner

220 × 144 mm
Pen and sepia wash over black chalk
Inscribed in lower right corner: *B. Morillo f*
Cabinet des Dessins, Musée du Louvre, Paris (no. 18434)

The elegant pose of this Angel is close to the central group of angels in *The Angels' Kitchen* (fig. 4). For further comment, see Cat. D10.

PROVENANCE, EXHIBITIONS AND REFERENCES
See Cat. D10

D12

D12

Angel with a Lance and Sponge

219 × 152 mm
Pen and sepia wash over red and black chalk on brown-toned paper
Inscribed in ink in lower right corner: *B. Morillo f*
Cabinet des Dessins, Musée du Louvre, Paris (no. 18432)

The Angel carries the lance and the pole used to hold up the sponge when Christ was on the cross. For further comment see Cat. D10.

PROVENANCE, EXHIBITIONS AND REFERENCES
See Cat. D10

D13

D13
The Crucifixion

407 × 356 mm
Red and black chalk on light brown paper
Inscribed on *verso* of mount:
This magnificent and almost unique study by Murillo belonged to the celebrated Conde de Aguila. His collection of Spanish drawings afterwards passed into the hands of Julian B. Williams, our vice consul at Seville, and who was by far the best judge of Spanish art in Europe: it was given to me at Seville by him in 1831, Rich[d] Ford.
Brinsley Ford, London

This drawing has been ascribed to Murillo since the late eighteenth century; Richard Ford's inscription on the back of the mount shows that his drawings as well as his paintings were appreciated by connoisseurs in the past.

The drawing is carefully composed; very delicate parallel lines in red chalk serve to establish the modelling of the body and, in some areas, red and black chalks are mixed to accentuate the shadows of the anatomy. The very light shading achieved by this technique augments the expression of suffering on Christ's face and adds to the illusion of reality. The drawing, still tinged with Murillo's strong naturalism, inevitably recalls Michelangelo's drawings of the same subject and is a good example of the artist's profound religious sensibility.

Brown dates this drawing in the 1670s and relates it to the *Crucifixion* (a Murillo-like composition) which is known through two versions, one in the Meadows Museum, Dallas and the other in the Hermitage, Leningrad; neither of these are accepted as originals by Angulo, although it is possible that both derive from a lost autograph Murillo for which this drawing was, perhaps, a preparatory sketch.

PROVENANCE
J. I. Espinosa y Tello de Guzmán, 3rd Conde de Aguila; J. Williams; R. Ford 1831

EXHIBITIONS
King's Lynn 1969, no. 32; London 1974, no. 167, pl. 8a; Princeton 1976–77, no. 56; Nottingham 1980, no. 54

REFERENCES
Angulo 1974, p. 104; Angulo 1981, II, nos. 1620, 1623, pls. 571, 572; Brown 1976, no. 56; Stirling-Maxwell 1847–48, III, p. 1446; IV, pl. 56; Waagen 1854, II, p. 224

D14

ADDITIONAL REFERENCES
Drawings by Old Masters from the 15th to the 20th century, Fermoy Art Gallery, Kings Lynn, 1969; *Richard Ford in Spain*, exhibition catalogue, Wildensteins, London, 1974

D14

The Virgin and Child with Joseph and Two Angels

166 × 159 mm
Red chalk with brown wash and touches of white lead (oxidized) on light brown paper
The Trustees of the British Museum, London (1895–9–15–891)

This is a good example of the complexity of Murillo's style as a draughtsman. He added a very faint, golden-toned transparent wash and touches of white lead also applied by brush, to red chalk or crayon drawn with tremulous, slightly smudged strokes, which endow the drawing with an effect of great richness.

It should be dated in Murillo's late period; the smudging of forms in the drawing achieve the same soft effect as his last paintings. The drawing bears no relation to any of the painter's Holy Families that have survived.

PROVENANCE
Cathedral Library, Seville; A. Fitzherbert, Baron St. Helens (1753–1839); 1840 acquired by Gibbs at Baron St. Helen's sale, London; J. Malcolm; 1895 donated by him to the Museum

EXHIBITIONS
Princeton 1976–77, no. 61

REFERENCES
Brown 1976, no. 61; Mayer 1915, p. 7, pl. 50

D15

D15

Vision of St. Antony of Padua

171 × 246 mm
Pen and sepia wash with touches of white lead over black chalk on light brown-toned paper
Inscribed in lower right corner: *Murillo*
Cabinet des Dessins, Musée du Louvre, Paris (RF 633)

This is an example of the rich pictorial technique of Murillo's late style. It is typical of the artist's method of work, whereby he established the figures almost exclusively by means of the brush, slightly reinforcing the image in pen, over smudged traces of black chalk. As Brown remarked, the use of toned paper with a delicate wash produces an atmospheric effect – the figures dissolving in space – very similar to the paintings of his last years.

The drawing is a preparatory study for a picture formerly in Berlin destroyed in the Second World War. Like most of Murillo's studies, it varies slightly from the painting. Curtis mentioned another drawing of the same composition in the collection of J.C. Robinson, London, but its present whereabouts is unknown (1883, no. 243).

PROVENANCE
Possibly C. Morse; His de la Salle; 1978 donated by him to the Musée du Louvre

EXHIBITIONS
Princeton 1976–77, no. 62

REFERENCES
Angulo 1981, II, no. 279; Brown 1976, no. 62; Curtis 1883, no. 243; Gómez Sicre 1949, pl. 63, 65; Mayer 1915, p. 7

ADDITIONAL REFERENCES
Dessins du Musée du Louvre, 1980, no. 347

D16

D16

The Christ Child Asleep on the Cross

180 × 135 mm
Red chalk, pen and bistre wash on white paper
Cabinet des Dessins, Musée du Louvre, Paris (no. 18428)

The drawing is a preparatory study for the picture in the Graves Art Gallery, Sheffield (Cat. 60). It is typical of Murillo's method of working; very detailed and finished, with nothing left to chance. The canvas is dated in the 1670s and the drawing is also typical of that period, both technically and stylistically. This composition was very popular in the eighteenth century and several copies of the painting are known; there is also an engraving by M. S. Carmona of a drawing by Maella.

PROVENANCE
J.I. de Espinosa y Tello de Guzmán, 3rd Conde de Aguila; J. Williams; F. H. Standish; Louis Philippe of Orléans; Musée du Louvre

EXHIBITIONS
London 1962, no. 108; Princeton 1976–77, no. 66

REFERENCES
Brown 1976, no. 66; Curtis 1883, p. 181, no. 157; Pérez Sánchez 1970, pp. 91–92, fig. 28; Stirling-Maxwell 1848, vol. 3, p. 1446

ADDITIONAL REFERENCES
Catalogue . . . of the Standish Collection, 1842, p. 48, no. 427

D17

D17

St. Thomas of Villanueva Adoring the Crucifix

205 × 110 mm
Pen and sepia wash over black chalk on yellowish white paper
Inscribed *Bartolomé Murillo fa*[t]
Brinsley Ford, London

This was identified by Angulo as a preparatory study for part of the altarpiece of St. Thomas of Villanueva in the church of San Agustín in Seville of *c.* 1665–70 (Cat. 42). It illustrates the episode when Christ informs the saint that he will die on the anniversary of the Virgin's birth. According to Brown, the style of the drawing would suggest a date around 1670. The differences between the drawing and painting (Museo de Bellas Artes, Seville) are slight, and the finished look of the study might perhaps indicate that it was a drawing to show the prospective client for his approval.

PROVENANCE
Richard Ford

EXHIBITIONS
Princeton 1976–77, no. 69; Nottingham 1980, no. 60

REFERENCES
Angulo 1962, p. 236, pl. 2; Angulo 1981, II, no. 57; Brown 1976, no. 69; Harris 1964, p. 337

D18

Roman Charity

220 × 180 mm
Pen and sepia wash over black chalk on yellowish paper
Inscribed: *Bartolomé Murillo fa*[t]
Boymans-van Beuningen Museum, Rotterdam (s–8)

This is a preparatory study for a painting by Murillo known from various sources. The original canvas may have belonged to the engraver, Tomás López Enguídanos, who reproduced it in a print of 1809 before selling it to the

D18

American collector, Richard Warsam Meade; it was destroyed in a fire at the Philadelphia Academy in 1845. Hernández Díaz has recently published a version in a private collection in Bilbao; Brown and Angulo consider this a copy, but they suggest as a possible original a small sketch in the collection of J. O'Connor Lynch.

The theme, common in seventeenth-century painting, particularly among Utrecht followers of Caravaggio, portrays the Roman matron, Pero, suckling her father, Cimon, who had been condemned to death by starvation, thereby saving his life (Valerius Maximus, *Factorum et Dictorum Mirabilium*, Book IX, V, 4). The theme is generally interpreted as an allegory of filial love, but it must not be forgotten that Caravaggio used it in his magnificent painting of the *Seven Acts of Mercy*, (Capodimonte, Naples) as the charitable act of 'feeding the hungry'. Hernández Perera has proposed that the engravings by Van Caukerken and A. Voet after the Rubens *Caritas Romana* in the Hermitage were prototypes for the composition: Harris has drawn attention to the differences between the Rubens and the Murillo, and between the drawing and the painting, where the young woman covers her father with her clothes, perhaps to suggest another act of mercy, 'clothing the naked'.

The drawing, with its tenuous and abbreviated technique, is an example of Murillo's mastery in obtaining luminous and spatial effects; it can be dated in the painter's late period, the 1670s.

PROVENANCE
Cathedral Library, Seville, 1840 acquired by Heath at Baron St. Helens sale, London; 1941 R.W. Koenigs: D. van Beuningen, who donated it to the Museum

EXHIBITIONS
Princeton 1976–77, no. 70

REFERENCES
Angulo 1981, III, no. 425; Harris 1964, fig. a; Hernández Díaz 1974, pp. 81–88; Hernández Perera 1957, pp. 55, 257; Pérez Sánchez 1970, pl. XXIX

ADDITIONAL REFERENCES
Valerius Maximus, *Factorum et Dictorum Mirabilium*, Book IX, V, 4

D19

D19

Virgin and Child

214 × 154 mm
Pen and sepia and light brown wash over red and black chalk
Inscribed in ink in upper right corner: *Murillo*
Cleveland Museum of Art (no. 86.66.), The Mr & Mrs Charles G. Prasse Collection

The drawing is a preparatory study for the painting of the same subject in the Metropolitan Museum, New York. The late date of the canvas, around 1670, also dates the drawing at about that time; it is typical of the rich and varied style and technique of Murillo's final period.

As in most of his drawings, there are slight variations in relation to the finished work; the Christ Child, who is turning his head towards the viewer in the final version, has his head slightly raised towards his mother in the drawing. Murillo's evolution as a draughtsman is demonstrated by comparing this drawing to the splendid *San Isidoro* (Cat. D3); the latter, although a forceful and vibrant sketch, was much more ordered and regular than this drawing with its variety of single, crossing and zig-zag strokes and lines. In this drawing, volume, light and movement are perfectly combined.

PROVENANCE
J. de Mons; F. Mont; Mr & Mrs C.G. Prasse, who donated it to the Museum in 1968

EXHIBITIONS
University of Kansas 1974, no. 26, pl. 26; Los Angeles 1976, no. 226; Princeton 1976–77, no. 79

REFERENCES
Angulo 1974[1], p. 105, fig. 18; Angulo 1981, II, no. 164; Brown 1976, no. 79; McKim Smith 1974, no. 26; Richards 1968, p. 235, fig. 1

D20

D20

Sleeping Woman

115 × 158 mm
Pen over black chalk on yellowish paper
Kunsthalle Kupferstichkabinett, Hamburg (no. 38581)

Brown has identified the subject as a sleeping Magdalen, and it is classified as such in the Hamburg museum. He has suggested that the faintly sketched vessel on the right of the figure is a jar of unguents, an iconographic attribute traditionally associated with the saint; and, because of the jumpy, interrupted pen strokes, he has proposed a late date for the sketch.

Angulo's identification, however, seems more convincing; he relates the drawing to the figure of the sleeping wife in *The Dream of the Patrician* (Cat. 36), painted in 1655 for the Seville church, Santa María la Blanca. It corresponds only in general terms and is reversed in the painting, perhaps to avoid the excessive similarity between her pose and that of the patrician.

Despite the rapid, forceful pen technique, the abbreviated shapes and lack of detail, Murillo succeeded in producing the same effect of calm, tranquil sleep that prevails in the painting.

PROVENANCE

J. A. Echevarría; 1891 B. Quaritch, who sold it to the Museum

EXHIBITIONS

Princeton 1976–77, no. 83; Madrid 1980, no. 182

REFERENCES

Angulo 1974[1], p. 102, fig. 6; Brown 1976, no. 83; Pérez Sánchez 1980, p. 182

D21

D21

The Immaculate Conception

234 × 149 mm
Pen
Inscribed: *Bartolome Murillo fa*[t]
The Trustees of the British Museum, London
(1946–7–13–1156)

This is an unusual version of the Immaculate Conception in that the Virgin is presented as a young girl. In his *Arte de la pintura* (II, p. 210) Pacheco counselled artists to depict the Virgin as a young girl of 12 or 13; advice which was not generally taken by painters. This drawing has been associated with the small oil sketch of the same subject in the Louvre, which Angulo accepts as an autograph Murillo, although it varies from the British Museum drawing (not in the Virgin's pose, which is very similar) in the group of child angels who support her. The style of the drawing is similar to that of others dated in the mid-1660s.

PROVENANCE
T. Phillipps; T.F.P. Fenwick, who donated it to the Museum in 1946

EXHIBITIONS
Kansas 1974, p. 51; Princeton 1976–77, no. 84; Nottingham 1980, no. 58

REFERENCES
Angulo 1969, p. 783; Angulo 1981, II, no. 116; Brown 1976, no. 84; McKim Smith 1974, p. 51; Pacheco 1649, II, p. 210

ADDITIONAL REFERENCES
A.E. Popham, *Catalogue of Drawings in the Collection formed by Sir Thomas Phillipps Bart.*, F.R.S., *Now in the Possession of his Grandson, T. Fitzroy Phillipps of Thirlestaine House, Cheltenham*, London 1935, p. 234, no. 2

D22

D22

The Penitent St. Peter

186 × 152 mm
Pen on yellowish white paper
Signed in lower left corner: *Murillo f* and *19*
The Trustees of the British Museum, London
(1946–7–13–1155)

This drawing corresponds to Murillo's later style – it may be as late as the early 1670s – when the pen strokes seem to become broader and slower, and some slight blotting occurs, producing areas of very dark shadow.

Murillo painted this subject, St. Peter repenting after his betrayal of Christ, on several occasions. Angulo has recently identified a late work painted for Justino de Neve, donated by the canon to the Hospital de los Venerables, today in the Townsend collection in Newick. The drawing does not seem to be directly related to this composition, but there are some similarities; a full robe envelopes the figure of the saint, who is seated in a landscape, his head raised and his hands clasped firmly together. It is impossible to reject entirely the supposition that the drawing was a preliminary sketch for this composition.

PROVENANCE
T. Phillipps; T.F.P. Fenwick, who donated it to the Museum in 1946

EXHIBITIONS
Princeton 1976–77, no. 86; Nottingham 1980, no. 50

REFERENCES
Angulo 1974[2], p. 160; Brown 1976, no. 86; McKim Smith 1974, p. 51; Popham 1935, p. 234, no. 1

ADDITIONAL REFERENCES
See Cat. D21; Popham 1935, p. 234, no. 1

D23

D23

Portrait of a Man Holding a Hat

144 × 101 mm
Pen over black chalk on yellowish paper
Inscribed: *Bartolome Murill(o)*
The Metropolitan Museum of Art, New York (no. 65.66.12), Rogers Fund

This drawing, rapidly executed and with a wonderful feeling of spontaneity, is a preparatory sketch for a portrait. Angulo has associated it with a portrait of a gentleman that was in the F. Kleinberger Collection (Mayer 1923, fig. 234), but Brown believes that it was for the portrait in the Cintas collection, New York. The figure, stouter than the figures in the two portraits, suggests that it may have been a preparatory drawing for a lost work. The vigorous, broken and involved lines suggest a fairly late date, around 1670.

PROVENANCE
J. Isaacs, New York; 1965 Sotheby's, who sold it to the Museum

EXHIBITIONS
Kansas 1974, no. 27; Princeton 1976–77, no. 87

REFERENCES
Angulo 1974[1], p. 107, fig. 29; Brown 1976, no. 87; McKim Smith 1974, no. 27; Mayer 1923[1], fig. 234

D24

The Immaculate Conception

193 × 130 mm
Pen over red chalk
Inscribed: *Barto(lome) Murillo fa*^{t}
Collection mark, Lugt Suppl. 2770a
Inscribed on the *verso*, a letter from Zurbarán to Murillo:

D24

. . . . . . mucho senti que c . . . . . . [de] *scuidase . . . . . . /la letra de los 32 pesos dijome le abia es*[crito?] */a fulano digo antonio pacheco que los diese/y abiame dicho que a domingo estensor y dicien/doselo o que me diese el dinero lo libraria yo alla/ me dio para domingo estensor esos dos renglones / que dice bastaran. Ud. me abise luego su efet* [o] *y me mande en que le sirva aqui en nuestro S*[eñor] */como deseo de madrid 27 de septiembre de 1* [. . .] */ Muchos recaudos al Sr. don Lorenco. S*r *bartolome morillo / Fran*co *Zurbarán*
Collection of The Hon. Alan Clark, M.P., Saltwood Castle, Kent.

The text of Zurbarán's letter, brought to light by Angulo, is fragmentary, but it refers to a debt the painter owed Murillo. Although the date is missing, the letter can be placed between 1658 and 1664, when Zurbarán died in Madrid; it is very interesting documentary proof of the acquaintance – and, perhaps, friendship – between the two artists. Brown thinks that *The Immaculate Conception* on the *recto* must be dated after 1664, or even as late as the end of the 1670s, because the technique and the style – the broken and somewhat tremulous strokes and the jumpy zig-zag of the pen – seem to imply a late date.

Although the sketch cannot be connected with any of Murillo's known paintings of the subject, Angulo relates it to the one in the Hermitage (to which the Hamburg Kunsthalle drawing [Cat. D7] is similar) because of the Virgin's pose and the composition's upward, dynamic feeling.

PROVENANCE
J. Rushout, 2nd Earl of Northwick; 1920 E.G. Spencer-Churchill sale; 1928 A.G.B. Russell; the Lord Clark of Saltwood

EXHIBITIONS
Royal Academy, London 1938, no. 479; Princeton 1976–77, no. 92; Nottingham 1980, no. 57

REFERENCES
Angulo 1962, p. 233–36; Brown 1976, no. 92; McKim Smith 1974, p. 51; Mayer 1936, p. 47; Pérez Sánchez 1970, p. 92, fig. 29; Richards 1968, p. 238, fig. 5

Bibliography

The bibliography is an abbreviated version of that given by Professor D. Angulo Iñiguez in his monograph on Murillo of 1981. Authors are listed alphabetically; catalogues are listed under the location of the exhibition

A., B.De 1914
A., B. De, 'Ribalta y Murillo', *Arte Español*, II, 1914–15, p. 315.

Abbad 1948
F. Abbad, *Las Inmaculadas de Murillo*, Barcelona, 1948.

Ainaud 1946
J. Ainaud, 'Pinturas de procedencia sevillana', Archivo Español de Arte, 1946, p. 54.

Alfonso 1883
L. Alfonso, *Murillo. El hombre. El artista. Las obras*, Barcelona, 1883.

Alvarez 1882
J. M. Alvarez, 'Noticias biográficas de Murillo', *Sevilla Mariana* II, 1882, pp. 384, 421.

Alvarez Miranda 1849
V. Alvarez Miranda, *Glorias de Sevilla*, 2 vols., Seville, 1849.

Amador de Los Rios 1864
J. Amador de Los Rios, *Sevilla pintoresca o descripción de sus más célebres monumentos artisticos*, including notes by D. Juan Colom, Seville, 1864.

Amerigo 1907
F. J. Amerigo, 'La Sagrada Familia, cuadro de Murillo', *Boletín Academia Bellas Artes*, 1907.

F. Ancell; *see* Lafond 1907.

Andrés 1971
G. De Andres, 'Relación anónima del siglo XVII sobre los cuadros de El Escorial', *Archivo Español de Arte*, 1971, pp. 49–64.

Angulo 1935
D. Angulo, 'La Academia de Bellas Artes de Méjico y sus pinturas españolas', *Arte en América y Filipinas*, II, 1935, pp. 1–75.

Angulo 1935–36
D. Angulo, 'Un San Juan atribuido a Murillo en la Academia de Méjico', *Arte en América y Filipinas*, 1935–36, p. 167.

Angulo 1940–1
D. Angulo, 'El San Francisco dei Murillo del Museo de Génova, *Arte Español*, 1940–41, pp. 312–13.

Angulo 1954
D. Angulo, 'Algunos cuadros españoles en museos franceses', *Archivo Español de Arte*, 1954, pp. 315–25.

Angulo 1959
D. Angulo, 'La Piedad de Murillo. El viaje del pintor a Madrid', *Archivo Español de Arte*, XXXII, 1959, pp. 146–49.

Angulo 1961[1]
D. Angulo, 'Miscelánea Murillesca', *Archivo Español de Arte*, XXXIV, 1961, pp. 1–24.

Angulo 1961[2]
D. Angulo, 'Murillo en Marchena: El retablo de San Agustín de Sevilla. Las copias de los cuadros de La Caridad', *Boletín de la Real Academia de la Historia*, 1961, p. 25.

Angulo 1961[3]
D. Angulo, 'El milagro de las flores de San Diego de Murillo', *Archivo Español de Arte*, XXXIV, 1961, p. 324.

Angulo 1962
D. Angulo, 'Murillo: varios dibujos de la Concepción y de Santo Tomás de Villanueva', *Archivo Español de Arte*, XXXV, 1962, pp. 231–6.

Angulo 1963
D. Angulo, 'Un Niño Jesús dormido y una Virgen de Murillo', *Archivo Español de Arte*, XXXVI, 1963, pp. 189–96.

Angulo 1964[1]
D. Angulo, 'Towards a revaluation of Murillo', *Apollo Magazine*, LXXIX, 1964, pp. 27–30.

Angulo 1964[2]
D. Angulo, 'Murillo: El retrato de Nicolás de Omazur adquirido por el Museo del Prado. Varios bocetos. La Adoración de Leningrado', *Archivo Español de Arte*, XXXVII, 1964, pp. 269–80.

Angulo 1966[1]
D. Angulo, 'Bartolomé Murillo. Inventario de sus bienes', *Boletín de la Real Academia de la Historia*, CLVIII, 1966, pp. 148–80.

Angulo 1966[2]
D. Angulo, 'Dos cuadros de Murillo que se precisa localizar', *Archivo Español de Arte*, XXXIX, 1966, pp. 85–87.

Angulo 1966[3]
D. Angulo, 'Un anónimo murillesco de la Pinacoteca de Munich', *Archivo Español de Arte*, XXXIX, 1966, pp. 191–92.

Angulo 1967
D. Angulo, 'La casa en que murió Murillo', *Archivo Español de Arte*, XL, 1967, pp. 264–66.

Angulo 1969
D. Angulo, 'Las pinturas de Murillo de Santa María la Blanca', *Archivo Español de Arte*, XLII, 1969, pp. 13–42.

Angulo 1970
D. Angulo, 'Un dibujo de Murillo para el cuadro de San Sebastián de Horta', *Archivo Español de Arte*, XLIII, 1970, pp. 407–08.

Angulo 1971
D. Angulo, 'Pintura del siglo XVII', *Ars Hispaniae*, 15, Madrid, 1971.

Angulo 1972[1]
D. Angulo, 'Quelques tableaux de Murillo', *Acts of the XXII International Conference on the History of Art*, Budapest, II, 1972, pp. 781–84.

Angulo 1972[2]
D. Angulo, 'Murillo: La profecía de Fray Julián, de Williamstown', *Archivo Español de Arte*, XLV, 1972, p. 55.

Angulo 1973[1]
D. Angulo, 'Los pasajes de Santo Tomás de Villanueva de Murillo en el Museo de Sevilla y la Colección Norton Simon de Los Angeles', *Archivo Español de Arte*, XLVI, 1973, pp. 71–75.

Angulo 1973[2]
D. Angulo, 'Una copia del retrato de Omazur de Murillo del Museo del Prado', *Archivo Español de Arte*, XLVI, 1973, p. 189.

Angulo 1973[3]
D. Angulo, 'El viaje de Murillo a Tierra Firme en 1633', *Archivo Español de Arte*, XLVI, 1973, pp. 354–58.

Angulo 1973[4]
D. Angulo, 'Murillo. El dibujo del Museo de Boston para el San Francisco Solano del Alcázar de Sevilla', *Archivo Español de Arte*, XLVI, 1973, pp. 435–36.

Angulo 1974[1]
D. Angulo, 'Algunos dibujos de Murillo', *Archivo Español de Arte*, XLVII, 1974, pp. 97–108.

Angulo 1974[2]
D. Angulo, 'Murillo. El San Pedro de los Venerables de Sevilla', *Archivo Español de Arte*, XLVII, 1974, pp. 156–60.

Angulo 1975[1]
D. Angulo, *Murillo y su escuela en colecciones particulares*, Caja de Ahorros, Seville, 1975.

Angulo 1975[2]
D. Angulo, 'La Virgen con el Niño de la Wallace Collection de Londres y Domingo Martínez', *Archivo Español de Arte*, XLVIII, 1975, p. 409.

Angulo 1976
D. Angulo, 'Casa de Venerables Sacerdotes', *Boletín de Bellas Artes*, Seville, 1976, p. 43.

Angulo 1981
D. ANGULO, *Murillo. Su vida, su arte, su obra*, 3 vols., Madrid 1981. Review by E. Harris, *Burlington Magazine* CXXIV, 1982, pp. 766–68.

Angulo 1982
D. ANGULO, 'Murillo', *Arte Hispalense*, Seville, 1982.

Arana de Varflora 1789
F. ARANA DE VARFLORA, (Fernando Valderrama), *Compendio Histórico descriptivo de Sevilla*, Seville, 1789, I, p. 99; II, p. 118; an earlier shorter edition 1766.

Arana de Varflora 1791
F. ARANA DE VARFLORA, *Hijos de Sevilla ilustres en santidad, letras, armas o dignidad*, Seville, 1791.

d'Argenville 1762
A. J. D'ARGENVILLE, *Abrégé de la vie des plus fameux peintres . . .*, Paris, 5 vols., 1762.

Arribas 1939–40
F. ARRIBAS, 'La protección al Patrimonio Artístico Nacional en el siglo XVIII', *Boletín Valladolid*, VI, 1939–40, p. 237.

Asencio 1882
M. ASENCIO, 'Murillo. Su inspiración providencial como pintor de la Inmaculada', Lecture given to the Academia Hispalense de Santo Tomás de Aquino, 11 December 1881, published in *Sevilla Mariana*, II, 1882, pp. 286, 332.

Ayala 1926
J. A. AYALA, 'Psicología de artistas: Murillo, Velázquez, Ribera', *Boletín Museo Murcia*, 5, 1926.

Banda 1957–58
A. DE LA BANDA, 'La Colección pictórica de la Infanta Luisa de Orléans', *Anales de la Universidad Hispalense*, 18, 1957–58.

Banda 1961
A. DE LA BANDA, 'Los estatutos de la Academia de Murillo', *Anales de la Universidad Hispalense*, 1961, pp. 107–20.

Barcia 1906
A. M. BARCIA, *Catálogo de la colección de dibujos originales de la Biblioteca Nacional de Madrid*, Madrid, 1906.

Barcia 1911
A. M. BARCIA, *Catálogo de la colección de pinturas del Excmo. Sr. Duque de Berwick y de Alba*, Madrid, 1911.

Barnard Castle 1967
Four Centuries of Spanish Painting, exhibition catalogue by Eric Young, Bowes Museum, Barnard Castle, 1967.

Baticle 1961
J. BATICLE, 'Le Dessin en Espagne au XVIIe siècle', *L'Oeil*, LXXXI, 1961, pp. 49–53, 82.

Baticle 1963
J. BATICLE, *Trésor de la peinture espagnole*, Paris, 1963.

Baticle 1964
J. BATICLE, 'Un tableau de Murillo', *Revue du Louvre*, 1964, pp. 93–96.

Baticle, Lacambre and Rissot 1981
J. BATICLE, J. LACAMBRE and C. RISSOT, *Catalogue sommaire illustré des peintures du Musée du Louvre: Ecole espagnole*, Paris, 1981.

Baticle and Marinas 1981
J. BATICLE and C. MARINAS, *La Galerie Espagnole de Louis Philippe, 1838–1848*; Paris, 1981.

Bell Scott 1873
W. BELL SCOTT, *Murillo and the Spanish School of Painting*, n.p., 1873.

Benjumea 1972
J. M. BENJUMEA, 'Descubrimiento en Sevilla de un Zurbarán, un Herrera y un Murillo', *Bellas Artes*, 16, 1972, p. 57.

Beroqui 1913–18
P. BEROQUI, 'Adiciones al Catálogo del Museo del Prado', *Boletín Soc. Castellana Excursiones*, 1913–18.

Beroqui 1930–32
P. BEROQUI 'El Museo del Prado. Apuntes para su historia', *Boletín Soc. Española Excursiones*, 1930, pp. 33, 112, 189, 252; 1931, pp. 20, 94, 190, 261; 1932, pp. 7, 85, 213.

Beroqui 1933
P. BEROQUI, *El Museo del Prado. Notas para su historia*, Madrid, 1933.

Beule 1861
E. BEULE, 'Murillo et l'Andalousie', *Revue des Deux Mondes*, 5.X.1861.

Borenius 1913
T. BORENIUS, 'Two still-life pictures by Murillo(?)', *Burlington Magazine*, XXIV, 1913, p. 74.

Boutelou 1875
BOUTELOU, *Estudio del San Antonio de Murillo*, Seville Alvarez, 1875.

Braham 1965
A. BRAHAM, 'The early style of Murillo', *Burlington Magazine*, CVII, 1965, pp. 445–51.

Braham 1970, *see* MacLaren and Braham 1970.

Braham 1981, *see* London 1981.

British Institution 1813–1823, *see* Dallaway 1824.

Brown 1970
J. BROWN, 'Hierogliphs of Death and Salvation: The Decoration of the Church of the Hermandad de la Caridad, Seville', *Art Bulletin*, LII, 1970, pp. 265–77.

Brown 1973
J. BROWN, 'Notes on Princeton Drawings: Bartolomé Esteban Murillo', *Record of the Art Museum*, Princeton University, XXXII, no. 2, 1973, pp. 28–33.

Brown 1974
J. BROWN, 'Pen Drawings by Herrera the Younger' in *Hortus Imaginum: Essays in Western Art*, edited by R.E.Enggass and M.Stokstad, Lawrence (Kans.), 1974.

Brown 1975[1]
J. BROWN, Review of 'Spanish Baroque Drawings in North American Collections', *Master Drawings* XIII, 1, 1975, pp. 60–63.

Brown 1975[2]
J. BROWN, 'Drawings by Herrera the Younger and a Follower', *Master Drawings*, XIII, 3, 1975, pp. 235–40.

Brown 1976
J. BROWN, *Murillo & His Drawings*, The Art Museum, Princeton University, 1976.

Brown and Elliott 1980
J. BROWN, J. H. ELLIOTT, *A Palace for a King, The Buen Retiro and the Court of Philip IV*, New Haven and London, 1980.

Buchanan 1824
W. BUCHANAN, *Memoirs of Painting, with a chronological history of the importation of pictures by the great masters into England since the French Revolution* 2 vols., London, 1824.

Burckhardt 1837
J. BURCKHARDT, 'Über Murillo' *Atlantis* IX, 1837, p. 482.

Burger 1865
W. BURGER, *Trésors d'Art en Angleterre*, Paris, 1865.

Busch 1957
K. BUSCH, 'Murillo: Die kleine Obshändlerin', *Westermanns Monatshefte*, 1957, VIII, p. 41.

Busuioceanu 1940
A. BUSUIOCEANU, 'A re-discovered painting by Murillo', *Burlington Magazine*, LXXVI, 1940, p. 55.

Calvert 1907
A. F. CALVERT, *Murillo, A Biography and Appreciation*, London and New York, 1907.

Caracas 1981
400 años de Pintura Española, exhibition catalogue by M. Díaz Padrón, M. Orihuela, L. Pan de Loraluce, Caracas, 1981.

Carnaid 1952
W. CARNAID, *Great Paintings from the National Gallery*, Washington, 1952.

Carriazo 1929
J. DE M. CARRIAZO, 'Correspondencia de don Antonio Ponz con el Conde del Aguila', *Archivo Español de Arte*, V, 1929, pp. 157–83.

Cascales 1929
J. CASCALES, *Las Bellas Artes en Sevilla. La Pintura, la escultura y la cerámica artística desde el siglo XIII hasta nuestros días*, Toledo, 1929.

Castro 1919–21
A. DE CASTRO, 'Autógrafo de don – sobre unos cuadros de Murillo que están en la iglesia de Santa Catalina en esta cuidad', *Boletín Museo Cádiz*, I, 1919–21, p. 26.

Causa 1964
R. CAUSA, *Murillo*, Buenos Aires, 1964.

Ceán Bermúdez 1800, 1965
J. A. CEAN BERMUDEZ, *Diccionario histórico de los más ilustres profesores de las Bellas Artes en España*, 6 vols., Madrid, 1800; reprinted 1965.

Ceán Bermúdez 1804
J. A. CEAN BERMUDEZ, *Descripción artística de la Catedral de Sevilla*, Seville, 1804.

Ceán Bermúdez 1805
J. A. CEAN BERMUDEZ, *Apéndice a la Descripción artística de la Catedral de Sevilla*, Seville, 1805.

Ceán Bermúdez 1806, 1968
J. A. CEAN BERMUDEZ, *Carta de D. Juan Agustín Ceán Bermúdez a un amigo suyo sobre el estilo y gusto en la pintura de la Escuela Sevillana y sobre el grado de perfección a que se elevó Bartolomé Esteban Murillo cuya vida se inserta, y se describen sus obras en Sevilla*, Cádiz 1806, reprinted Seville, 1968.

Ceán Bermúdez 1819, 1968
J. A. CEAN BERMUDEZ, *Diálogo sobre el Arte de la Pintura (Murillo)*, Seville, 1819, reprinted in F. Tubino, *Murillo*, 1864, p. 278; reprinted with Ceán Bermúdez 1806 in 1968.

Ceán Bermúdez 1826, *see* Madrazo 1826.

Céan Bermúdez 1863
J. A. Cean Bermudez, *Descripción de la Catedral de Sevilla*, annotated edition, Seville, 1863.

Charmet 1971
R. CHARMET, 'Murillo un genie à retrouver', *Jardin des Arts*, CXCIV, 1971.

Chaves 1894
M. CHAVES, 'Bartolomé Esteban Murillo', *Páginas Sevillanas*, 1894, pp. 208–11.

Chaves 1904
M. CHAVES, 'El hijo de Murillo', *Cosas nuevas y viejas. Apuntes sevillanos*, Seville, 1904.

Cheix 1882
I. CHEIX, 'La fe del artista', *Sevilla Mariana*, II, 1882, p. 417 (poem).

Cook 1834
S. COOK, *Sketches in Spain during the years 1829, 30, 31 and 32*, 2 vols., London, 1834.

Cook and Hall 1926
E. COOK, E. HALL, *Catalogue of the Pictures in the Gallery of Alleyn's College of God's Gift at Dulwich*, London, 1926.

Coronado 1882
C. CORONADO, 'Las Vírgenes de Murillo', *Sevilla Mariana*, II, 1882, pp. 300–05.

Cortegana 1957
J. CORTEGANA, 'Restauración del gran cuadro de Murillo. La Visión de San Antonio de Padua', *Archivo Hispalense*, LXXXI, 1957, pp. 107–10.

Costa 1972
J. COSTA, *Murillo*, Barcelona, n.d. [1972].

Courcelle 1972
J. Y. P. COURCELLE, *Iconographie de Saint Augustin. Les cycles du XVIe et du XVIIe siècle*, Paris, 1972.

Crombie 1967
T. CROMBIE, 'The Spanish Exhibition at the Bowes Museum', *Apollo Magazine*, LXXXVII, 1967, p. 152.

Crosa 1912
B. S. CROSA, 'Los Murillos de Macharaviaya', *Arte Español*, 1912–13, p. 329.

Cruzada Villamil 1867
G. CRUZADA VILLAMIL, 'Neuvas noticias de la vida y obras de Murillo', *Arte en España*, VI, 1867, p. 5.

Cumberland 1787
R. CUMBERLAND, *Anecdotes of Eminent Painters in Spain during the 16th and 17th centuries*, 2 vols., London, 1787.

Curtis 1883
C. B. CURTIS, *Velázquez and Murillo. A Descriptive and Historical Catalogue of the Works*, London, New York, 1883; reprinted Ann Arbor, 1973.

Dallaway 1824
J. DALLAWAY, *The British Institution. An account of all the pictures exhibited in the British Institution from 1813 to 1823*, London 1824.

Dalton 1863
H. DALTON, *Murillo und seine Gemälde in der Kgl. Ermitage zu St. Petersburg*, St. Petersburgh, 1863.

Davies 1819
E. DAVIES, *The Life of Bartolomé E. Murillo, Compiled from the Writings of Various Authors*, London, 1819.

Denucé 1932
J. DENUCÉ, *Inventories of the Art Collections in Antwerp in the 16th and 17th centuries*, Antwerp, 1932.

Díaz de Lamarque 1882[1]
A. DIAZ DE LAMARQUE, 'A la Inmaculada Virgen María en el segunde centenario de Murillo', *Sevilla Mariana*, II, 1882, p. 458 (poem).

Díaz de Lamarque 1882[2]
A. DIAZ DE LAMARQUE, 'La Aurora de Murillo', *Sevilla Mariana*, II, 1882, p. 466.

Domenech 1929–30
R. DOMENECH, 'Murillo' *Libro de Oro de la Exposición Iberoamericana*, 1929–30, pp. 145–48.

Domínguez 1930
L. L. DOMINGUEZ, *La Caridad de Sevilla: Mañara, Murillo y Valdés Leal*, Madrid, 1930.

Domínguez Bordona 1936
J. DOMÍNGUEZ BORDONA, 'Noticias de pinturas elegidas por orden de Godoy', *Archivo Español de Arte*, XII, 1936; p. 272.

Domínguez Ortiz 1946
A. DOMÍNGUEZ ORTIZ, 'Orto y ocaso de Sevilla', *Archivo Hispalense*, 1946.

Dorival 1951
B. DORIVAL, 'Callot, modèle de Murillo', *Revue des Arts*, 1951; pp. 94–101.

Dorival 1973
B. DORIVAL, 'La Pintura en las colecciones francesas del siglo XVIII', *Congreso de Granada*, 1973.

Dotor 1964
A. DOTOR, *Murillo*, Madrid, 1964.

Drossong 1898
A. DROSSONG, 'Die "Portiuncula" des Murillo', *Illustrierte Zeitung*, no. 2896, 29, XII, 1898, p. 904.

Edinburgh 1951
An Exhibition of Spanish Paintings from El Greco to Goya, exhibition catalogue by Ellis Waterhouse, Edinburgh, 1951.

Elizalde 1955
J. ELIZALDE, *Las Inmaculadas de Murillo*, Madrid, 1955.

Elliott 1963, 1972
J. H. ELLIOTT, *Imperial Spain*, London, 1963; second edition, 1972.

Ewald-Schübeck 1965
F. EWALD SCHÜBECK, 'Estudios sobre la técnica de los pintores españoles y especialmente sobre los cuadros de Murillo', *Archivo Español de Arte*, XXXVIII, 1965, pp. 43–57.

Fernández Espino 1860
J. FERNÁNDEZ ESPINO, 'Al insigne pintor Bartolomé Esteban Murillo. Oda.', *Revista de Ciencias, Literatura y Artes*, VI, 1860, pp. 690–699.

Filhol 1804–1815
FILHOL, *Galerie du Musée Napoleon* I, 2 vols., 1804–15.

Fischer 1953
D. J. FISCHER, *Murillo as genre painter*, New York, 1953 (Doctoral Thesis), résumé in *Marsyas*, VI, 1953, p. 81.

Ford 1830–32, 1855, 1966
R. FORD, *A Handbook for Travellers in Spain*, London 1830–32; revised edition, 2 vols., 1855; reprinted 1966, 3 vols.

Ford 1848
R. FORD, reviews of publications by Sir Edmund Head (1847) and William Stirling (1848), *Quarterly Review*, LXXXIII, No. CLXV, 1848.

Ford 1853
R. FORD, Articles on the Standish Sales, *The Athenaeum*, 1853, May, pp. 14, 21, 28; June, pp. 4, 11.

Garcia Herraiz 1974
E. GARCIA HERRAIZ, 'Murillo: San Agustín lava los pies de Cristo peregrino', *Archivo Español de Arte*, 1974, p. 335.

Garnelo 1917
J. GARNELO, 'Cuadro que representa a San Antonio atribuido a Murillo', *Boletín Academia Bellas Artes*, 1917, p. 5.

Gautier 1864
T. GAUTIER, *Esteban Bartolomé Murillo. Les Dieux et les demi-dieux de la peinture*, Paris, 1864.

Gavard 1839–41
C. GAVARD, Galerie Aguado, *Choix des principaux tableaux de la Galerie de M. le Marquis de las Marismas del Guadalquivir par –. Notices sur les peintres par Louis Viardot*, Paris, n.d. [1839–1841].

Gaya Nuño 1958
J. A. GAYA NUÑO, *La pintura española fuera de España*, Madrid, 1958.

Gaya Nuño 1978
J. A. GAYA NUNO, *L'opera completa di Murillo*, Milan, 1978; Spanish translation 1978.

Gestoso y Pérez 1899–1902
J. GESTOSO Y PEREZ, *Sevilla Monumental y artística*, 3 vols., Seville 1889–1902.

Gestoso y Pérez 1896
J. GESTOSO Y PEREZ, *Catálogo de las obras que forman la exposición de la pintura sevillana en virtud de acuerdos de su Excmo. Ayuntamiento*, Seville, 1896.

Gestoso y Pérez 1899–1908
J. GESTOSO Y PEREZ, *Diccionario de los artífices que florecieron en Sevilla desde el siglo* XIII *al* XVIII *incluído*, 3 vols., Seville, 1899–1908.

Gestoso y Pérez 1909
J. GESTOSO Y PEREZ, *Una requisa de cuadros en la Catedral de Sevilla*, Seville, 1909.

Gestoso y Pérez 1910
J. GESTOSO Y PEREZ, *Exposición de retratos*, Seville, 1910.

Gestoso y Pérez 1912[1]
J. GESTOSO Y PEREZ, 'Notice . . . des principaux artistes flamands qui travaillerent à Seville depuis le XVIe siècle jusqu'à la fin du XVII', *Les Arts anciens de Flandre*, IV, Brussels, 1912.

Gestoso y Pérez 1912[2]
J. GESTOSO Y PEREZ, *Catálogo de las pinturas y esculturas del Museo Provincial de Sevilla*. Seville, 1912.

Gómez Imaz 1891[1]
M. GOMEZ IMAZ, 'La Santa Isabel de Murillo. Carta a D.Pedro de Madrazo, *Heraldo de Madrid*, 17-V; 22-VII-1891.

Gómez Imaz 1891[2]
M. GOMEZ IMAZ, 'La Santa Isabel de Murillo. Exposición del Excmo. Ayuntamiento de Sevilla', *El Universal*, 5-IX-1891.

Gómez Imaz 1896, 1972
M. GOMEZ IMAZ, *Inventario de los cuadros sustraídos por el Gobierno intruso en Sevilla el año 1810*, Seville, 1896; another edition 1916; reprinted 1972.

Gómez Imaz 1897
M. GOMEZ IMAZ, 'Cuadro de Murillo', *El Porvenir*, 5–XII, 1897.

Gómez Imaz 1902
M. GOMEZ IMAZ, *Exposiciónes que la Hermandad de la Santa Caridad de Sevilla ha dirigido al Ministro de Fomento e Instrucción Pública en los años 1891, 1901 y 1902 en demanda del cuadro de su propiedad, la Santa Isabel de Murillo*, Seville, 1902.

Gómez Imaz 1911
M. GOMEZ IMAZ, *Exposición que la Hermandad de la Caridad de Sevilla dirige al Excmo. Ministro de Fomento en demanda del cuadro du su propiedad Santa Isabel de Murillo*, Seville 1911.

Gómez Sicre 1949
J. GOMEZ SICRE, *Spanish Drawings:* XV–XIX *Centuries*, New York, 1949.

González de León 1844
F. GONZALEZ DE LEÓN, *Noticia artística y curiosa de todos los edificios . . . de Sevilla*, 2 vols., Seville, 1844.

Gradmann 1939
E. GRADMANN, *Spanische Meisterzeichnungen*, Frankfurt, n.d. [1939].

Guerra 1954
GUERRA, ARCADIO, 'Cómo salió de España "La Caridad Romana" de Murillo', *Archivo Español de Arte*, 1954, pp. 336–39.

Guerrero 1950
J. GUERRERO, 'Murillo y Assereto', *Archivo Español de Arte*, XXIII, 1950, pp. 133–44.

Guerrero 1952
J. GUERRERO, 'Los grabados que inspiraron la "Santa Isabel" de Murillo', *Archivo Español de Arte*, XXV, 1952, pp. 323–30.

Guerrero 1952
J. GUERRERO, 'La capilla de los pintores de la Hermandad de San Lucas', *Archivo Hispalense*, XVI, 1952, I.

Guinard 1939
P. GUINARD, 'Zurbarán et la découverte de la peinture espagnole en France sous Louis Philippe', *Homage à Martinenche*, Paris, 1939.

Guinard and Baticle 1950
P. GUINARD and J. BATICLE, *Histoire de la peinture espagnole du* XIIe *au* XIX *siècle*, Paris, 1950.

Guinard and Baticle 1967
P. GUINARD and J. BATICLE, *Les peintres espagnols*, Paris, 1967.

Gutierrez 1846
GUTIERREZ DE LA VEGA, 'A la memoria de Murillo', *Semanario Pintoresco*', n.p., 1846, p. 213.

Haley 1960
G. HALEY, 'Some Aspects of Religious Life in 17th Century Seville', *The Art Institute of Chicago Quarterly*, LIV, 2, 1960, p. 15.

Hamburg 1966
Spanische Zeichnungen von El Greco bis Goya, exhibition catalogue by W.Stubbs, Kunsthalle, Hamburg, 1966.

Haraszti-Takács 1968
M. HARASZTI-TAKÁCS, Murillo és Kortásai Szépmüveszeti Múzeum, Budapest, 1968.

Haraszti-Takács 1978
M. HARASZTI-TAKÁCS, *Murillo*, Budapest, 1978.

Harris 1951
E. HARRIS, 'Spanish Painting from Morales to Goya in The National Gallery of Scotland', *Burlington Magazine*, XCIII, 1951, pp. 310–17.

Harris 1953
E. HARRIS, 'Spanish Paintings from the Bowes Museum', *Burlington Magazine*, XCV, 1953, pp. 22–24.

Harris 1964
E. HARRIS, 'A Caritas Romana by Murillo', *Journal of the Warburg & Courtauld Institutes*, XXVII, 1964, pp. 337–39.

Harris
E. HARRIS, 'Murillo en Inglaterra', forthcoming article in *Goya*.

Hautecour 1926
L. HAUTECOUR, *Musée National du Louvre, Catalogue de peintures exposés dans les galleries.* II. *École italienne et école espagnole*, Paris, 1926.

Hazanas 1918
J. HAZANAS, *Vázquez de Leca*, Seville, 1918.

Head 1848
E. HEAD, *A Handbook of the History of the Spanish and French Schools of Painting*, London, 1848.

Hernández Díaz, Sancco and Collantes 1938
J. HERNANDEZ DIAZ, A. SANCCO and F. COLLANTES, *Catálogo . . . Provincia de Sevilla*, 4 vols., Seville, 1938.

Hernández Díaz 1945
J. HERNANDEZ DIAZ, 'Nuevos datos de Velázquez, Murillo y Valdés', *Archivo Hispalense*, IV, 1945, p. 225.

Hernández Díaz 1967
J. HERNANDEZ DIAZ, *Museo Provincial de Bellas Artes*, Seville, 1967.

Hernández Perera 1959
J. HERNANDEZ PERERA, 'La Caridad Romana de Murillo', *Archivo Español de Arte*, XXXII, 1959, pp. 257–60.

Herrera 1882
L. HERRERA, 'A Murillo: Soneto', *Sevilla Mariana*, 1882, II, p. 314.

Jordan 1967
W. JORDAN, *The Virginia Meadows Museum. Recent Acquisitions*, Dallas, 1967.

Jordan 1968[1]
W. JORDAN, 'A Museum of Spanish Painting in Texas', *The Art Journal*, XXVII, 1968, pp. 288–96.

Jordan 1968[2]
W. JORDAN, 'Murillo's Jacob laying the peeled rods before the flocks of Laban', *Art News*, LXVII, 1968, p. 31.

Jordan 1974
W. JORDAN, *The Meadows Museum: A Visitor's Guide*, Dallas, 1974.

Justi 1891–92
C. JUSTI, 'Murillo', *Zeitschrift für bildenden Kunst*, 1891, pp. 153, 261; 1892, pp. 32, 154.

Justi 1898
C. JUSTI, 'Ein Bildnis König Ferdinands des Heiligen von Murillo', *Zeitschrift für christhichen Kunst*, XI, 1898, p. 268.

Justi 1903
C. JUSTI, *Velázquez und sein Jahrhundert*, Bonn, 1903; Spanish translation Madrid, 1953.

Justi 1904
C. JUSTI, *Murillo*, second edition, Leipzig, 1904

Justi 1908
C. JUSTI, 'Bildnisse Königs Ferdinands', *Miscellaneen*, Berlin, 1908, I, p. 40.

Kansas 1974
Spanish Baroque Drawings in North American Collections, exhibition catalogue by Gridlay McKim Smith, University of Kansas, 1974.

Knackfuss 1896
H. KNACKFUSS, *Murillo*, Leipzig, 1896.

Kubler and Soria 1959
G. KUBLER and M. SORIA, *Art and Architecture in Spain and Portugal and their American Dominions 1500–1800*, Harmondsworth, 1959.

Kubler 1970
G. KUBLER, 'El San Felipe de Heraclea de Murillo y los cuadros del claustro chico', *Archivo Español de Arte*, XLIII, 1970, pp. 11–31.

Lafond 1907, 1946
P. LAFOND, *Murillo*, Paris, 1907; another edition Buenos Aires, 1946, with an appendix by F. Ancell, 'Murillo en América'.

Lafuente Ferrari 1937
E. LAFUENTE FERRARI, 'Dibujos de maestros andaluces', *Archivo Español de Arte*, XIII, 1937, pp. 37–59.

Lafuente Ferrari and Friedländer 1935
E. LAFUENTE FERRARI and MAX J. FRIEDLÄNDER, *El realismo en la pintura del siglo* XVII*: Países Bajos y España*, Barcelona, 1935.

Lafuente Ferrari 1946
E. LAFUENTE FERRARI, *Breve Historia de la Pintura Española*, Madrid, 1946.

Lamarque 1882
J. LAMARQUE, 'El pintor de la Inmaculada', *Sevilla Mariana*, II, 1882, p. 471 (poem).

Langasco 1938
C. LANGASCO, 'Sette Murillo dispersi?' *Liguria*, VII, 1938, pp. 11, 17.

Latour 1855
A. LATOUR, *Etudes sur l'Espagne. Seville et l'Andalousie*, 2 vols., 1855 (Chapter 5 of Vol. II, 'Murillo et l'école de Seville').

Latour 1860
A. LATOUR, 'Una Virgen de Murillo. Anécdota. Poesia de . . . traducida librements por D. José Fernández Espino', *Revista de Ciencias, Literatura y Arte*, VII, 1860, p. 502.

Lefort 1875
P. LEFORT, 'Murillo et ses éleves', *Gazette des Beaux Arts*, 1875, I, pp. 35, 176, 315; II, p. 251.

Lefort 1892
P. LEFORT, *Murillo et ses éleves*, Paris, 1892.

Lefort 1893
P. LEFORT, *La peinture espagnole*, Paris, 1893.

León 1805
A. LEON, *Libro historial de Convento de los Capuchinos de Sevilla* (manuscript), 1805.

León 1915
L. LEON, 'Murillo y la crítica moderna', *Bética*, Seville, February 1915, p. 15.

León y Domínguez 1882
J. M. LEON Y DOMINGUEZ, 'El sueño del pintor de la Concepciones', *Sevilla Mariana*, 1882, II, p. 394.

Lipschutz 1961
I. H. LIPSCHUTZ, 'El despojo de obras de arte en España durante la Guerra de la Independencia', *Arte Español*, 1961, p. 215.

Lipschutz 1972
I. H. LIPSCHUTZ, *Spanish Painting and the French Romantics*, Harvard, Cambridge, 1972.

London 1895–96
Spanish Art, exhibition organized by Sir Charles Robinson, The New Gallery, London, 1895–96.

London 1901
Exhibition of the Works of Spanish Painters, exhibition catalogue by A.G. Temple, Guildhall Gallery, London, 1901.

London 1913–14
Spanish Old Masters, exhibition catalogue by M.W. Brockwell, Grafton Galleries, London, 1913–14.

London 1920–21
Exhibition of Spanish Paintings, catalogue notes by F. J. Sánchez Cantón, Royal Academy of Arts, London, 1920–21.

London 1931
Old Masters by Spanish Artists, exhibition catalogue, Tomás Harris Galleries, London, 1931.

London 1938
Exhibition of Seventeenth Century Art in Europe, exhibition catalogue, Royal Academy of Arts, London, 1938.

London 1947
An Exhibition of Spanish Paintings, exhibition catalogue by N. MacLaren, The Arts Council, The National Gallery, London, 1947.

London 1950
Paintings and Silver from Woburn Abbey, exhibition catalogue, Royal Academy of Arts, London, 1950.

London 1951
Two Great Masterpieces and other Paintings, exhibition catalogue, Frank T. Sabin, London, 1951.

London 1976
The Golden Age of Spanish Painting, exhibition catalogue, Royal Academy of Arts, London, 1976.

London 1978
Spanish Drawings from the Witt Collection, exhibition catalogue by P. Troutman, Courtauld Institute Galleries, London, 1978.

London 1981
El Greco to Goya. The Taste for Spanish Paintings in Britain and Ireland, exhibition catalogue by A. Braham, The National Gallery, London, 1981.

López Alonso 1958
A. LOPEZ ALONSO, *Murillo en el Museo del Prado*, Madrid, 1958.

López Estrada 1973
F. LOPEZ ESTRADA, 'Los "Murillos" de la Pinacoteca de Munich', *Archivo Hispalense*, 1973, p. 329.

Los Angeles 1976
Old Master Drawings in American Collections, exhibition catalogue by E. Feinblatt, Los Angeles County Museum of Art, 1976.

Lothe 1961–62
LOTHE, 'Un cuadro de Murillo en Suiza', *Goya*, 1961–62, p. 393.

Lozoya 1945
M. LOZOYA, *Historia del Arte Hispánico*, Barcelona, IV, 1945.

Lozoya 1967
M. LOZOYA, ¿ Un precedente de la Sagrada Familia del Pajarito?', *Archivo Español de Arte*, 1967, p. 83.

Lucke 1877
H. LUCKE, 'B.E. Murillo', *Kunst and Künstler*, 1877, p. 14.

Luna 1973
J. J. LUNA, 'Inventario y almoneda de algunas pinturas de la colección de Isabel de Farnesio', *Boletín Sem. Arte Valladolid*, 1973, p. 365.

MacLaren 1947, *see* London 1947.

MacLaren 1952
N. MACLAREN, *The National Gallery Catalogues, The Spanish School*, London 1952.

MacLaren and Braham 1970
N. MACLAREN and A. BRAHAM, *The National Gallery Catalogues, The Spanish School*, revised edition, London, 1970. Review by A.E. Pérez Sánchez, *Archivo Español de Arte*, XLIV, 1971, p. 197.

Madoz 1845–50
P. MADOZ, *Diccionario geográfico-estadístico-histórico de España*, Madrid, 1845–1850 (see vol. X, 1847).

Madrazo 1826–36
J. MADRAZO, *Colección litográfica de cuadros del Rey de España ...*, text by D. J. A. Ceán Bermúdez and D. J. Musso Valiente, 3 vols., Madrid, 1826–36.

Madrazo 1945
M. MADRAZO, *Historia del Museo del Prado, 1818–1868*, Madrid, 1945.

Madrazo 1872
P. MADRAZO, *Catálogo desciptivo e histórico del Museo del Prado*, Madrid, 1872.

Madrazo 1884
P. MADRAZO, *Viaje artístico de tres siglos por las colecciones de cuadros de los Reyes de España*, Barcelona, 1884.

Madrid 1819–72
Catalogo del Museo del Prado, 1819–72.

Madrid 1927
Exposición Franciscana, VII *Centenario de la muerte de San Francisco de Asís*, exhibition catalogue, Madrid, 1927.

Madrid 1972
San José en el Arte español, exhibition catalogue, Madrid, 1972.

Madrid 1980
El Dibujo español de los siglos de Oro, exhibition catalogue by A.E. Pérez Sánchez, Madrid, 1980.

Madrid 1982
Pintura española en el colecciones centroeuropeas, exhibition catalogue, Museo del Prado, Madrid, 1982.

Mâle 1951
E. MALE, *L'Art réligieux de la fin du* XVI*e du* XVII*e siècle et du* XVIII*e siècle*, Paris, 1951.

Manchester 1957
European Old Masters, exhibition catalogue, Manchester, 1957.

Matute 1886
J. MATUTE, *Adiciones y correcciones a los Hijos de Sevilla de Arana*, Seville, 1886.

Matute 1886
J. MATUTE, *Noticias relativas a la Historia de Sevilla que no constan en sus Anales, Ano 1828*, Seville, 1886, III.

Matute 1886–87
J. MATUTE, *Hijos de Sevilla señalados en santidad, letras, artes o dignidad*, 2 vols., Seville, 1886–87.

Matute 1886–88
J. MATUTE, 'Adiciones y correcciones al tomo IX del Viaje a España de D. Antonio Ponz', *Archivo Hispalense*, 1886–88, I–IV.

Matute 1887
J. MATUTE, *Anales eclesiásticos y seculares de la Ciudad de Sevilla . . . desde el año del 1701 . . . hasta el de 1800*, 3 vols., Seville, 1887.

Mayer 1908[1]
A. L. MAYER, in *Monatschefte für Kunstwissenschaft*, I, 1908, p. 520.

Mayer 1908[2]
A. MAYER, 'Murillos Arbeiten für die Sevillaner Kathedrale', *Jahrbuch der preussische Kunstsammlungen*, XLIII, 1908.

Mayer 1911
A. MAYER, *Die Sevillaner Malerschule*, Leipzig, 1911.

Mayer 1913[1]
A. MAYER, *Murillo*, Klassiker der Kunst, Stuttgart, Berlin, 1913; 2nd ed. 1923.

Mayer 1913[2]
A. MAYER, *Geschichte der Spanischen Malerei*, Leipzig, 1913.

Mayer 1914
A. MAYER, 'An unknown portrait by Murillo', *Burlington Magazine*, XXIV, 1914, pp. 231–32.

Mayer 1915
A. MAYER, *Handzeichnungen Spanischer Meister. 150 Skizzen und Entwurfen des 16 bis 19 Jahrhunderts*, New York, 1915.

Mayer 1918
A. MAYER, 'Die Spanischen Zeichnungen in der Kunsthalle zu Hamburg', *Zeitschrift für bildenen Kunst*, XIX, 1918, p. 109.

Mayer 1920
A. MAYER, 'La coleccion de dibujos espanoles en el Museo de Hamburgo', *Boletín de la Real Academia de la Historia*, 1920, p. 130.

Mayer 1921[1]
A. MAYER, *The Work of Murillo*, New York, 1921.

Mayer 1921[2]
A. MAYER, *Murillo, der Maler der Betteljungen und Madonnen*, Munich, 1921.

Mayer 1922
A. MAYER, *Geschichte der Spanischen Malerei*, Leipzig, 1922.

Mayer 1923[1]
A. MAYER, *Murillo*, Klassiker der Kunst, Stuttgart, second edition, 1923.

Mayer 1923[2]
A. MAYER, *Jusepe de Ribera*, Leipzig, 1923.

Mayer 1923[3]
A. MAYER, 'Josef und die Frau des Potiphar von Murillo', *Der Cicerone*, 1923, II.

Mayer 1923[4]
A. MAYER, 'Retratos españoles en el extranjero: Carreño, Murillo y Nicolás Bussi', *Boletín de la Real Academia de la Historia*, III, 1923, p. 123.

Mayer 1924
A. MAYER, 'Zum Werk von Velázquez und Murillo', *Zeitschrift für bildenden Kunst*, 1924, p. 24.

Mayer 1924–25
A. MAYER, Review of *Murillo* by Montoto, 1923, *Zeitschrift für bildenden Kunst*, L. 1924–25, p. 118.

Mayer 1925
A. MAYER, 'Two unknown paintings by Murillo', *Apollo Magazine*, XI, 1925, p. 220.

Mayer 1926[1]
A. MAYER, 'Three Paintings by Murillo', *Burlington Magazine*, XLVIII, 1926, p. 251.

Mayer 1926[2]
A. MAYER, 'Cuadros españoles en el mercado internacional', *Arte Español*, VIII, 1926, pp. 53–54, 173.

Mayer 1927[1]
A. MAYER, 'Unbekannte Spanier. Ein unbekanntes Frühwerk von Murillo', *Cicerone*, XIX, 1927, p. 217.

Mayer 1927[2]
A. MAYER, 'Notas sobre algunas pinturas en Museos provinciales de Francia', *Boletín de la Real Academia de la Historia*, 1927, p. 160.

Mayer 1928
A. MAYER, *Historia de la Pintura Española*, Madrid, 1928.

Mayer 1929
A. MAYER, 'Laban in search of his Household Gods', *Apollo Magazine*, IX, 1929, pp. 79–80.

Mayer 1931
A. MAYER, 'Murillo' in Thieme Becker, *Allgemeines Lexikon der bilbenden Kunstler*, Leipzig, XXV, 1931, p. 286.

Mayer 1932[1]
A. MAYER, 'Zur Austellung der Spanischen Gemälde des Grafen Contini in Rome', *Pantheon*, 1932, pp. 203–08.

Mayer 1932[2]
A. MAYER, 'The Exhibition of the Castle Rohoncz Collection in the Munich New Pinakothek', *Apollo Magazine*, XII, 1932, II, p. 89.

Mayer 1932[3]
A. MAYER, 'Arte español en el extranjero', *Revista Española de Arte*, 1932, p. 22.

Mayer 1932[4]
A. MAYER, 'Los cuadros de Murillo en colleciónes de Amberes del siglo XVII', *Archivo Español de Arte*, VIII, 1932, p. 275.

Mayer 1934
A. MAYER, 'Anotaciones a obras murillescas', *Boletín de la Soc. Española de Excursiones*, 1934, p. 14.

Mayer 1936
A. MAYER, 'Anotaciones al arte y a las obras de Murillo', *Revista Española de Arte*', V, 1936, p. 46.

Mayer 1936–40
A. MAYER, 'Anotaciones a cuadros de Velázquez, Zurbarán, Murillo y Goya en el Prado y en la Academia de San Fernando', *Boletín de la Real Academia de la Historia*, 1936–40, p. 41.

Mayer 1938
A. MAYER, 'Murillo und seine Italienischen Barockvorbilder', *Critica d'Arte*, XV, 1938, p. 120.

Mayer and Longhi 1930
A. MAYER and R. LONGHI, *The Old Spanish Masters from the Contini Bonacossi Collection*, Rome, 1930.

McKim Smith 1974 *see* Kansas 1974

Méndez Casal 1936
MÉNDEZ CASAL, Pintura antigua española en Escandinavia', *Revista Española de Arte*, 1936, p. 8.

Minor 1882
E. MINOR, *Murillo*, London, 1882.

Montana 1962
J. MONTANA, 'Pintura profana de Murillo', *Archivo Español de Arte*, XXXV, 1962, p. 271–73.

Montesa 1927
M. DE MONTESA, 'Exportación de obras de arte en tiempo de Carlos III', *Arte Español*, VII, 1927, pp. 301–02.

Montesa 1951
M. DE MONTESA, 'El Cazador de Murillo', *Arte Español*, 1951, p. 158.

Montoto 1882
L. MONTOTO, 'La última tarde', *Sevilla Mariana*, 1882, p. 428.

Montoto 1922–24
S. MONTOTO, 'Un modelo de la Inmaculadas de Murillo', *Boletín Museo Cádiz*, II, 1922–24, p. 106.

Montoto 1923
S. MONTOTO, *Murillo*, Seville, 1923.

Montoto 1945
S. MONTOTO, 'Nuevos documentos de Bartolomé Esteban Murillo', *Archivo Hispalense*, 1945, p. 319.

Montoto 1946
S. MONTOTO, 'La biblioteca de Murillo', *Bibliografía Hispánica*, July 1946, p. 465.

Morgado 1882
M. MORGADO, 'Apariciones de la Santísima Virgen a varios Santos representados por Murillo', *Sevilla Mariana*, 1882, p. 369.

Mundler 1965
O. MUNDLER, 'Die Spanische Schule in München und der neue Katalog der Pinakothek', *Recenslonen und Mitteilungen über bildenden Kunst*, IV, 1965.

Munich 1982
Von El Greco bis Goya, exhibition catalogue, Haus der Kunst, Munich, 1982.

Muñoz 1942
A. MUÑOZ, *Murillo*, Novara, 1942.

Murray 1980
P. MURRAY, *Catalogue of the Dulwich Picture Gallery*, London, 1980.

Nottingham 1980
The Golden Age of Spanish Art, exhibition catalogue by E. Harris and P. Troutman, Nottingham University Gallery, 1980.

Oertel 1968
R. OERTEL 'Die Taufe Christi von Murillo', *Jahrbuch der Preussischer Kulturbesitz*, 1968, pp. 215–17.

Ortiz de Zúñiga 1677, 1795–96
D. ORTIZ DE ZUÑIGA, *Anales eclesiasticos y seculares de la más noble y muy leal ciudad de Sevilla . . . desde el año de 1246 hasta el de 1671*, Seville, 1677. Annotated edition by D. Antonio Maria Espinosa y Carzel, 5 vols., Madrid, 1795–96.

'P' 1922–24
'P' (unsigned article), 'Desgraciado accidente ocurrido a Murillo en el convento de Capuchinos de Cádiz y que ocasiono su fallecimiento', *Boletín Museo Cádiz*, II, 1922–24, p. 103.

Pacheco 1649, 1956
F. PACHECO, *El arte de la pintura, su antigüedad y grandeza*, Seville, 1649, another edition, Madrid, 1866; another edition, ed. F. Sánchez Cánton, 1956.

Palacios 1914–15
E. PALACIOS, 'Murillo', *Coleccionismo*, XXII, 1914, p. 13; XXIII, 1915, pp. 25, 29.

Palomino 1715–24, 1947
A. PALOMINO, *Museo Pictórico y Escala Optica*; I, *Theorica de la pintura*, 1715; II, *Practica de la pintura*, 1724; III, *El Parnaso español pintoresco laureado*, 3 vols., Madrid, 1715–24; reprinted 1795–97, 1947.

Pantorba 1947
B. PANTORBA, *Murillo*, Madrid, 1947.

Pantorba 1961
B. PANTORBA, 'A new Painting by Murillo', *Burlington Magazine*, CIII, 1969, p. 109.

Paris 1963
Trésors de la peinture espagnole, exhibition catalogue, Musée du Louvre, Paris, 1963.

Paris 1976
La peinture espagnole du siècle d'or de Greco à Velázquez, exhibition catalogue by A. E. Pérez Sánchez, Petit Palais, Paris, 1976.

Pemán 1952
C. PEMAN, *Catálogo de las pinturas. Museo de Bellas Artes de Cádiz*, 1952.

Pemán 1957
C. PEMAN, 'La restauración de la Visión de San Antonio de Murillo y el estilo murillesco', *Archivo Hispalense*, 1957, p. 45.

Pemán 1958[1]
C. PEMAN, 'Restauración de una obra de Murillo.', *Archivo Español de Arte*, XXXI, 1958, pp. 67–69.

Pemán 1958[2]
C. PEMAN, 'Noticia sobre la restauración del San Antonio de Murillo en 1876', *Archivo Hispalense*, 1958, I.

Pemán 1962
C. PEMAN, 'Murillo comparado con Zurbarán', *Revista de Estudios Extremenos*, 1962, p. 639.

Pérez Sánchez 1964
A. E. PEREZ SANCHEZ, *Inventario de la pinturas. Real Academia de Bellas Artes*, Madrid, 1964.

Pérez Sánchez 1967
A. E. PEREZ SANCHEZ, *Pintura italiana del siglo* XVII *en España*, Madrid, 1967.

Pérez Sánchez 1969
A. E. PEREZ SANCHEZ, *Catálogo de la Colección de Dibujos del Instituto Jovellanos de Gijón*, Madrid, 1969.

Pérez Sánchez 1964
A. E. PEREZ SANCHEZ, *Pintura Italiana*, Madrid, 1970.

Pérez Sánchez 1970[1]
A. E. PEREZ SANCHEZ, *Gli spagnoli da El Greco a Goya* (Disegni dei Maestri), Milan, 1970.

Pérez Sánchez 1972
A. E. PEREZ SANCHEZ, *Museo del Prado. Catálogo de dibujos, I. Dibujos españoles: siglos* XV–XVII, Madrid, 1972.

Pérez Sánchez 1980
A. E. PEREZ SANCHEZ, *El dibujo español de los Siglos de Oro*, Madrid, 1980.

Ponz 1772–94, 1947
A. PONZ, *Viaje de España, en que se da noticia de la cosas apreciables y dignas de saberse que hay en ella*, Madrid, 1772–94; reprinted, 1947.

Princeton 1976
Murillo and his Drawings, exhibition catalogue by J. Brown, Princeton University, 1976.

Princeton 1982
Painting in Spain 1650–1700, exhibition catalogue by E. Sullivan and N. A. Mallory, Princeton University, 1982.

Quilliet 1816
F. QUILLIET, *Dictionnaire des peintres espagnols*, Paris, 1816.

Quintero 1933[1]
P. QUINTERO, 'La Virgen de la Serrana de Murillo y la del Palacio Corsini', *Boletín Museo Cádiz*, XVII, 1933, p. 9.

Quintero 1933[2]
P. QUINTERO, 'Virgen de la Faja', *Boletín Museo Cádiz*, XVII, 1933, II, p. 13.

Reveil 1828–34
REVEIL, *Musée de Peinture et de Sculpture . . . dessiné et gravée a l'eau forte par Reveil avec de notices par Duchesne*, 16 vols., Paris, 1828–34.

Ricci 1913
S. RICCI, *Description raisonée des peintures du Louvre, I, Italie et Espagne*, Paris, 1913.

Richards 1968
L. S. RICHARDS, 'Bartolomé Esteban Murillo: A drawing for a Virgin and Child', *Bulletin of the Cleveland Museum of Art*, V, 1968, p. 235.

Richardson 1948
E. P. RICHARDSON, 'Murillo's Flight into Egypt', *Bulletin of the Detroit Institute of Arts*, XXVII, 4, 1948, pp. 78–80.

Saltillo 1926
MARQUES DE SALTILLO, 'El Gobierno intruso y la riqueza artística de Sevilla', *Boletín R. Academia Sevillana de Bellas Letras*, X, 1926, pp. 41–48.

Saltillo 1928
MARQUES DE SALTILLO, 'El Murillo de la Casa de Alba', *La Epoca*, Madrid, no. 27751, 8–XII–1928.

Saltillo 1933
MARQUES DE SALTILLO, *Mr Frederick Quilliet Comisario de Bellas Artes, del Gobierno intrusio 1809–14*, Madrid, 1933.

Saltillo 1947
MARQUES DE SALTILLO, *La Heráldica en el arte*, Madrid, 1947.

Sánchez Cantón 1930
F. J. SANCHEZ CANTON, *Dibujos españoles*, 5 vols., Madrid, 1930.

Sánchez Cantón 1936
F. J. SANCHEZ CANTON, *Fuentes literarias para la historia del Arte Español*, Madrid, 1936, vol. IV.

Sánchez Cantón 1937[1]
F. J. SANCHEZ CANTON, 'El supuesto retrato de Gabriel Murillo, "clérigo"', *Archivo Español de Arte*, XIII, 1937, p. 74.

Sánchez Cantón 1937[2]
F. J. SANCHEZ CANTON, 'La venta de cuadros en 1801: La Concepción de Aranjuez y El Descendimiento de Montpellier', *Archivo Español de Arte*, XIII, 1937, pp. 165–67.

Sánchez Cantón 1937[3]
F. J. SANCHEZ CANTON, 'Más sobre Luciano Bonaparte, coleccionista', *Archivo Español de Arte*, XIII, 1937, pp. 261–62.

Sánchez Cantón 1940
F. J. SANCHEZ CANTON, 'La Inmaculada "Soult" en Madrid', *Semana*, 24–XII–1940.

Sánchez Cantón 1952, 1972
F. J. SANCHEZ CANTON, *Museo del Prado, Catalogo de los cuadros*, Madrid, 1952; another edition 1972.

Sánchez y Peña 1743
SANCHEZ Y PEÑA, *Adiciones al libro de don Pablo de Espinosa intitulado Teatro de la Santa Iglesia*, Seville, 1743.

Sancho Corbacho 1946
A. SANCHO CORBACHO, 'Una supuesta colaboración entre Velázquez y Murillo', *Archivo Hispalense*, 1946, p. 117.

Schubeck 1965
F. SCHUBECK, 'Estudios Sobre la técnica de los pintores españoles y especialmentre sobre los cuadros de Murillo', *Archivo Español de Arte*, XXXVIII, 1965, pp. 53–57.

Seville 1897
Catalogo de las pinturas y esculturas del Museo de Sevilla, catalogue by Boutelou, Gestoso, Mattoni and Bilbao, Seville, 1897.

Seville University 1927–46
Documentos para la Historia del Arte en Andalucia, 10 vols., Seville University, 1927–46.

Seville 1982
La epoca de Murillo. Antecedentes y consecuentes de la pintura, exhibition catalogue by E. Valdivieso and J. M. Serrera, Seville, 1982.

Soehner 1963
H. SOEHNER, *Gemälde Katalog. Spanische Meister*, Munich, 1963.

Sonnenburg 1980
H. SONNENBURG, 'Zur Maltechnik Murillos', *Maltechnik-Restauro*, 3, 1980.

Soria 1948[1]
M. SORIA, 'Flemish sources of the Spanish Baroque', *The Art Bulletin*, XXX, 1948, pp. 249–59.

Soria 1948[2]
M. SORIA, 'Murillo's boy and girl companion pieces', *Burlington Magazine*, XC, 1948, p. 22.

Soria 1959, *see* Kubler and Soria 1959

Soria 1960
M. SORIA, 'Murillo's Christ and St. John the Baptist', *The Art Institute of Chicago Quarterly*', LIV, 2, 1960, p. 14.

Sota 1882
R. SOTA and E. GARCIA VALERO, 'Murillo, pintor de la vida de la Santísima Virgen', *Illustración Bética*, XXIII, 1882.

Sotos 1972
C. SOTOS, 'El retablo de San Agustín de Sevilla', *Archivo Español de Arte*, XLV, 1972, pp. 287–95.

Standish 1840
F. H. STANDISH, *Seville and its vicinity*, London, 1840.

Standish Collection 1842
Catalogue . . . de la Collection Standish: Catalogue des tableaux, dessins et gravures de la Collection Standish legués au Roi par M. Franck Hall Standish, Paris, 1842.

Stechow 1966
W. STECHOW, 'B.E. Murillo. Laban searching for his stolen Household Gods in Rachel's Tent', *The Bulletin of the Cleveland Museum*, LIII, 1966, p. 367.

Stirling-Maxwell 1848, 1891
W. STIRLING-MAXWELL, *Annals of the Artists of Spain*, 4 vols., London, second edition 1891; first edition (W. Stirling) 1848.

Stirling-Maxwell 1873
W. STIRLING-MAXWELL, *Essay Towards a Catalogue of Prints Engraved from Works of Velázquez and Murillo*, London, 1873.

Suida 1930
W. SUIDA, 'Spanische Gemälde der Sammlung Contini-Bonacossi', Belvedere, IX, 1930, pp. 142–4.

Sullivan and Mallory 1982, *see* Princeton 1982

Tokyo and Osaka 1980
Velázquez y la Pintura española de su tiempo, exhibition catalogue, Tokyo and Osaka, 1980.

Toreno 1872
CONDE DE TORENO, *Historia del levantamiento, guerra y revolución en España*, Madrid, 1872.

Tormo 1914
E. TORMO, 'La Inmaculada y el arte español', *Boletín Español de Arte*, 1914, pp. 108, 176.

Tormo 1929
E. TORMO, *Cartillas excursionistas. Academia de San Fernando*, Madrid, 1929.

Torre Farfán 1663
F. TORRE FARFAN, *Templo panegírico al certamen poético que celebró la Hermandad insigne del Santísimo Sacramento estrenando la gran fábrica del Sagrario Nuevo . . . en obsequio del Breve concedido por la Santidad de N. Padre Alejandro* VII . . ., Seville 1663.

Torre Farfán 1666
F. TORRE FARFAN, *Fiestas que celebró la Iglesia de Santa María la Blanca en celebridad del Breve de Alexandro* VII *en favor de la Concepción de María y al estreno del templo*, Seville, Juan Gómez de Blas, 1666.

Torre Farfán 1672
F. TORRE FARFAN, *Fiestas de la Sta. Iglesia . . . de Sevilla, al nuevo culto del Señor Rey San Fernando*, Seville, 1672.

Townsend 1791, 1792
J. TOWNSEND, *A Journey through Spain in the Years 1786 and 1787*; 3 vols., London 1791, reprinted 1792.

Trapier 1941
E. DU GUE TRAPIER, 'Notes on Spanish Drawings', *Notes Hispanic*, I, 1941, pp. 1–61.

Trapier 1966
E. DU GUE TRAPIER, 'A "Christ Child as the Good Shepherd" attributed to the School of Murillo in the Hispanic Society's Collection', in *Homenaje a Rodríguez Moñino*, Madrid, II, 1966, pp. 273–76.

Troutman 1956
P. TROUTMAN, *A Handbook of the Drawings in the Witt Collection*, Courtauld Institute of Art, London, 1956.

Tubino 1864
F. M. TUBINO, *Murillo, su época, su vida, sus cuadros*, Seville, 1864.

Valdivieso 1978
E. VALDIVIESO, *Catálogo de las pinturas de la Catedral de Sevilla*, Seville, 1978.

Valdivieso 1980
E. VALDIVIESO, 'Juan de Roelas', *Archivo Hispalense*, 1980.

Valdivieso and Serrera 1979
E. VALDIVIESO and J. SERRERA, *Catálogo de las pinturas del Palacio Arzobispal de Sevilla*, Seville, 1979.

E. Valdivieso and J. M. Serrera 1982, *see* Seville 1982.

Valencina 1908[1]
A. VALENCINA, *Reseña histórica de la Provincia Capuchina de Andalucía*, 5 vols., Seville, 1906–08.

Valencina 1908[2]
A. VALENCINA, *Murillo y los Capuchinos*, Seville, 1908.

Velázquez and Sánchez 1864
E. VELAZQUEZ and J. SANCHEZ, *Bartolomé Esteban Murillo*, La Cruz del Rodeo, Seville, 1864.

Velázquez 1926
E. VELAZQUEZ, *El taller de Murillo y su comercio con América*, Veracruz, 1926.

Vienna 1982
Von Greco bis Goya, exhibition catalogue, Kunstlerhaus, Vienna, 1982.

Vignau 1903–05
M. VIGNAU, 'Napoli y la Coleccion de cuadros del exconvento del Rosario', *Revista de Archivos*, 1903, pp. 372–76; 1904, pp. 192–99, 1905; pp. 152–96.

Villot 1849
F. VILLOT, *Notice des tableaux exposés dan les galeries du Musée National du Louvre. Ecole d'Italie et d'Espagne*, Paris, 1849.

Viñaza 1889–94
CONDE DE LA VIÑAZA, *Adiciones al Diccionario histórico de D. Juan Agustín Ceán Bermúdez*, Madrid, 1889–94.

Waagen 1838
G. F. WAAGEN, *Works of Art and Artists in England*, 3 vols., London, 1838.

Waagen 1854
G. F. WAAGEN, *Treasures of Art in Great Britain*, 4 vols., London, 1854.

Waagen 1867
G. F. WAAGEN, *Galleries and Cabinets of Art in Great Britain*, London, 1867.

Waterhouse 1946
E. K. WATERHOUSE, 'Fancy Pictures', *Burlington Magazine*, LXXXVIII, 1946, p. 134.

Waterhouse 1947
E. K. WATERHOUSE, 'The exhibition from Althorp House at Messrs Agnew's', *Burlington Magazine*, LXXXIX, 1947, p. 78.

Waterhouse 1951, *see* Edinburgh 1951.

Waterhouse 1953
E. K. WATERHOUSE, 'Some notes on the Exhibition of Works of Art from Midland Houses', *Burlington Magazine*, XCV, 1953, pp. 305–09.

Waele 1889
J. WAELE and J. P. RICHTER, *Catalogue of the Collection of the Earl of Northbrook*, 1889.

Young 1973
E. YOUNG, 'A drawing of the Annunciation by Murillo', *Burlington Magazine*, CXV, 1973, pp. 604–07.

Young 1980
E. YOUNG, *Die grössen Meister der Malerei, Bartolomé Murillo*, 1980, Spanish edition 1982.

Zarco 1934
ZARCO, 'Cuadros reunidos por Carlos IV, siendo príncipe, en su Casa de Campo de El Escorial', *Religion y Cultura*, El Escorial, 1934.

Index of Lenders

Index of Paintings and Drawings by Murillo

Works in the exhibition are indicated by their catalogue number in bold type: references to paintings and drawings not in the exhibition are indicated by page or figure number.

Paintings

Drawings

Photographic Acknowledgements

The exhibition organizers would particularly like to thank the Museo del Prado, Juan Oronoz S.A. and David Manso for their assistance in providing photographs of works in Spanish and other European collections. The following also kindly made photographs available. All other photographs were provided by the owners of the paintings.

Courtauld Institute of Art D13, D17
National Gallery fig. 74
Photographie Giraudon fig. 7

Royal Academy Trust

The Trustees and Appeal Committee of the Royal Academy Trust wish to express their gratitude to the many companies and individuals who have already given their support to the appeal. Among many others they would like to extend their thanks to:

Akai
Allied-Lyons PLC
Anglia Television Limited
The Arthur Andersen Foundation
James Archibald
Associated British Foods
Bank of England
Barclays Bank PLC
B.A.T Industries p.l.c.
The Baring Foundation
The Benham Charitable Settlement
BICC plc
Blue Circle Industries plc
The BOC Group
The British Electric Traction Company PLC
British Airways
British National Oil Corporation
British Olivetti Limited
British Petroleum Company PLC
Brooke Bond Group plc
Capital Radio
The Cleary Foundation
The John S. Cohen Foundation
Commercial Union Assurance Company plc
Coopers & Lybrand
Coutts and Co.
The De La Rue Jubilee Trust
Eagle Star Insurance Group
Finance for Industry plc
The Fishmongers' Company
The Garfield Weston Foundation
The General Electric Company plc
The Jack Goldhill Charitable Trust
The Goldsmiths' Company
Her Majesty's Government
Roger de Grey, RA
The Haberdashers' Company
Dr. and Mrs Armand Hammer
Mrs Sue Hammerson, OBE
The Hammerson Group of Companies
L.G.Harris and Company Limited
Hayward Tyler
The Hedley Foundation
H.J.Heinz Charitable Trust
Hill Samuel Group PLC
Hogg Robinson Group
IBM United Kingdom Group
IC Gas
The Idlewild Trust
Imperial Chemical Industries PLC
Imperial Tobacco Limited
International Thomson Organisation
The Kaye Organisation
Kleinwort, Benson Limited
Lazard Brothers & Co. Limited
Lex Service PLC
Lloyds Bank Plc
The Corporation and Members of Lloyd's and Lloyd's Brokers
The Manifold Trust
McCann Erickson Advertising Limited
Metal Box p.l.c.
Midland Bank plc
The Miller and Tiley Charitable Trust
The Peter Minet Trust
The Moorgate Trust Fund
Mobil Oil Company Limited
Morgan Grenfell & Co. Limited
National Westminster Bank PLC
The Normanby Charitable Trust
Norwich Union Insurance Group
Sir Duncan Oppenheim
Ove Arup Partnership
H.R.Owen Limited
P & O Steam Navigation Company
S. Pearson and Son plc
Peerless Pump
The Pilgrim Trust
R.V.Pitchforth, RA
The Plessey Company plc
The Rank Organisation Plc
The Rayne Foundation
Reed International PLC
Leopold de Rothschild Charitable Trust
Royal Insurance p.l.c.
Royal Oak Foundation, Inc., New York
RTZ Services Limited
The Sainsbury Family Charitable Trusts
J. Henry Schroder Wagg & Co. Limited
William Scott, CBE, RA
Shell UK Limited
Sir Richard Sheppard, CBE, RA
The Skinners' Company
Standard Chartered Bank
Mr and Mrs Dennis C Stanfill
Sun Alliance & London Insurance Group
Taylor Woodrow Charitable Trust
Technical Indexes Limited
Sir Jules Thorn Charitable Trust
Thomas Tilling plc
Thorn EMI plc
Trafalgar House Public Limited Company
Trustee Savings Banks (Holdings) Limited
Unilever PLC
A.F. Wallace Charitable Trust
S.G. Warburg & Company Limited
Wartski
The Weinberg Family Charitable Trust
Whitbread & Company PLC
Wilde Sapte
Winsor and Newton (part of the Reckitt & Colman Group)
Sir John Woolf

(18.XI.82)

The Friends of the Royal Academy

PATRON H.R.H. The Duke of Edinburgh, KG, KT

The Friends of the Royal Academy receive the following privileges
FRIENDS £15.50 annually
FRIENDS (Concessionary) £12.50 annually for full-time Museum Staff and Teachers
£10.00 annually for Pensioners and Young Friends under the age of 25 years

Gain free and immediate admission to all Royal Academy Exhibitions with a guest or husband/wife and children under 16.
Obtain catalogues at a reduced price.
Enjoy the privacy of the Friends' Room in Burlington House.
Receive Private View invitations to various exhibitions including the Summer Exhibition.
Have access to the Library and Archives.
Benefit from other special arrangements, including lectures, concerts and tours.

COUNTRY FRIENDS £10.00 annually for Friends living more than 75 miles from London
Gain free and immediate admission to Royal Academy Exhibitions on 6 occasions a year with a guest or husband/wife and children under 16.
Receive all the other privileges offered to Friends.

ARTIST SUBSCRIBERS £25.00 annually
Receive all the privileges offered to Friends.
Receive free submission forms for the Summer Exhibition.
Obtain art materials at a reduced price.

SPONSORS £500 (corporate), £150 (individual) annually
Receive all the privileges offered to Friends.
Enjoy the particular privileges of reserving the Royal Academy's Private Rooms when appropriate and similarly of arranging evening viewings of certain exhibitions.
Receive acknowledgement through the inclusion of the Sponsor's name on official documents.

BENEFACTORS £5,000 or more
An involvement with the Royal Academy which will be honoured in every way.

Further information and Deed of Covenant forms are available from
The Friends of the Royal Academy, Royal Academy of Arts, Piccadilly, London W1V 0DS

Benefactors and Sponsors

BENEFACTORS
Mrs. Hilda Benham
Lady Brinton
Mr. and Mrs. Nigel Broackes
Keith Bromley, Esq.
The John S. Cohen Foundation
The Colby Trust
Michael E. Flintoff, Esq.
The Lady Gibson
Jack Goldhill, Esq.
Mrs. Mary Graves
D. J. Hoare, Esq.
Sir Antony Hornby
George Howard, Esq.
Irene and Hyman Kreitman
The Landmark Trust
Roland Lay, Esq.
The Trustees of the Leach Fourteenth Trust
Hugh Leggatt, Esq.
Mr. and Mrs. M. S. Lipworth
Sir Jack Lyons, CBE
The Manor Charitable Trustees
Lieutenant-Colonel L. S. Michael, OBE
Jan Mitchell, Esq.
The Lord Moyne
Mrs. Sylvia Mulcahy
G. R. Nicholas, Esq.
Lieutenant-Colonel Vincent Paravicini
Mrs. Vincent Paravicini
Richard Park, Esq.
Phillips Fine Art Auctioneers
Mrs. Denise Rapp
Mrs. Adrianne Reed
Mrs. Basil Samuel
Eric Sharp, Esq., CBE
The Revd. Prebendary E. F. Shotter
Dr. Francis Singer
Lady Daphne Straight
Mrs. Pamela Synge
Harry Teacher, Esq.
Henry Vyner Charitable Trust
Charles Wollaston, Esq

CORPORATE SPONSORS

Barclays Bank International Limited
Bourne Leisure Group Limited
The British Petroleum Company Limited
Christie Manson and Woods Limited
Citibank
Consolidated Safeguards Limited
Courage Limited
Davidson Pearce Limited
Delta Group p.l.c.
Esso Petroleum Company Limited
Ford Motor Company Limited
The Granada Group
Arthur Guinnes Son and Company Limited
Guinness Peat Group
House of Fraser Limited
Alexander Howden Underwriting Limited
IBM United Kingdom Limited
Imperial Chemical Industries PLC
Investment Company of North Atlantic
Johnson Wax Limited
Lex Service Group Limited
Marks and Spencer p.l.c.
Mars Limited
The Worshipful Company of Mercers
Merrett Syndicates Limited
Midland Bank Limited
The Nestlé Charitable Trust
Ocean Transport and Trading Limited (P. H. Holt Trust)
Ove Arup Partnership
Philips Electronic and Associated Industries Limited
The Rio Tinto-Zinc Corporation PLC
Rowe and Pitman
The Royal Bank of Scotland Limited
J. Henry Schroder Wagg and Company Limited
The Seascope Group
Shell UK Limited
Thames Television Limited
J. Walter Thompson Company Limited
Ultramar PLC
United Biscuits (U.K.) Limited

INDIVIDUAL SPONSORS

The A.B. Charitable Trust
Mrs. John W. Anderson II
Ian Fife Campbell Anstruther, Esq.
Mrs. Ann Appelbe
Dwight W. Arundale, Esq.
Edgar Astaire, Esq.
The Rt. Hon. Lord Astor of Hever
The Rt. Hon. Lady Astor of Hever
Miss Margaret Louise Band
A. Chester Beatty, Esq.
Mrs. E. D. Blythe
Godfrey Bonsack, Esq.
Peter Bowring, Esq.
Mrs. Susan Bradman
Cornelis Broere, Esq.
Jeremy Brown, Esq.
Simon Cawkwell, Esq.
W. J. Chapman, Esq.
Major A. J. Chrystal
Alec Clifton-Taylor, Esq.
Henry M. Cohen, Esq.
Mrs. Elizabeth Corob
Mrs. Yvonne Datnow
Raymond de Prudhoe, Esq.
Raphael Djanogly, Esq. JP
Thomas B. Dwyer, Esq.
Mrs. Gilbert Edgar
Brian E. Eldridge, Esq.
Aidan Ellis, Esq.
Eric Ford, Esq.
Victor Gauntlett, Esq.
Lady Gibberd
Peter George Goulandris, Esq.
J. A. Hadjipateras, Esq.
Mrs. Penelope Heseltine
Geoffrey J. E. Howard, Esq.
Mrs. Patricia D. Howard
Roger Hughes, Esq.
Mrs. Manya Igel
J. P. Jacobs, Esq.
Mrs. Christopher James
Alan Jeavons, Esq.
Irwin Joffe, Esq.
S. D. M. Kahan, Esq.
David J. Kingston, Esq.
Peter W. Kininmonth, Esq.
Owen Luder, Esq.
A. Lyall Lush, Esq.
Mrs. Graham Lyons
Jeremy Maas, Esq.
Ciarán MacGonigal, Esq.
Dr. Abraham Marcus
Peter Ian McMean, Esq.
Princess Helena Moutafian, MBE
David A. Newton, Esq.
Raymond A. Parkin, Esq.
Mrs. M. C. S. Philip
Dr. L. Polonsky
Cyril Ray, Esq.
Mrs. Margaret Reeves
The Rt. Hon. Lord Rootes
The Hon. Sir Steven Runciman
The Master, The Worshipful Company of Saddlers
Sir Robert Sainsbury
R. J. Simia, Esq.
Christina Smith
Steven H. Smith, Esq.
Thomas Stainton, Esq.
Cyril Stein, Esq.
James Q. Stringer, Esq.
Mrs. A. Susman
Mrs. G. M. Susman
The Hon. Mrs. Quentin Wallop
Sidney S. Wayne, Esq.
Frank S. Wenstrom, Esq.
David Whithead, Esq.
David Wolfers, Esq. MC
Brian Gordon Wolfson, Esq.
Lawrence Wood, Esq.

There are also anonymous Benefactors and Sponsors